Playing a Jewish Game

—◄o►—

Gentile Christian Judaizing
in the First and Second Centuries CE

Studies in Christianity and Judaism /
Études sur le christianisme et le judaïsme : 13

Studies in Christianity and Judaism / Études sur le christianisme et le judaïsme
publishes monographs on Christianity and Judaism in the last two centuries before
the common era and the first six centuries of the common era, with a special interest in studies of their interrelationship or the cultural and social context in which
they developed.

Studies in Christianity and Judaism /
Études sur le christianisme et le judaïsme : 13

Playing a Jewish Game

—◄o►—

Gentile Christian Judaizing
in the First and Second Centuries CE

Michele Murray

Published for the Canadian Corporation for Studies in Religion /
Corporation Canadienne des Sciences Religieuses
by Wilfrid Laurier University Press
2004

We acknowledge the financial support of the Government of Canada through the Book Publishing Industry Development program for our publishing activities. We acknowledge the Government of Ontario through the Ontario Media Development Corporation's Ontario Book Initiative.

National Library of Canada Cataloguing in Publication

Murray, Michele, 1964-
    Playing a Jewish game: Gentile Christian judaizing in the first and second centuries CE / Michele Murray.

(Studies in Christianity and Judaism = Études sur le christianisme et le judaïsme ESCJ; v. 13).
Includes bibliographical references and indexes.
ISBN 0-88920-401-2

    1. Church history—Primitive and early church, ca. 30-600. 2. Christianity and other religions—Judaism. 3. Judaism—Relations—Christianity. 1. Canadian Corporation for Studies in Religion. 11. Title. 111. Series: Studies in Christianity and Judaism ; 13.

BR195.J8M87 2004   270.1   C2003-907123-5

© 2004 Canadian Corporation for Studies in Religion /
Corporation Canadienne des Sciences Religieuses

Cover design by Leslie Macredie. Cover photographs by Patricia Coyne of the entrance to the largest excavated synagogue in the world, Sardis, Turkey, dated to . the third and fourth centuries CE. Text design by PJWoodland.

∞
Printed in Canada

Order from:
Wilfrid Laurier University Press
Wilfrid Laurier University
Waterloo, Ontario, Canada N2L 3C5
www.wlupress.wlu.ca

To Daniel

Contents

◄○►

Acknowledgements

◄◦►

T HE FIRST STEP ALONG THE LONG JOURNEY leading to the publication of this book was taken in Jerusalem. It was there, in a course taught by Professor Isaiah Gafni at the Hebrew University of Jerusalem, that I was introduced for the first time to the topic of Jewish-Christian relations in the early centuries of the Common Era. A few years later, in a class with Visiting Professor John Gager, my interest in the topic was further fired. At the University of Toronto's Centre for the Study of Religion, I entered fully into the study of Jewish-Christian relations in antiquity during doctoral studies leading to a dissertation on Gentile Christian judaizers. This book, a revision of the dissertation, could not have been completed without the help and support of many people.

To Professor Peter Richardson, my doctoral supervisor, I owe a great debt. In addition to being an outstanding course instructor, and thereby a mentor for how to teach, he provided constructive criticism and timely encouragement through each stage of the PhD process, and subsequently. Professors John Corbett and Leif Vaage read various drafts of my work, correcting errors and providing references along the way. Professors Michel Desjardins and Stephen Wilson likewise contributed to the dissertation by offering helpful suggestions for improvement.

I certainly could not have begun this project without the emotional and financial support of my parents, Lorie and Roy Murray: it was they who encouraged me to undertake my first trip to the Middle East—little could they have known the lasting impact of that visit. Roz Murray, Ruth and Eric Miller, and Sheldon Lewkis offered support, friendship (and sometimes a much-needed glass of port). Among friends at the University of Toronto who contributed in important ways were especially Ken Derry, Keir Hammer, Phil Harland, Lesley Lewis, Elaine Myers, Tony Michael, Cheryl Nafziger-Leis, and Dana Sawchuk. Several of my colleagues at Bishop's University—particularly Pat Coyne, Jamie Crooks, George Englebretsen, Kerry Hull, Norm Jones, David Seale, Dale Stout, Andy Stritch, and Harvey White—have substantially contributed to the provision of a most agreeable working environment. I especially wish to thank Professor Pat Coyne, who thoroughly read the entire manuscript twice, and through this and many conversations on the topic of Gentile judaizing, helped to make this book a better final product. My student Chloe Riley contributed by assisting in final proofreading.

For financial assistance toward the publishing process, I am grateful to the Senate Research Committee at Bishop's University for a publication grant. I would also like to thank those at Wilfrid Laurier University Press for their help, including Brian Henderson, Carroll Klein, Leslie Macredie, and Susan Quirk.

Finally, last but not least, my husband, Daniel Miller, contributed towards the completion of this project in several different ways: reading and editing many drafts of my writing, making intelligent suggestions for improvement, and being at times counsellor and at times comedian— often in the wee hours of the morning, when self-doubts loomed large. It is to him that this book is dedicated, with much love.

◄o►

The New Revised Standard Version of the Bible has been used through-out the text.

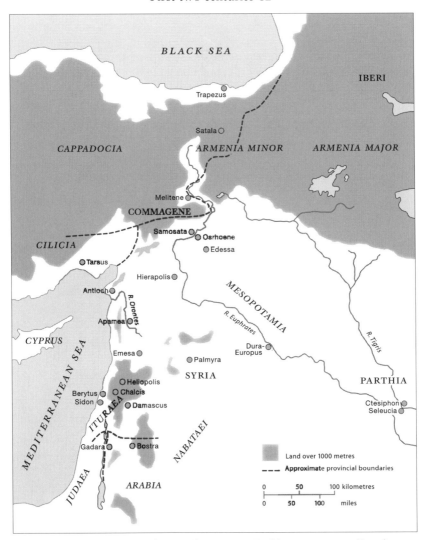

Adapted from: Martin Goodman, *The Roman World 44 BC-AD 180* (London: Routledge, 1997), p. 243.

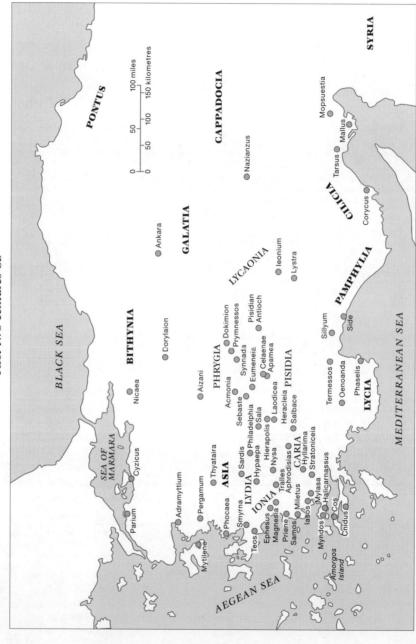

MAP OF ASIA MINOR
First two centuries CE

BLACK SEA

PONTUS

SEA OF MARMARA

Parium
Cyzicus
Nicaea

BITHYNIA

Dorylaion

CAPPADOCIA

Nazianzus

Ankara

GALATIA

LYCAONIA

Ieonium
Lystra

100 miles
150 kilometres
50   100
50   100
0   0

SYRIA

Mopsuestia

Mallus
Tarsus

CILICIA

Corycus

Adramyttium

Pergamum

Thyataira

ASIA

Aizani

PHRYGIA

Dokimion
Prymnessos

Acmonia
Sebaste   Synnada
Sala   Eumeneia
Laodicea   Celaenae
Apamea

Pisidian
Antioch

PISIDIA

Sillyum

PAMPHYLIA

Side

Phocaea

Smyrna
Teos

Sardis
Hypaepa
Hierapolis
Nysa

Philadelphia

Heracleia   Salbace

Termessos

Oenoanda
Phaselis

LYCIA

Mytilene

Ephesus
Magnesia
Tralles
Priene
Samos
Iasos
Miletus

LYDIA

IONIA

Aphrodisias

CARIA

Hyllarima
Stratoniceia

Mylasa
Halicarnassus

Myndos
Cos
Chidus

Amorgos
Island

AEGEAN SEA

MEDITERRANEAN SEA

Adapted from: Paul R. Trebilco, *Jewish Communities in Asia Minor* (Cambridge University Press), 1991, p. xvi.

CHAPTER I

Introduction: Judaizing and the Early Development of Christianity

◄o►

U NTIL APPROXIMATELY THIRTY or forty years ago, scholars in the field of Christian origins tended to treat Judaism and Christianity as historically and conceptually separate movements with few interactions and little in common.[1] Judaism and Christianity were understood to be virtually monolithic communities, and the existence of diverse groups within each community was given minimal, if any, attention. If scholars did address these differences, they frequently treated them as though they were erroneous deviations from the authentic forms of each religion. They had a propensity to describe the separation of Christianity from Judaism as taking place shortly after the destruction of the Jewish Temple in 70 CE, and to treat both movements as though their boundaries and identities were sharply defined in reaction to this traumatic event. Interaction between Christians and Jews in the early centuries of the Common Era was rarely acknowledged or seriously discussed.

By contrast, recent early Christian scholarship has shown an appreciation for the pluralism and rich diversity of Judaism and Christianity and has reflected an interest in advancing new interpretations of the history of the relationships among Jewish and Christian communities.[2] Scholars have come to understand that modern notions of Jewish and Christian identities as distinct and rigid categories ought not to be projected into antiquity. There is acknowledgement, moreover, that the boundaries between the two broadly identified communities were more fluid than was formerly held, and that each religious community expressed itself in a wide variety of ways in belief and practice. In particular, scholarly perceptions of how the history of early Christianity developed and how definitions of the terms "orthodoxy" and "heresy" ought to be applied to this history, have changed significantly. In many geographical areas "heresies" were actually the primary forms of Christianity; the voices of alleged heretics were deliberately suppressed by other Christians who eventually triumphed in the struggle for dominance. There is recognition that, in order to appreciate more fully the diversity and vitality of nascent Christianity, the muted voices of so-called heretics—who had been part of the variegated Christian movement—must be heard.[3]

Notes to Chapter 1 start on page 153

This study contributes toward the current discussion by addressing one of the largely neglected points of contact in the spectrum of Jewish-Christian relations in the first two centuries CE. It argues that significant strands of early Christian literature, which have been interpreted as expressing anti-Jewish sentiment, were actually directed against *Gentile Christians*[4]— more significantly, Gentile Christian *judaizers*—rather than against Jews or Jewish Christians,[5] as is usually understood. These Gentile Christian judaizers combined a commitment to Christianity with adherence in varying degrees to Jewish practices without viewing such behaviour as contradictory. From the perspective of certain Christian leaders, these Christian community members were "playing a Jewish game" by living like Jews and adhering to certain Jewish practices and dangerously blurring the boundaries between Christianity and Judaism. There were attempts to suppress this phenomenon, and Gentile Christian judaizers became the target of anti-Jewish rhetoric found within various early Christian writings. Certain passages of *adversus Judaeos* material—often understood to be reflective of conflict between Christians and Jews—is more accurately to be understood as expression of an *intra muros* debate *among Christians*.

By examining the phenomenon of Gentile Christian judaizing within broader Jewish-Christian relations in the early centuries of the Common Era, this study enables the suppressed voices of Gentile Christian judaizers, once part of the rich diversity of nascent Christianity, to be heard. One of the central goals of this exploration, therefore, is to contribute toward a more carefully defined and nuanced understanding of the larger picture of Jewish-Christian relations in antiquity. I owe much to a small number of scholars: John Gager (1985), Lloyd Gaston (1986), and more recently Stephen Wilson (1995), who have discussed certain pieces of evidence for Gentile Christian judaizing and have laid a solid foundation for a more comprehensive study of the phenomenon. Such a comprehensive study naturally follows the paths that have already been trod by other scholars; this exploration analyzes some of the same documents as they have, and at times reaches similar conclusions. My objective is not comprehensive, detailed analyses of the individual documents; most of these have been the subjects of extensive analysis in their own right. The present study's task is to draw all possible references to Gentile Christian judaizers together and to consider the evidence in its geographical context for the first time in a single study. In addition, the inclusion of documents that have not been investigated before in terms of their relevance to Gentile Christian judaizing will, obviously, enhance current knowledge of this phenomenon.

The Term "Judaizer" in the Context
of Nascent Christianity

"Judaizer" is a noun derived from transliteration via Latin of the
Greek verb *ioudaizein* (ἰουδαΐζειν), "to judaize." Frequently, this term has
been used incorrectly by scholars to refer to Jews or, more typically, Jewish Christians who actively engaged in persuading non-Jews—usually
Pauline Christians—to follow part or all of the Jewish law. According to
this understanding, the initial success of the "judaizers" provoked the
strong opposition of the apostle Paul, whose animosity toward them is
expressed in his letters, particularly the one addressed to the Galatian
churches. This view rests on the assumption that the history and development of early Christianity was shaped primarily by conflict between two
separate and distinct groups: Pauline Gentile Christians and certain Jewish Christians who regarded observance of the Mosaic law (including such
practices as circumcision, Sabbath observance, and the distinction between
clean and unclean meats) as obligatory for *all* Christians, whether of Jewish or Gentile origin.

Likewise, angry statements from post-Pauline ecclesiastical leaders usually have been understood to be directed toward Jews or Jewish Christians
who put pressure on Gentile Christian members of the church to observe
Torah. For example, in the *Epistle of Barnabas,* the author vigorously
criticizes several Jewish customs, including circumcision, food laws and
Sabbath observance, stressing throughout his writing that the Mosaic law
was never meant to be taken literally (9.4; 10.9; 15.6-8). Elsewhere the
author bitterly complains that "some" members of his Christian congregation hold the view that "the covenant is both theirs and ours" (ἡ διαθήκη
ἐκείνων καί ἡμῶη, *Barn.* 4.6); that is, these Christians believe that the
covenant belongs equally to Christians and Jews. These statements are
generally understood to be directed against Jewish Christians. The Book
of Revelation provides another example of what is regularly perceived to
be hostility directed toward Jews or Jewish Christians. The author casti-
gates "those who say that they are Jews, and are not" as members of the
"synagogue of Satan" (συναγωγή τοῦ Σατανᾶ) in messages addressed to
churches in Smyrna and Philadelphia (Rev. 2:9 and 3:9). Similarly, in one
of his letters to various Christian communities located throughout Asia
Minor, Ignatius issues the following warning about "judaizing" to his
readers in Magnesia: "It is monstrous (ἄτοπόν) to talk of Jesus Christ and
to practise Judaism (ἰουδαΐζειν). For Christianity did not base its faith
on Judaism, but Judaism on Christianity..." (Magn. 10.3). Most New
Testament scholars have interpreted Ignatius' hostility to be directed toward
Jewish Christians.

The typical interpretation of the above passages as being directed against Jewish Christians has been challenged recently by a small number of scholars (Gaston 1986: 33–44; Gager 1985). They have argued that this polemic was the reaction of ecclesiastical leaders to the strong attraction to Judaism and observance of Jewish customs exhibited by certain *Gentile* Christians within their own communities. These scholars assert that the correct understanding of the meaning of the term "judaizers" in the context of the Roman world is Gentiles who "live like Jews" by observing various components of the Mosaic law, such as keeping the Sabbath or certain food laws, without fully converting to Judaism and becoming Jews.

This interpretation of the term as referring to the *actions of Gentiles* is more consistent with its ancient usage. Shaye Cohen notes that in *War* 2.463 Josephus uses the term to refer to Gentiles in the cities of Syria who "sided with the Jews in their political struggles" or who "adopted Jewish customs and manners" (1999: 185). Josephus writes that Syrian cities were divided into two rival groups: Syrians and Jews. The Syrians killed as many Jews as they could, but there was another group that they were uncertain about: "For, though believing that they had rid themselves of the Jews, still each city had its judaizers (τοὺς ἰουδαΐζοντας), who aroused suspicion; and while they shrunk [*sic*] from killing offhand this equivocal element in their midst, they feared these neutrals as much as pronounced aliens" (*War* 2.463). According to Josephus, Syrian authorities were aware of Gentiles who sympathized with the Jews to such an extent that they were seen as possible security hazards.[6] Cohen draws a useful comparison between ἰουδαΐζειν and the verb λακωνίζειν, which can mean to imitate the Lacedaemonians in manners, dress, etc., or to side with the Lacedaemonians (1987: 418 n.27). He notes that ancient Greek has many verbs with the stem *-izein* that are compounds of the name of a region or ethnic group: these verbs "have three basic meanings: a) to give political support (a political meaning); b) to adopt the customs and manners (a cultural meaning); c) to speak a language (a linguistic meaning)," and some verbs have a combination of these meanings (1999: 175–78; 1993: 31). This observation highlights the intransitive meaning of the verb and the fact that the imitative action is carried out by someone who *is not originally or naturally a part of the group being imitated.* Thus, ἰουδαΐζειν refers to the actions of Gentiles, not Jews.[7]

Having established that the verb "to judaize" and its various forms are properly defined as referring to *Gentile* behaviour, hereafter in this study I will not employ the redundant phrase "Gentile Christian judaizing" but will use "Christian judaizing" or "Christian judaizers" instead.

Christian Judaizing in Nascent Christianity

Chronological Parameters

IN THE PAST, SCHOLARS HAVE OFTEN MADE two disparate assumptions concerning the chronological parameters of Christian judaizing: 1) it was a phenomenon that existed only during the apostolic period, rapidly diminishing by the end of the first century because of the increasing presence of Gentiles in the church (Munck 1959: 134), or 2) it was a new development combated by John Chrysostom in fourth-century CE Antioch, as indicated in his vituperative sermons against Gentile Christian members of his church who attended synagogue and were attracted to Jewish customs and religious rites (Ruether 1974: 170; Taylor 1995).

Johannes Munck, one of the earliest scholars to countenance seriously the idea that some early Gentile Christians were attracted to Judaism and Jewish customs, is an advocate of the first perspective. Munck argues that judaizing was a phenomenon prompted in part by Paul's positive teachings about Jewish Christianity and Jerusalem, which made some Gentile Christians insecure about their status compared with that of Jewish Christians, and in part by Gentile Christians' reading the Hebrew scriptures and becoming convinced that it was necessary for them to observe the Jewish law in order to receive God's promises (1959). Munck asserts that Christian judaizing existed only during the time of the apostles: "Certainly the Judaizers' demands of circumcision and observance of the Law are not put forward after the time of the apostles" (1959: 134). He furthermore holds the view that the judaizing movement, as a "Gentile Christian heresy" had existed "only within the Galatian churches" (1959: 279-80).

A recent proponent of the second view is Miriam Taylor, who claims that evidence for the occurrence of Christian judaizing in the early church simply does not exist prior to the Constantinian period; for her, "anti-Jewish" rhetoric was merely a theological abstraction (1995: 30). She accuses scholars who argue that judaizing did occur in the first and second centuries CE of dealing more with unfounded assumptions than reality, suggesting that "[t]he sparseness of the evidence for judaizing in the pre-Constantinian period has forced scholars to formulate their theories on the basis of the later evidence which is then read back and presumed to apply in the earlier period as well" (1995: 30). She furthermore denies that judaizing behaviour among Christians has anything to do with a living Jewish community: "judaizing appears to have been chiefly an internal phenomenon with no apparent connection either to the drawing power of contemporary Judaism, or to positive pressures exerted by the Jews" (Taylor 1995: 29).[8]

This study challenges both of these assumptions regarding the chrono-logical parameters of Christian judaizing. I argue that evidence for the genesis and early manifestations of Christian judaizing is found in Paul's letter to the Galatians and, therefore, that judaizing was an issue with which the first generation of Christians had to struggle. In fact, the exis-tence of Christian judaizing extended well beyond apostolic times in the regions of Syria and Asia Minor and was not manifest only in the Galat-ian Christian communities. I also demonstrate that pre-Constantinian lit-erary evidence for judaizing may indeed be found in documents which date from the first and second centuries CE. I show that "anti-Jewish" dis-course was not simply a theological abstraction but an ecclesiastical response to a concrete situation in certain early Christian communities that illuminates aspects of actual Jewish-Christian relations in antiquity. Evidence for Christian judaizing in the fourth century, post-Constantinian period (of which Chrysostom's writings are a characteristic example), is, therefore, more correctly to be viewed as a *continuation* of a phenomenon that was already manifest in first and second century CE Christian commu-nities.

Geographical Parameters

The pivotal (1934) study of Walter Bauer, *Rechtglaubigkeit und Ketzerei im ältesten Christentum* (trans. 1971), effectively demonstrates how the emergence and manifestations of early Christianity differed from one geo-graphical area to the next. Thus, the local contexts of textual evidence and the variations among locales ought not to be ignored. While Gaston, Gager and Wilson have considered evidence for Christian judaizing from various geographical settings, they have not sufficiently considered varia-tions in the textual evidence among these different regions. Gager, for example, suggests that the phenomenon of "judaizing Christians" was one that "seems to have been particularly prevalent and persistent in Syria, but it was by no means limited to one region of the Empire," and mentions that it occurred in Asia Minor as well, without commenting on the simi-larities or differences exhibited in the two regions (1985: 132). Likewise Stephen Wilson concludes after his brief treatment of the topic that the problem of Christian judaizing "seems to have been widespread in time and space," without expanding on possible distinctions visible among the dif-ferent geographical settings (1995: 166). I address this lacuna by examin-ing Christian judaizing in the two geographical domains of Syria and Asia Minor between c.50 CE and 160 CE, taking account of discrepancies between the two where they exist.[9]

This time frame includes the destruction of the Temple in Jerusalem, the spread of Christianity beyond the borders of Palestine to Syria and Asia

Minor and the Bar Kochba revolt, all of which had a significant impact on Jewish-Christian interaction. I reconsider certain texts that have already been a part of the debate concerning the existence of Christian judaizing and introduce new documents relevant to the discussion. It is my contention that the cumulative evidence from these texts attests incontrovertably to the existence of Christian judaizing within early Syrian and Asia Minor Christian communities during the period in question.

Methodology

THE BEST APPROACH FOR INVESTIGATING Christian judaizing in this period is through analysis of the criticism levelled against Jewish customs by leaders of Christian communities, where it can be determined that Gentile Christians would have comprised at least a major part of the community. The texts surveyed are those considered to have addressed congregations composed predominantly of Christians of Gentile origins, and Gentile presence can be determined through evidence provided by the texts themselves. For example, warnings against returning to idolatrous worship, or becoming circumcised, point toward a Gentile readership. The lack of archaeological evidence for a Jewish community in the immediate area of the document might also be used to argue for a Gentile audience, although absence of evidence is not, of course, evidence of absence.

At times the intended target of the polemic is clear (for example, Justin Martyr in his *Dialogue with Trypho* inveighs explicitly against Gentile Christians who observe parts of the Mosaic law within his church community [47: 4]), but for the most part it is not. Those who originally composed many anti-Jewish passages, and those who read them, knew very well against whom the polemic was directed. I contend that the target was Gentile Christians who manifested what was considered to be excessive attachment to Jewish custom but that this understanding was lost over time. Left with, essentially, one side of an argument, modern readers must analyze this polemic and reconstruct the socio-historical context of the documents—fill in the other side of the debate, so to speak—by "mirror-reading" the criticism with the goal of understanding accurately who (and what behaviour) was being criticized. While essential, the method of mirror reading is considered controversial by some, and therefore needs to be applied with care. The task of reconstructing the socio-historical context is all the more challenging when dealing with polemical material that can distort the "mirror."

A few scholars have elucidated the inherent risks of mirror reading for Paul's letters, and observations generally relevant to this study may be drawn from their cautionary comments (Lyons 1985; Barclay 1987). For example, one factor that makes interpretation difficult is that the opponents of the author may not have embraced exactly what is nominally disputed by the author in the documents. Indeed, in order to present the adversaries in a bad light and increase the efficacy of the vilification for readers, the author may have exaggerated or twisted the facts. Certain aspects of the dispute might be purposely polarized, and the opponent might be caricatured. John Barclay points out a further potential pitfall of mirror reading: some scholars have tended to portray, for example, Paul's opponents using descriptions that make the opponents sound suspiciously like the scholars' own theological adversaries: "I suspect this is why, in Protestant circles, Paul's opponents have so often been described as legalistic and mean-minded Jewish Christians, with a streak of fundamentalist biblicism: in exegeting and supporting Paul one can thereby hit out at Jews, Catholics and fundamentalists all at once!" (1987: 81).

The shortcomings of the technique of mirror reading should not be exaggerated, however, since the approach can be effective if applied judiciously (Murphy-O'Connor 1996: 195; Barclay 1987). While it would be imprudent to underestimate the distorting effects of polemic, it would be equally ill-advised to assume that an author would *wholly* misrepresent (or invent) the behaviour denounced in the text, *particularly if the purpose of the text is to influence the behaviour of its readers in a specific way.* The author would need to write in such a way that readers of the text could recognize what the author was referring to.

The alternative to a prudent application of mirror reading is to conclude that virtually nothing could be known about the historical circumstances in which the criticism in question was written. Rather than resort to such a scholarly "agnosticism," I would subscribe to Barclay's view that, when applied with caution and with certain "logical criteria," this methodology can be effective (1987: 84). For example, Barclay argues that when assertions or commands are made by an author, we may assume that among the readers is someone who is *at least* in danger of overlooking or neglecting what the author has stipulated and *at most* has explicitly denied it or is purposely deriding it. If a denial or prohibition is made, *at least* someone may be prone to accept what the author denies, or to do what he prohibits, and *at most* someone has explicitly asserted it, or already flagrantly disobeyed the prohibition (Barclay 1987: 84). If the tone of the statement reflects "emphasis and urgency" and is repeated often by the author, clearly the issue is important and perhaps central.[10]

In accordance with these stipulations, evidence in early church documents that can be determined to be pointing to the criticism or encouragement of Christian judaizing in Syria and Asia Minor during the first and second centuries CE is explored with a view to addressing the following questions: What motivated certain Gentile Christians to become judaizers? Who desired Gentile Christians to judaize? Which Jewish customs were involved? Throughout this study, the socio-cultural and religious contexts of the documents are re-examined to elucidate the sociological and historical circumstances underpinning the reaction to or encouragement of Christian judaizing. The texts discussed include canonical documents, both early (e.g., Galatians) and late (e.g., Revelation); non-canonical documents of an orthodox nature (e.g., *Epistle of Barnabas,* the *Didache*, the letters of Ignatius) as well as literature of a "heterodox" nature (e.g., Marcion's writing, the *Pseudo-Clementine* literature) and the Apologists (e.g., Justin Martyr's *Dialogue with Trypho*, Melito's *Peri Pascha*).

The existence of Christian judaizers complicates the portrait of Jewish-Christian relations by adding another dimension, for not only were there Jewish Christians and Gentile Christians, there were Gentile Christians who lived like Jews. Christian judaizing offers evidence of how diverse interactions were between Christians and Jews, and attests to the indistinct, fluid boundaries among members of each group. This investigation inevitably contributes to the discussion of the development of Christian identity. Early ecclesiastical leaders' reactions to the judaizing phenomenon helped to determine, to a significant extent, what constituted "proper" Christian behaviour as distinct from Judaism. Warnings and criticism of Christian judaizing reflect a determined effort on behalf of the church leadership to forge a Christian identity fully differentiated from Judaism and would, ultimately, contribute to the eventual "parting of the ways" of Christianity and Judaism.

CHAPTER 2

Gentile Attraction to Judaism
in the Roman Empire

◄◦►

EXTANT TEXTUAL AND EPIGRAPHIC DATA indicate that the Jewish way of life had considerable appeal among Gentiles in the Roman Empire in the first and second centuries CE, particularly among the aristocratic class of Roman society, including the imperial family. The purpose of this chapter is twofold: first I discuss the phenomenon of non-Christian judaizing in the Roman Empire in the first and second centuries CE, then I consider how pagans became attracted to Judaism and the complicated question of whether Judaism was a missionary religion. Investigation of Gentile attraction to Judaism in the first and second centuries CE provides a context for my particular focus on the appeal of Judaism for Gentile *Christians* during this period.

Gentile Attachment to Judaism in
the First Centuries CE

MANY GENTILES IN THE GRECO-ROMAN world found themselves attracted to Judaism, expressing their attachment to Judaism through a variety of different behaviours. While literary and epigraphic evidence indicates that some Gentiles underwent the full conversion process and became Jews, others expressed their adherence to Judaism by voluntarily adopting certain Jewish customs or by supporting the Jewish community through benefactions or political support (Cohen 1999: 140–74).

Gentiles were attracted to Judaism for a wide assortment of reasons. Some scholars speculate that Gentiles may have considered the long history of the Jews and their possession of an ancient text to be attractive qualities (Feldman 1993: 177–200). In contrast to the current North American appeal of the "new and improved," the Greco-Roman world valued older things as more trustworthy and desirable—"since ancient times were closest to the gods" (Cicero, *De Natura Deorum* 3.1.5–4.10).[1] The possibility of associating with a close-knit community with a clear set of ethical guidelines probably appealed to some Gentiles, while the Jewish reputation among certain Greek writers as a wise and philosophical people—

Notes to chapter 2 start on page 154

in part probably because of their emphasis on study of their ancient texts—
likewise would have attracted certain individuals to Judaism. Pythago-
ras's condemnation of the use of images is attributed in Diogenes Laertius,
Lives of the Philosophers (1.6-9), to Jewish influence, while references to
the Jews as philosophers by birth were made by the historian Megasthenes
(*Indica,* apud: Clement of Alexandria, *Stromata* 1.15; 72.5; Stern, *Authors*
no. 14) and the philosophers Theophrastus (*De Pietate,* apud: Porphyrius,
De Abstinentia 2.26; Stern, *Authors* no. 4) and Clearchus of Soli (*De
Somno,* apud: Josephus, *Against Apion* 1.176-83; Stern, *Authors* no. 15).
The connection between wisdom and the ability to express oneself well was
emphasized in antiquity and garnered the Jews praise from non-Jewish
writers: first-century CE literary critic Pseudo-Longinus, for example,
expresses admiration for the literary style of Jewish scripture in his *De
Sublimitate* (9.9: see Stern, *Authors* no. 148; Feldman 1993: 214).

Literary evidence from the first and second centuries CE demonstrates
that Gentiles did convert to Judaism. Philo speaks warmly of converts
and states that they should be welcomed into the fold as equals (*Virtues*
20.103-104). First-century Jewish historian Flavius Josephus writes that
Jews "were constantly attracting to their religious ceremonies multitudes
of Greeks, and these they had in some measure incorporated with themselves" (κἀκείνους τρόπῳ τινὶ μοῖραν αὐτῶν πεποίηντο; *War* 7.45) probably through conversion (*contra* Goodman 1994: 87, no. 58). Josephus
provides at least seven instances of conversion to Judaism in *Antiquities,*
for example in the person of Fulvia, an aristocratic Roman woman (*Ant.*
18.81-82), and in the members of the royal household of Adiabene (*Ant.*
20.17-96; Cohen 1987).

Roman writers also attest to Gentile conversion to Judaism. Dio Cassius writes that, because, in 19 CE, "the Jews had flocked to Rome in great
numbers and were converting many of the natives to their ways" (καὶ
συχνοὺς τῶν ἐπιχωρίων ἐς τὰ σφέτερα ἔθη μεθιστάντων), the emperor
Tiberius banished most of them from Rome (*Roman History* 57.18.5a; also
Tacitus, *Annals* 2.85; Josephus, *Ant.* 18.83-84). Tacitus states that "circumcision was adopted by [Jews] as a mark of difference from other men.
Those who come over to their religion adopt the practice, and have this
lesson first instilled into them, to despise all gods, to disown their coun-
try, and set at nought parents, children, and brethren" (*Histories* 5.5).[2] In
a passage that has incorrectly been used as evidence for the existence of
an aggressive Jewish missionary movement in Rome, Horace writes in
Satires 1.4.142-43: "then would a big band of poets come to my aid—for
we are the big majority—and we, like the Jews, will compel you to join
our throng." (*Satires* 1.4.142-43).[3]

Epigraphic evidence from funerary inscriptions in Rome and Asia Minor records the existence of converts to Judaism. Seven Jewish inscriptions from Rome refer to proselytes (*CIJ* #68, 202, 222, 256, 462, 532 in Leon 1995: 263ff). One dated to the third or fourth century CE clearly identifies Crescens Sincerius Iud(a)eus as *proselytos* (*CIJ* #68; Noy 1993: 392, #491). Another inscription in Latin simply states: *Mannacius sorori Crysidi dulcissime proselyte*, "Mannacius, for his most sweet sister, Crysis, a proselyte" (Noy 1993: 199, #224; Leon 1989: 296, #222; Kraemer 1989: 38ff; also Kraabel 1982). It may have been customary for pagan converts to Judaism to take on a Jewish name in addition to their own, as is demonstrated in an inscription that may date to the second century CE: "Veturia Paulla ... placed in her eternal home, who lived 86 years, 6 months, a proselyte for 16 years under the name of Sarah, mother of the synagogues of Campus and Volumnius. In peace her sleep" (#523). This woman apparently converted to Judaism at the age of seventy, and subsequently assumed leadership roles in two synagogues (Kraemer, ed., 1988: 289; Noy 1993: 457, #577)—a rather remarkable achievement!

A number of Gentiles observed a variety of Jewish customs and traditions and attended synagogue services without converting fully to Judaism. Inscriptions from Aphrodisias, Sardis and Miletus identify a group of people with exclusively Greek names as God-fearers (θεοσεβής) (Reynolds and Tannenbaum 1987: 48–67; Siegert 1973; *CIJ* #228, 748). Although the term θεοσεβής has a double meaning—in that it can refer either to Jews (i.e., a "pious" Jew) or to Gentiles (i.e., God-fearing Gentiles)—it seems in some of these cases to be referring to Gentiles who supported the Jewish community in some capacity (and perhaps attended synagogue meetings) without converting outright.

An inscription discovered in the outlying area of the ancient city of Aphrodisias in south-central Turkey, dated to the early third century CE, is understood by many scholars to be such evidence and has quieted most of the scepticism concerning the existence of "God-fearers."[4] Its message reveals that residents of Aphrodisias, both Jewish and Gentile, participated together to establish a soup kitchen for the benefit of the poor of the city.[5] In the inscription are two lists. The second list bears fifty-two names that are primarily Gentile—except, possibly, Eusabbathios—and they are introduced by the words "and as many as are God-fearers" (καὶ ὅσοι θεοσεβεῖς) (Reynolds and Tannenbaum 1987: 7). These Gentiles, nine of whom are also identified as city councillors (βουλευτής), apparently contributed to the soup kitchen; Murphy-O'Connor suggests that they were called God-fearers (θεοσεβής) as "a gracious compliment to their moral character" and not necessarily as an indication that they participated in the

synagogue (1992: 423; Overman 1992: 145-52). The first list is introduced by the words "Below (are) listed the (members) of the decany of the
students (or disciples or sages) of the law, also known as those who fer-
vently (or continuously) praise God," and is followed by names that are
primarily Jewish (Reynolds and Tannenbaum 1987: 5; Murphy-O'Connor
1992: 421). Of these names, three are identified as proselytes. Two others with Gentile names (Emmonios and Antonios) are identified as
θεοσεβής; significantly, these two are distinguished from the three proselytes who have Jewish names and, clearly, they were involved in the Jewish group devoted to study and prayer. Thus Emmonios and Antonios
were "God-fearers"—Gentiles who did not convert to Judaism but interacted in some capacity with the Jewish community, perhaps as participants in synagogue worship (Murphy-O'Connor 1992: 423). It appears
that Jews made room in their synagogues for Gentiles who had a curiosity and interest in their ways and worship—just as in their Temple in
Jerusalem where, until its destruction in 70 CE, the largest court on the
premises was for Gentile participants in the Temple cult.

Josephus proudly, and probably with some exaggeration, testifies to
the dissemination of Jewish religious observances in the pagan world,
declaring that "there is not one city, Greek or barbarian, nor a single
nation, to which our custom of abstaining from work on the seventh day
has not spread, and where the fasts and the lighting of lamps and many
of our prohibitions in the matter of food are not observed" (*Against Apion*
2.282).[6] In *War* (2.462-63), Josephus describes the situation in Syrian
cities just prior to the outbreak of the Jewish war against Rome in 66 CE:

> The whole of Syria was a scene of frightful disorder; every city was divided
> into two camps, and the safety of one party lay in their anticipating the
> other. They passed their days in blood, their nights, yet more dreadful, in
> terror. For, though believing that they had rid themselves of the Jews, still
> each city had its judaizers, who aroused suspicion (τοὺς ἰουδαΐοντας εἶχον
> ἐν ὑποψίᾳ); and while they shrunk [*sic*] from killing offhand this equivocal
> element in their midst (καὶ τὸ παρ' ἑκάστοις ἀμφίβολον), they feared these
> neutrals [or, better, "mixed"] as much as pronounced aliens (καὶ μεμιγμένον
> ὡς βεβαίως ἀλλόφυλον ἐφοβεῖτο).[7]

Between the "two camps" of Jews and Greeks in each city was the unpre-
dictable, ambiguous group of judaizers, whom the Syrian Greeks did not
kill but did treat as foreigners. These were a "mixed" element, Greek in
origin but sympathetic to the Jews and, therefore, the Syrians treated them
with suspicion. In the first century, the Greek people of the city of Damascus encountered a similar problem. Planning to kill the Jews of their
city, they assembled them in the gymnasium to implement their plan: "their

only fear was of their own wives who, with few exceptions, had all become subject to (or been brought under) the Jewish religion (ὑπηγμένας τῇ Ἰουδαϊκῇ θρησκείᾳ), and so their efforts were mainly directed to keeping the secret from them" (*War* 2.559-60).[8]

The Roman satirist Juvenal (c.55-140 CE) criticizes Gentile attraction to Judaism in his fourteenth satire. He bitterly laments how, frequently, children not only inherited the weaknesses of their parents but were even more deeply affected by the inherited vice than the previous generation had been. At one point, Juvenal complains (*Satires* 14.96-106) about the effect a judaizing father has on his child:

> Some, whose lot it was to have Sabbath-fearing fathers, worship nothing but clouds and the *numen* of the heavens, and think it as great a crime to eat pork, from which their parents abstained, as human flesh. They get themselves circumcised, and look down on Roman law, preferring instead to learn and honour and fear the Jewish commandments, whatever was handed down by Moses in that arcane tome of his—never to show the way to any but fellow-believers (if they ask where to get some water, find out if they're foreskinless). But their fathers were the culprits: they made every seventh day taboo for all life's business, dedicated to idleness.

Juvenal provides a vivid and detailed description of two different positions within the spectrum of Gentile attraction to Judaism. While the father judaized by means of observing a small number of Jewish rites (such as the Sabbath and abstention from eating pork), the son quite immerses himself in Judaism, to the point, perhaps, of making a full conversion (i.e., he becomes circumcised and honours the Jewish law). Juvenal's problem with Judaism is that it is foreign and anti-Roman (a *barbara superstitio*) and he gives expression to the negative attitude found in contemporary Roman literary circles regarding Jewish abstinence from pork, interaction with non-Jews, and the Sabbath (e.g., Tacitus, *Histories* 5.5). The satirist mocks in particular the fact that a son of a Roman would choose to observe Jewish law over and above Roman law (Gager 1985: 58-59). From Juvenal's perspective, by their actions this father and son are traitors to law and order, the most essential components of Roman society; for him this behaviour is baffling and worthy of derision.

The Appeal of Judaism among the Powerful

JUDAISM'S APPEAL IN THE ROMAN EMPIRE extended to people from the upper echelons of society. An inscription from Acmonia in Phrygia, dated to the 80s or 90s CE, refers to the restoration of a synagogue originally built by a woman named Julia Severa in the 50s or 60s CE (Trebilco 1991: 59; CIJ #766). Numismatic and epigraphic evidence shows that Julia Severa was involved in the Imperial cult of the city during the reign of Nero, serving as a high priestess (ἀρχιέρεια) and a judge or president of games (ἀγωνοθέτης). Given the fact that she was a priestess of a pagan cult, it is likely that Julia Severa was a Gentile patroness of the Jewish community who financed the building of a synagogue rather than an apostate Jew who held an authoritative role in a pagan religion but nonetheless donated money to build a synagogue (Trebilco 1991: 59; Wilson 2000: 364). That the Jewish community at Acmonia obtained the patronage of Julia Severa is significant, for she was clearly a woman of high standing. Her first husband, Servenius Capito, was a powerful man, and their son, L. Servenius Cornutus, served in the Senate under Nero and, in 73 CE, was legatus to the proconsul of Asia. Another relative of the family, C. Iulius Severus, served as a consul (Trebilco 1991: 59-60; Stern 1964: 158 n.24; Walton 1929). In Severa, the Jews of Acmonia would have had a significant and powerful ally.

Another local dignitary (probably some time in the third century CE) who favoured the Jewish community in Phocea with a donation to the synagogue was Tation, daughter of Straton son of Empedon. She constructed the assembly hall and the enclosure of the open courtyard with her own funds, "as a gift to the Jews" (Lifshitz 13; CIJ #738). In recognition of her generosity, the Jewish community gave her a golden crown and the privilege of sitting in the seat of honour in the synagogue.

Luke, writing in the final decades of the first century CE, refers to a Gentile who built a synagogue. The author reports that the Jews of Capernaum say that a centurion "loves our people and it is he who built our synagogue for us" (Luke 7:5). While the story as it appears in the gospel of Luke may not be historical—the parallel account in Matthew 8:5-13 does not mention a connection between the centurion and a synagogue—it reflects what Luke thought plausible. Other examples of Gentiles from the upper class who are drawn to Judaism include the Ethiopian eunuch described in Acts 8:27 who "had come to Jerusalem to worship," and was a man of high standing who served as a court official of Candace, queen of the Ethiopians, "in charge of her entire treasury." Cornelius, a Roman centurion of the Italian Cohort, is described by the author of Acts as "a devout man who feared God" (φοβούμενος τὸν θεόν) (Acts 10:2). He was a man who "prayed constantly to God" (Acts 10:1-2) and was "well spoken of by the whole Jewish nation" (Acts 10:22). Some caution is advisable, since part of Luke's purpose is to present Christianity as a movement benign to the Roman authorities, and this motive may underlie his identifying the first Gentile convert to Christianity as a Roman centurion. There is nothing in this story or the others, however, to indicate that the author thought that his readers would not have believed the Gentiles' connection to Judaism.

Certain senatorial families in the first century CE had connections with Judaism. Stern and Feldman each conjecture that one possible judaizer from the senatorial aristocracy was Pomponia Graecina, the wife of Aulus Plautius, who lived until about 83 CE (Stern 1987: 383; Feldman 1993: 310). According to Tacitus, in 57 CE this "distinguished lady...was accused of some foreign superstition (*externae superstitionis rea*) and handed over to her husband's judicial decision" (Tacitus, *Ann.* 13.32). The most that can be said about this piece of evidence, however, is that involvement in Judaism *may* be meant (Leon 1995: 252). The example of Fulvia is more secure evidence for direct association of a person of elevated social status with Judaism. She is described as "a woman of high rank who had become a Jewish proselyte" (τῶν ἐν ἀξιώματι γυναικῶν καὶ νομιμοις προσεληλυθυῖαν τοῖς Ἰουδαϊκοῖς), who was swindled by a group of Jewish thieves out of gold and purple that she had intended for the temple authorities in Jerusalem (Josephus, *Ant.* 18.81-82). Her husband, Saturninus, who reported the incident to the Emperor Tiberius, may have been a member of the senate (Stern 1964: 161). A further example of Jewish influence among leading administrators is found in Acts (13:6-12): by the story's conclusion, the proconsul of Cyprus, Sergius Paulus, has been convinced by Paul's words and becomes a Christian. Significantly for our purposes, the proconsul initially is described by Luke as keeping company with Bar-Jesus, whom Luke describes as a Jewish false prophet.

Attraction to Judaism extended to certain members of the imperial families of Rome. Poppaea Sabina, initially the mistress and later the wife of Emperor Nero, used her influence on behalf of Jews on two occasions (Josephus, *Ant.* 20.191; *Life* 16). Josephus describes Poppaea as a θεοσεβής who "pleaded on behalf of the Jews" (*Ant.* 20.195). There is much debate among scholars over the degree to which Poppaea was an adherent of Judaism. The problem rests on the interpretation of the word θεοσεβής. Many scholars understand this term to be synonymous with the Lukan references to "those who fear God" (φεβούμενοι τὸν θεόν, Acts 10:2, 22, 35; 13:16, 26) and "those who revere God" (σεβόμενοι τὸν θεόν, Acts 13:43, 50; 16:14; 17:4, 17; 18:7). As noted in the discussion of the Aphrodisias inscription, the term θεοσεβής has a double meaning: it can refer to "pious" Jews or Gentiles, and to Gentile sympathizers who were attracted to Judaism but did not fully convert.

The ambiguity of the term necessitates careful evaluation of its meaning according to the context in which the term is found. Josephus calls Poppaea a θεοσεβής right after his description of how she had "pleaded on behalf of the Jews" (*Ant.* 20.195) regarding the wall erected by the Jews to block the invasive gaze of King Agrippa into the Temple. After stating that Nero judged in favour of the Jews after having heard the case presented by both sides (Josephus, *Ant.* 20.195), Josephus immediately writes: "in this [Nero] showed favour to his wife Poppaea, who was a θεοσεβής"—rendered "a worshipper of God" by Feldman (1965: 105). Certainly the context of these comments about Poppaea suggests that, in Josephus' view, Poppaea's intervention on behalf of the Jews was representative of a special connection with the Jewish community. He describes her not as a convert to Judaism but as a "pro-Jewish" Gentile.[9] Some might argue that allowance needs to be made for the possibility that this view of Poppaea was simply wishful thinking on the part of Josephus.[10] But, with both Nero and Poppaea held in very low esteem by the time Josephus wrote *Antiquities*, there would appear to be little benefit in making a spurious claim linking Poppaea with Judaism, either for Josephus himself, or for the reputation of Judaism (also Mason 1996: 5).

If Poppaea found Judaism intriguing in some way, she certainly was not unique among upper-class women. Luke mentions that the Jews in Pisidian Antioch "incited the devout women of high standing" (Acts 13: 50), and that "not a few of the leading women" were present in the synagogue at which Paul preached in Thessalonica (Acts 17: 4), as well as in a synagogue in Beroea (Acts 17:12). Likewise, Fulvia, Julia Severa, Tation, and the women of Damascus who were drawn to Judaism were all women of high social standing.[11] Indeed, attraction to Judaism and attendance at synagogue meetings could very well have been "fashionable" activities for upper-class pagan women in the first century CE (Henderson 1903: 467; Williams 1988: 111).[12]

Interestingly, in the apocryphal Acts of Pilate, the following statement is made by Pilate: "You know that my wife is pious (θεοσεβής) and prefers to practice Judaism (ἰουδαΐζει) with you" (2.1). Perhaps aware of the sympathy of noble Roman women toward Judaism, the author makes Pilate's wife a judaizer. There is little agreement among scholars as to when the document was written, but a date sometime in the late first or early second century CE for the story, when an author would likely have had access to the four gospels and been familiar with Gentile attraction to Judaism, seems a reasonable proposal—especially if the reference to the "Acts of Pontius Pilate" in Justin Martyr's *First Apology* (1.35, 38) is indeed to this document.

Another Jewish connection with the imperial family came via the relationship between Titus, elder son of Emperor Vespasian, and Berenice, a great-granddaughter of Herod the Great and daughter of Agrippa i. Titus became smitten with Berenice during his campaign against the Jews in 66-70 CE, and, in 75 CE, she came to Rome as his mistress (Tacitus, *History* 2.2; Suetonius, *Titus* 7; Dio Cassius 66.15, 18; see Crook 1951: 162-75). Her stay in Rome was tense, as she was not well-liked: "she was ostentatious, wore huge diamonds, and behaved in an arrogant fashion, claiming privileges which did not belong to her" (Benko 1971: 64; see Juvenal, *Satires* 6: 156; also Kraft 1971: 88). In *War*, Josephus emphasizes the Jewishness of Berenice and her brother Agrippa. Josephus had been in correspondence with the latter from Rome (*Life* 364-67). In *Antiquities*, though, he turns on them, hinting at an incestuous relationship between Berenice and her brother (*Ant.* 20.145; Crook 1951: 163 n. 9).[13] Queen Berenice may have exerted a political influence in Rome that was unlikely to have won support among the populace. Quintilian, during his discussion of biased judges who presided over cases "where their own interests were involved," reveals that "I myself, when I appeared on behalf of Queen Berenice, actually pleaded before her" (*Institutio* 4.1.19). According to Suetonius, Titus "sent Queen Berenice away from Rome, which was painful for both of them," presumably because their relationship had caused a stir in that city (*Titus* 7).

Gentile interest in Judaism continued to penetrate the highest aristocratic circles of the Roman empire during the reign of Emperor Domitian (81-96 CE); the devastating loss of the Jews to the Romans in 70 CE did not quell interest in Judaism. Flavius Clemens, a Roman consul and cousin of Domitian, was executed in c.95 CE and his wife Domitilla was banished when, according to Dio Cassius, both were charged with "atheism [ἀθεότης], a charge on which many others who drifted [εξοκέλλοντες] into Jewish ways [τὰ τῶν Ἰουδαίων ἤθη] were condemned. Some of these were put to death, and the rest were at least deprived of their property" (*Roman History*, 67.14.2). Prior to this, because he had no sons of his own, Domitian had named the two sons of this couple as his successors, changing their names to Vespasian and Domitian (Suetonius, *Domitian* 15).

The charge of atheism (ἀθεότης) was levelled, in fact, against both Christians and Jews at times. In *First Apology*, Justin Martyr combats the charge of "atheism" targeting Christians. Indeed, in Christian tradition, Flavius Clemens and Domitilla are presented as martyrs from the period of Domitian's persecution of the Christians. The earliest testimony is that of Eusebius, who presents Domitilla as the niece of Clemens instead of his wife, and explains that she was banished to the island of Ponita for being a Christian (Eusebius, *Hist. eccl.* 3.18, 4-5). The first source that presents Clemens as a Christian is that of Syncellus, written in the ninth century CE (Stern 1980: 381). Given the fact that Judaism was a religion protected by Roman law, some scholars have suggested that perhaps those who faced persecution for adhering to "Jewish customs" were actually Christians and not Jews (Benko 1971: 67; Reicke 1965: 224-25).

This argument, ultimately, is not persuasive. In *Against Apion* (2.148), Josephus notes that Apollonius reviles Jews "as atheists" (ὡς ἀθέους); (Keresztes 1979: 262). Leon and Feldman each note that, although Dio does not refer to Christians, it is certain that by his time (150-235 CE) he could distinguish between Jews and Christians (Feldman 1993: 332). Leon states: "[t]hat the well-known Christian catacomb of Domitilla was dug on the private estate of a certain Flavia Domitilla is an unquestioned fact. Still, the definite statement in Dio, a historian who surely knew the difference between Judaism and Christianity, seems to compel the conclusion that Clemens and Domitilla were convicted as judaizers" (Leon 1995: 35).[14] It is, furthermore, significant that ancient Christian sources do not identify Clemens as a Christian prior to the ninth century.

According to Suetonius, Domitian's agents collected the *fiscus Iudaicus*, or Jewish tax, "with a peculiar lack of mercy" (*Domitian* 12). Two categories of people were delineated as targets for taxation: those who concealed their Jewish extraction and had not been paying the tax (*dissimulata origine imposita genti tributa non pependissent*); and those who lived as Jews without professing Judaism (*improfessi Iudaicam viverent vitam*). The first group included born Jews who felt themselves to be distant from Judaism and had not paid the tax to the fiscus; the second group included Gentiles who lived like Jews but had not fully converted to Judaism and, hence, did not consider themselves to be Jews. It is notable that judaizers were a large enough group for Domitian to target for fiscal gain.

Emperor Nerva, who succeeded Domitian in 96 CE, instituted a more benevolent administration for gathering the Jewish tax. According to Dio Cassius, under his rule, "no persons were permitted to accuse anybody... of adopting the Jewish mode of life" (τοῖς δὲ δὴ ἄλλοις...οὔτ' Ἰουδαϊκοῦ βίου καταιτιᾶσθαί τινας συνεχώρησες (*Roman History* 68.1, 2). A special coin memorialized this action; it reads FISCI IVDAICI CALVMNIA SVBLATA S.C., surrounding a date palm, the emblem of Judea (Carson 1990: 35; Mattingly and Sydenham 1926: plate VII. 124; Meshorer 1997: 131-32; Richardson and Shukster 1983).[15]

The considerable degree of Gentile attraction to Judaism in the first century CE, in Rome and other areas of the Roman Empire, penetrated different social levels, including people from the general populace but particularly those from the aristocratic class. It is especially intriguing that plausible Jewish connections can be traced to members of the families of three emperors: Nero (54-68 CE) via his mistress Poppaea; Titus, through his association with Berenice, Herod the Great's great-granddaughter; and Domitian (81-96 CE), who condemned to death his cousin Flavius Clemens and banished Clemens' wife Domitilla, the parents of Domitian's successors and his closest surviving relatives, for being associated with Judaism. The fact that Herod the Great's children and grandchildren were raised and educated in the imperial household in Rome probably contributed toward cultivating this connection with Judaism.

The evidence, moreover, demonstrates that attraction to Judaism was expressed in diverse ways. Wealthy Roman aristocrat Fulvia (Josephus, *Ant.* 18.81-82) underwent conversion to Judaism. The God-fearers mentioned in the Aphrodisias inscription, and Julia Severa from Acmonia, stopped short of full conversion and, perhaps in addition to other Jewish observances, were attached to the synagogue. Josephus and Juvenal note the pervasiveness of Gentile observance of a number of Jewish rituals (such as maintaining the Sabbath and food laws) in *Against Apion* 2.282 and *Satires* 14.96-106. The Damascene women described by Josephus (*War* 2.559-60) and Nero's mistress and wife Poppaea furthermore expressed their respect for Judaism by siding with the Jews and supporting their causes.

How Did Attraction to Judaism Occur?

THE QUESTION OF WHETHER JUDAISM was a "missionary religion" in terms of Jews self-consciously seeking converts during the period of Christian origins has been debated often.[16] Such scholars as McKnight (1991) and Goodman (1992, 1994) have argued persuasively that a distinction ought to be made between the passive reception of converts or interested pagans, and the desire to convert the non-Jewish world to Judaism.[17] Indeed, the presence of pagan attraction or association with Judaism in antiquity does not imply a strong missionary effort toward Gentiles by Jews. What it does imply is non-Jewish exposure to Jewish tradition.

Pagan exposure to Jewish lifestyles primarily occurred through social networks and interpersonal connections between Gentiles and Jews rather than through self-conscious, aggressive tactics, as part of an institutionally organized missionary effort on the part of Jews. In his recent foray into the sphere of Christian origins, sociologist Rodney Stark asserts that "[t]he basis for successful conversionist movements is growth through social networks, through a *structure of direct and intimate interpersonal attach-*

EVIDENCE OF GENTILE ASSOCIATION WITH JUDAISM

	Persons of non-Jewish origin	Manifestation(s) of attraction or association with Judaism	How exposure to Judaism might have occurred	Source(s)
a	multitudes of Greeks	use of Jewish customs	attraction to Jewish customs from living in proximity to Jews	Josephus (*War* 7.45)
b	Romans	follow Jewish ways	Jews who "had flocked to Rome in great numbers" to convert and were later banished by Tiberius	Dio Cassius (*Roman History* 57, 18.5a)
c	more than 50 Gentiles	contribute to soup kitchen with Jews; convert to Judaism; involved in prayer group	involvement in civic duty with Jews, exposure by living in same city with Jews	Aphrodisias (inscription)
d	Roman sons	"worship nothing but clouds"; avoid eating pork; are circumcised	influence of kin (i.e., Sabbath-fearing fathers)	Juvenal (*Satires* 14.96–106)
e	Titus (17–81 CE)	brings Queen Berenice to live with him in imperial household	personal relationship	Tacitus (*Histories* 2.2); Suetonius (*Titus* 7); Dio Cassius (*Roman History* 66.15, 66.18)
f	royal household of Adiabene	convert to Judaism	Ananias, a travelling Jewish merchant; an unnamed Jew who instructed Queen Helena; Eleazar from Galilee, who came to pay respects to king	Josephus (*Ant.* 20.17–96)

ments" (Stark 1996: 20). He further explains that "typically people do not *seek* a faith; they *encounter* one through their ties to other people who already accept this faith. In the end, accepting a new religion is part of conforming to the expectations and examples of one's family and friends" (Stark 1996: 56). These comments are applicable to the phenomenon of pagan exposure, attraction and conversion to Judaism in antiquity.[18]

From among all of the examples cited that provide evidence of Gentile attraction to Judaism, six offer explanations for how the pagan individuals discussed came into contact with Judaism. In the above table, for five of the groups of persons discussed—a, c, d, e, f—exposure to Judaism occurred through interpersonal attachments rather than impersonal mass campaigns for new converts.

In example (a), Josephus states that Jews "were constantly attracting to their religious ceremonies multitudes of Greeks, and these they had in some measure incorporated with themselves" (*War* 7.45). The statement implies that the Gentiles were attracted by the lifestyle maintained by the Jews living in their midst, not by proselytizing efforts made by Jews to draw them in. As Goodman has observed, "[o]ne would expect a great deal to be said about such a mission in the works of Philo and Josephus if Jews wished all Gentiles to take so momentous a step. But in fact these authors have little about proselytes and nothing about a mission to win them" (1992: 70-71). Regarding (d), Wolfgang Wiefel states that the Jewish "tendency toward proselytism, still active in the second half of the [first] century, is described in these words by Juvenal" (1999: 99). While Juvenal provides evidence for the dissemination of Jewish customs in Rome through parental influence—including not eating pork, becoming circumcised, and observing the Sabbath—he does not tell us why or how the father became involved in Jewish practices in the first place. The last part—"never to show the way to any but fellow-believers"—in fact suggests that the Jews were reluctant to share their "secrets" with non-Jews. McKnight suggests, in fact, that Juvenal's words can be taken as evidence that Judaism was *not* missionary in character (1991: 113). Indeed, Juvenal's description demonstrates how pagan attraction to Judaism was facilitated through intimate interpersonal connections with friends or, in this case, family members, who already were attached in some way to Judaism.[19]

The only statement among these examples that indicates that Jews aggressively sought new converts among pagans is (b). Dio Cassius is said by John of Antioch (seventh century CE) to have written the following in the early third century CE: "As the Jews flocked to Rome in great numbers and were converting many of the natives to their ways, [Tiberius] banished most of them" (*History of Rome* 57.18.5a). There are, however, a number of problems associated with this statement. While Dio Cassius states that the Jews were expelled for actively converting non-Jews to Judaism, this explanation is missing in earlier histories by Josephus, Tacitus, and Suetonius who nevertheless comment on the expulsion. Josephus describes the rather curious story about an aristocratic Roman proselyte named Fulvia (*Ant.* 18.81-84) who is cheated by unscrupulous Jews who are after her money and that this is the cause of the expulsion. It has been argued that Tacitus, who reports on the proscription of Egyptian and Jewish rights and the expulsion of 4,000 enfranchised slaves "tainted with that superstition,"(*Ann.* 2.85) simply did not know the real reason for the expulsion (Georgi 1986: 92–93). This argument seems odd, since Tacitus was formerly a supervisor of foreign cults and would have been interested in precisely this type of reason for the event; therefore, if conversion were the cause, Tacitus is unlikely to have been ignorant of it. Suetonius (*Tiberius* 36) also writes nothing about proselytizing tactics as the causal factor for the expulsion:

> [Tiberius] abolished foreign cults, especially the Egyptian and the Jewish rites, compelling all who were addicted to such superstitions to burn their religious vestments and all their paraphernalia. Those of the Jews who were of military age he assigned to provinces of less healthy climate, ostensibly to serve in the army; the others of the same race or of similar beliefs he banished from the city, on pain of slavery for life if they did not obey.

The information attributed to Dio Cassius must be seen in light of descriptions given by other authors for the banishment of the Jews by Tiberius in 19 CE. He is the only historian to suggest that non-Jewish interest in Judaism was caused by Jews actively seeking converts. Significantly, the statement itself is not found in the manuscript traditions of Dio Cassius, but in only one quotation by the seventh-century Christian writer John of Antioch. Goodman rightly suggests, if the statement is indeed a verbatim quotation from Dio Cassius—which is not certain—it is possible that it more accurately reflects Jewish involvement in missionary activities in the third century CE when Dio Cassius wrote rather than the situation in the first century CE, about which he was writing (1994: 83).[20]

The Conversion of the Royal House of Adiabene

THE STORY OF THE CONVERSION of the royal house of Adiabene at Charax Spasinou, a small kingdom on the Tigris river (i.e., [f] in the table above), in the first half of the first century CE, is told proudly by Josephus (*Ant.* 20.34–48). It is frequently used by scholars as evidence for the existence of aggressive Jewish missionaries and proof that Judaism of antiquity organized self-conscious missionary efforts. The story need not necessarily be understood in this way, however: it more effectively illustrates how exposure of non-Jews to Judaism was generated naturally, through personal interaction between Jews and pagans.

Josephus describes how "a certain Jewish merchant named Ananias visited the king's wives and taught them to worship God after the manner of the Jewish tradition" (*Ant.* 20.34). He also records that Queen Helena "had likewise been instructed by another Jew and had been brought over to their laws" (δὲ καὶ τὴν᾽ Ελένην ὁμοίως ὑφ᾽ ἑτέρου τινὸς ᾽Ιουδαίου διδαχθεῖσαν εἰς τοὺς ἐκείνων μετακεκομίσθαι νόμους (*Ant.* 20.35). Unfortunately, Josephus does not offer further information concerning this Jewish instructor; he states that, "when Izates had learned that his mother was very much pleased with the Jewish religion, he was zealous to convert to it himself" (*Ant.* 20.38). In his zeal, Izates wished to become circumcised. Queen Helena persuaded him not to do so, however, because she feared that it would negatively impact his political prospects and the merchant Ananias agreed with Helena's counsel (*Ant.* 20.41). Despite this advice, Izates continued to desire to be circumcised, and when another Jew "named Eleazar, who came from Galilee and who had a reputation for being extremely strict when it came to the ancestral laws, urged him to carry out the rite" (*Ant.* 20.43), he did so.

This narrative *is* evidence that individual Jews taught Gentiles about Judaism. It is imprudent, however, to build a whole typology of organized missionary activity from this story like that of the Christians described in Acts, as some scholars have done.[21] In his description of the two Jewish teachers of the royal family, Josephus does not say anything about their travelling specifically to convert others to Judaism. Indeed, he describes Ananias as a merchant who was presumably on a business trip, and makes it clear that Eleazar had come to Adiabene to pay respects to the king's family (*Ant.* 20.44; see Goodman 1992: 57; Goodman 1994: 84).

The story of the conversion in Adiabene demonstrates how pagans might have become exposed to Jewish traditions through personal relations occurring as a result of business or social connections, or through travel. Multitudes of people journeyed on Roman roads and by sea during the early centuries, including those involved in trade, such as merchants and buyers, bankers and shipowners, as well as governmental workers, such as mail deliverers, and military personnel. While commerce and government comprised a large number of travellers, other reasons to travel included health (i.e., to the sanctuaries of Asclepius or to the *aquae*, the mineral springs), observing or participating in international Greek games and spectacles sponsored by the Roman emperors (e.g., Titus inaugurated the Colosseum with one hundred days of exhibitions), and holidaying (Casson 1974: 130-37). Ananias and Eleazar travelled for business and social reasons and, along their way, instructed interested non-Jews about Judaism.

Gentile attraction to Judaism does not imply a vigorous missionary effort by Jews, but simply exposure to Jewish lifestyles. Two modern examples are relevant to this discussion, one involving "indianizing" by non-native Americans (Hallowell 1963), and the other regarding the attraction of African-Americans to the religion of Islam. Pasto (1994: 5) states:

> European contact with native Americans produced a fairly widespread phe-
> nomenon of colonialists "going Indian." In some cases this involved an
> adoption process whereby the European became an "Indian." However, in
> other cases we find groups of Europeans taking on some native American
> rituals and ideas and calling themselves Indians....None of this is a result
> of active missionization by native Americans.[22]

The adherence of African-Americans to Islam provides a similar example. Pasto observes that "although the impetus may have come from an
Islamic missionary preacher, the development of the Nation of Islam was
largely independent of mainstream Islam. There was never any major
effort by other Muslims to convert Africans in America" (1994: 5).

Did the attachment of aristocrats to Judaism—perhaps on account of
a particular "fashion trend"—have an effect on the subjects of the Roman
Empire? Did it serve as an example to be emulated by the masses? Did the
harsh reaction of Domitian toward Flavius Clemens and Domitilla stem
from his fear that attraction to Judaism would spread if these two prominent judaizers remained in Rome? According to Suetonius, Augustus
praised his grandson Gaius for not worshipping in the temple in Jerusalem
during his journey through the east (*Augustus* 93). Perhaps, as Cohen
suggests, "the emperor felt that worship at the temple might encourage
'judaizing' among the Romans" (1987: 415).

As Stark states, "the network assumption is not compatible with an
image of proselytizers seeking out most converts along the streets and
highways, or calling them forth from the crowds in the marketplaces"
(1996: 56-57). Non-Jewish attraction to Judaism, expressed through full
conversion or through the adoption of various Jewish customs by Gentiles,
does not necessarily imply that Judaism had a clear missionary impulse that
impelled individual Jews to draw others into their movement. What it
does imply is, simply, that pagans were exposed to Jewish traditions and
ways of life. The evidence presented in this chapter demonstrates that this
exposure occurred mainly by means of personal connections between Jews
and Gentiles. The adoption of various Jewish practices occurred naturally
through social contact as neighbours rather than through organized pur-
suit of converts by Jews. Non-Jewish attraction to Judaism was the result
of Jews and Gentiles living in proximity to one another.[23] The dispersion
of many Jewish communities throughout the Roman Empire meant that
Gentiles and Jews often shared the same city. Gentiles had Jewish friends
and maybe relatives, and they would have had opportunities to participate
in Jewish festivals and to attend synagogue services. As shown here, pagan

exposure to Judaism took place through informal contact made between Jews and Gentiles who shared the same social world as fellow travellers, business associates, neighbours, and friends.

◄o►

CHAPTER 3

Christian Judaizing in Galatia:
Paul's Letter to the Galatians

◄○►

PAUL'S LETTER TO GALATIA abounds with polemic directed against what he perceives to be views discordant with his own. The frequently vehement tone of his arguments reveals that he understands these opposing views to represent very real threats to the Christian communities to which he writes, and to his own identity as a leader of these communities. Whereas Paul's negative statements about certain aspects of the Jewish Law have been understood by later generations of Christians and scholars to target Jews, Jewish Christians, or Judaism, in the original context of the letter they were meant to correct the practices of *Gentile* Christians.

Paul's letters are occasional, that is, they were written in order to address historical circumstances and problems specific to individual communities. He and the recipients of his correspondence were well aware of the circumstances that prompted the letters. For modern readers, however, these factors are largely opaque. The ambiguous nature of many of the details provided in the letters has led to a wide variety of scholarly reconstructions of the historical circumstances behind each of the letters, as well as numerous suggestions as to the origin and essence of each of the disagreements. In order to reconstruct the historical context of each of the letters, understanding the nature of the crisis reflected in each letter and what Paul's opponents might have argued is of pivotal importance. While Paul's rivals may indeed have written letters or speeches, they are not extant. The only access we have to the teachings and perspectives of Paul's adversaries, therefore, is through his criticism of them. The ensuing treatment here focuses on the parts of the letter to the Galatians containing Paul's polemic against his enemies in Galatia with the intention of reconstructing the identities and positions of these opponents.

The Presence of Christian Judaizers in Galatia

TO PARAPHRASE SHAKESPEARE, something was rotten in the province of Galatia. The letter to the Galatians is one of Paul's most emotionally

---

Notes to chapter 3 start on page 157

charged pieces of correspondence with the struggling communities of early
Christians in Asia Minor (Betz 1979: 11-12). It may also be one of Paul's
earliest letters, probably written between c. 52-56 CE after the Jerusalem
conference while Paul was at Ephesus (see Murphy-O'Connor 1996: 180;
Roetzel 1998: 96).[1] According to Paul, opponents have infiltrated the community and are compelling Gentile Christians to adhere to Jewish customs. Some of the Galatian Gentile Christians have submitted to circumcision and are observing other aspects of the Mosaic law as well. For Paul,
this behaviour represents a fundamental threat to the truth regarding faith
in Christ that he preached and under which most of the Gentiles in Galatia initially converted to Christianity.

While it is impossible to arrive at a complete picture of what each situation was like, in order to understand the circumstances addressed by Paul
in his letters, and against whom he argues, one must attempt to understand
the environment in which he writes. This means examining the particular
sociological and historical contexts behind Paul's comments to the Galatian community; in the words of John Elliott, one must cultivate a "sociological imagination" (1981: 5) to understand the socio-historical circumstances that prompted the writing of the letter to the Galatians.[2]

I argue here that an accurate reconstruction of the crisis reflected in
Paul's letter to the Galatians is one in which Christian judaizers are among
the primary agitators and opponents of Paul.[3] Attention is paid to Paul's
argumentation against the teaching of his opponents in Galatians; concomitantly, the following questions are explored: To whom does Paul address
his letter? What is the meaning of Ἰουδαΐζειν in Galatians 2:14? Who
"compelled" Gentile Christians in Galatia to observe the Mosaic law?
and Why did Gentile Christians in Galatia observe the Mosaic law?

To Whom Does Paul Address His Letter?

PAUL IS INCENSED THAT MEMBERS of the Galatian community, which he
himself had founded, are deserting his own teachings "and are turning to
a different gospel" (εἰς ἕτερον εὐαγγέλιον) (Gal. 1:6). The recipients of the
letter had undergone initiatory baptism "into Christ" (3:27) and were
once pagans "enslaved to beings that by nature are not gods" (4:8). They
are now being confused by a corrupt version of the gospel (1:7). While the
Galatians had rejoiced and warmly welcomed Paul when he initially came
to stay with them, their enthusiasm toward him apparently had waned, for
he asks: "What has become of the good will you felt? For I testify that, had
it been possible, you would have torn out your eyes and given them to me"

(4:15). The letter furthermore reflects the fact that male Gentile Christians in Galatia are being persuaded to become circumcised (2:3; 5:2-12; 6:12, 15). It is clear that the recipients of the letter are Gentile Christians, and that they are Paul's central focus.

In 5:2-3 readers learn for the first time that, in turning from Paul's teaching and accepting a "different gospel," Gentile Christians are becoming circumcised,[4] when Paul states: "Listen! I, Paul, am telling you that if you have yourselves circumcised (ὅτι ἐὰν περιτέμνησθε),[5] Christ will be of no benefit to you. Once again I testify to every person who receives circumcision (παντὶ ἀνθρώπῳ περιτεμνομένῳ) that he is obliged to obey the entire law." Paul tries to convince the Galatians of the logical outcome of a decision to submit to circumcision: once they are circumcised, they are obligated to keep the whole law. Given that many Jews did not in fact keep the law in its entirety, Paul's statement is somewhat confusing. Perhaps he was compelled to make the statement in 5:2-3 because he perceived the Galatian Gentile Christians to be unaware that if they became circumcised on the understanding that this step was necessary for their salvation, they thereby became legally obligated to the rest of Judaic law. He may have felt that the Gentile Christians were ignorant of the full significance of their action either because the people teaching the Galatians to become circumcised were themselves ignorant of this step's implications, or because they were deliberately attempting to mislead the Galatians. In order to dissuade Gentile Christians in Galatia from submitting to circumcision, Paul argues that becoming circumcised is an indication of a desire to be "subject to the law" (4:21) and "justified by the law" (5:4).

Paul addresses his letter to Gentile Christians who are observing Jewish customs, and he understands this behaviour as an attempt to become justified through Jewish law and thereby compromise their faith in Jesus. In 6:12, Paul states: "It is those who want to make a good showing in the flesh that try to compel you to be circumcised" (οὗτοι ἀναγκάζουσιν ὑμᾶς περιτέμνεσθαι) (Gal. 6:12). Paul also tells the Galatians that though the ones putting the pressure on the Gentiles to be circumcised do not keep the law themselves, they nevertheless "want you to be circumcised" (θέλουσιν ὑμᾶς περιτέμνεσθαι) (Gal. 6:13).[6] Paul's adversaries, as one scholar suggests, "were now urging the Galatians to accept circumcision as the rite by which they could become sons of Abraham and participants in the blessings of the Abrahamic covenant" (Burton 1921: 274).

When Paul was with the Galatians last, they were "running well," but now their situation has completely changed and they are being prevented from "obeying the truth" (5:7). The introduction of a new teaching into the Galatian churches caused internal controversy and strife among members, for Paul warns members of the communities "if you bite and devour one another, take care that you are not consumed by one another" (5:15). In Paul's view, communal unity is of crucial importance, thus in his eyes the situation in the Galatian churches is dire indeed.

The Meaning of Ἰουδαΐζειν in Galatians 2:14

IN GALATIANS 2:11–14, PAUL DESCRIBES a serious disagreement between him and Peter that had occurred at an earlier unspecified time in Antioch, Syria. Paul relates that Peter would eat with Gentiles—presumably Gentile Christians—in Antioch but, on the arrival of a particular group of men "from James" (2:12), he ceased this contact with Gentiles. Paul suggests that Peter acted as he did from "fear" of these men, whom he refers to later as "the circumcised" (2:12) (φοβούμενος τοὺς ἐκ περιτομῆς)—a group likely composed of Jewish Christians from Jerusalem who were influenced by James. In Paul's view, Peter was aware of the truth—that is, that Gentile Christians did not need to become law observant and that fellowship between Christians of Jewish origin and Gentile origin was harmless and in fact desirable—but was feigning obedience to the law (τῇ ὑποκρίσει) from his concern about how the people from James would judge his interaction with Gentiles. Paul, deeply annoyed by Peter's inconsistent behaviour, tells how "the other Jews" collaborated with Peter by similarly withdrawing from sharing table fellowship with Gentile Christians, so that "even Barnabas" was influenced (v. 13). The consequence of the Jewish Christians' separation from the Gentile Christians was that the Gentile Christians in Antioch, with whom Peter initially ate, were put in an awkward position and felt pressured to observe Jewish law (i.e., to judaize). According to Paul, Peter, who acted out of fear, may have been ignorant of the repercussions his behaviour would have on Gentile Christians.[7]

In verse 14, Paul reports that he asked Peter: "If you, though a Jew, live like a Gentile and not like a Jew, how can you compel the Gentiles to live like Jews" (ἀναγκάζεις Ἰουδαΐζειν)?[8] Here we encounter the term pertinent to our understanding of what was occurring in Galatia: Ἰουδαΐζειν (to judaize). As explained earlier, the meaning of this verb describes the phenomenon of Gentiles observing certain components of the Mosaic law without converting to Judaism. Esler argues that Paul's use of the term means "to become a Jew or to live like a Jew, but in either case to be circumcised, given the ways…in which Paul ties the two situations together" (1994: 61). But looking more broadly at the use of the term reveals that judaizing does not *necessarily* entail circumcision, although it *may* include it. Josephus' use of the term shows that circumcision was not automatically assumed to be a part of judaizing behaviour when he describes how Metilius, the commander of the Roman garrison and sole survivor of a vicious battle, "saved his life by entreaties and promises to judaize *as far as circumcision*" (emphasis added; τοῦτον γὰρ ἱκετεύσαντα καὶ μέχρι περιτομῆς ἰουδαΐζειν) (*War* 2:454).[9] To "judaize," then, can refer to Gentiles who adopt some of a variety of Jewish customs, without necessarily undergoing circumcision.[10]

In Galatians 2:11-14, Paul addresses Peter's behaviour and the consequences of his actions in Antioch. From Paul's perspective, by withdrawing from Gentile table fellowship, Peter was sending a message to the Gentile believers of Antioch. The message to Antiochene Gentile Christians was that they were to judaize (ἰουδαΐζειν), by observing the rules of *kashruth*—and perhaps other Jewish practices in addition. In my view, the primary reason why Paul includes the story of what transpired in Antioch between him and Peter is that he saw in it a similarity with what was occurring in Galatia. Esler argues that Paul included the story because in both Antioch and Galatia, Gentiles were being pressured to undergo circumcision. But the verb "to judaize," as discussed above, does not necessarily include circumcision but the adoption of a range of Jewish customs in varying degrees. I would suggest that a more precise interpretation is that, in both places, Gentiles were experiencing pressure to judaize and that, in Galatia, circumcision was involved while, in Antioch, the pressure revolved around following food laws. In both venues, Christians were behaving inconsistently with "the truth of the gospel" (2:14)—that is, that which Paul had taught them—with the result being Christian judaizers.

Some of the Gentile Christians in Galatia were seeking justification through means other than faith alone; they were "deserting" Paul's teachings and turning to a different, perverted gospel (1:6,7) which involved submitting to pressure to "live like Jews" (2:14), including becoming circumcised (2:3; 5:2-12; 6:12,15) and observing other Jewish customs (4:10), while others contemplated doing so.[11] Members of the community also were observing the Jewish calendar, "observing special days, and months, and seasons, and years" (ἡμέρας παρατηρεῖσθε καὶ μῆνας καὶ καιροὺς καὶ ἐνιαυτούς; 4:10). It is likely that the "days" referred to are the Sabbaths, the "months" are the monthly celebrations of the new moon, the "seasons" include such annual festivals of Passover and Tabernacles, and the "years" are the sabbatical year and the year of jubilee (Lightfoot 1890: 171; Burton 1921: 232-33; Richardson 1969: 91 n.2). Paul fears that his work among these individuals was in vain. In order to counteract this behaviour,

Paul argues that "a person is justified not by the works of the law but through faith in Jesus Christ" (2:16), and that justification comes through "faith in Christ, and not by doing the works of the law, because no one will be justified by the works of the law" (2:16). Paul saw further inconsistency in the fact that those who were putting pressure on the Gentiles to be circumcised were not following the laws themselves (6:13).

Judaizing in Antioch and in Galatia—if that was the phenomenon underlying his letter—caused Paul tremendous pain because in both places it produced internal imbalance within the Christian community and caused a rift between him and Peter, and between him and the Galatians. In Antioch, Syria, Jewish Christians, by implication of their actions, intimidated Gentile Christians to live like Jews. In Galatia, Jewish Christians probably were factors again, but Christian judaizers were the primary antagonists, as we shall now see.

Who Compelled Gentile Christians in Galatia to Judaize?

IT IS CLEAR THAT THOSE who are pressuring the Galatian Gentiles to submit to circumcision (and other Jewish customs) are fellow Christians, since Paul refers to their teachings as a "different gospel" (Gal. 1:6) and states that his opponents "are confusing [the Galatians] and want to pervert the gospel of Christ" (1:7), that is, Paul's teaching. The fact that Paul's opponents are also believers in Jesus intensifies his anger and sense of betrayal.[12] The degree of Paul's anger over this "perversion" of the gospel is reflected in his casting of a curse on whoever would "proclaim...a gospel contrary to what we proclaimed to you" (1:8), and then repeating the curse in the next verse.

Most modern scholars have viewed Paul's opponents as Jewish Christians, probably from Judea, who urged Gentile Christians to keep the Jewish law (or in other words, convert to Judaism) in addition to confessing faith in Jesus as Messiah.[13] F.C. Baur argues in his 1845 monograph *Paulus, der Apostel Jesu Christi* that Paul's opponents were zealous Jewish Christians from Jerusalem who disapproved of Paul's teachings and sought to impose the requirements of the law on Gentiles so that their conversion would be complete; he further states that they were the same "men from James" who caused problems in Antioch between Peter and Paul (Gal. 2:12). Baur's thesis—known as the "Tübingen hypothesis"—has had an enduring effect on modern scholarship.[14] Evidence contained in the letter itself, however, strongly suggests that, among the primary instigators causing problems among the Galatian Gentiles, were *non*-Jews.[15]

The concluding paragraph of the letter (Galatians 6:11-18) is a post-script added by Paul in his own handwriting. Consistent with letter-writing conventions of the time, the addition of an autographed postscript assured recipients that the letter was authentic and conveyed information that the sender forgot to include in the body of the letter. Most importantly for purposes of this study, the postscript summarized the significant points of the letter (Weima 1994: 160; Betz 1979: 312).[16] The postscript is a crucial part of the letter, for it is in the postscript that some of the most revealing information about the identity of Paul's opponents in Galatia is discovered.[17]

In two of the most important verses, Paul writes: "It is those who want to make a good showing in the flesh that try to compel you to be circumcised—only that they may not be persecuted for the cross of Christ. Even the circumcised (οἱ περιτεμνόμενοι) do not themselves obey the law, but they want you to be circumcised so that they may boast about your flesh" (Gal. 6:12-13). The interpretation of these verses is complicated. Two crucial questions arise: Who are "the circumcised" of verse 13, who argue for the circumcision of Galatian Gentiles but are not obeying the law themselves? and Are they the same people Paul refers to in verse 12, whose motivation for pressuring the Galatian Gentiles to become circumcised is the avoidance of persecution?[18]

The existence of a textual variation in verse 13 makes answering these questions difficult, but not impossible. There is textual evidence for both the present participle οἱ περιτεμνόμενοι and the perfect participle οἱ περιτετμημένοι.[19] The perfect form, "those who have been circumcised," likely refers to Jews who were circumcised according to Jewish tradition on the eighth day after birth. Although found in P[46], a highly respected and early text, as well as in other manuscripts, it is likely a later scribal correction of the present tense. The present form, "those who receive circumcision" [i.e., are being circumcised], appears in more manuscripts and is generally preferred as the more original reading. This is because the meaning of the present participle is understood to refer to Gentiles undergoing circumcision; this form is more likely to have been considered confusing by a scribe, necessitating alteration.[20] The original reading of verse 13, then, is "Even those who receive circumcision [i.e., are being circumcised] do not themselves keep the law, but they desire to have you circumcised that they may glory in your flesh." The existence of the present tense of the same verb in Galatians 5:2, 3 and 6:12, further strengthens the argument that the present participle is the original form in verse 13 as its sense is "to get circumcised," or "to receive circumcision"—that is, it refers to someone undergoing circumcision, rather than to a circumcised person (Burton

1921: 353). Other parts of the letter also point to Gentile opponents. While Paul's bitter comment: "I wish those who unsettle you would castrate themselves!" (Gal. 5:12) could apply to Jews, it is more effective and relevant to the situation if applied to Gentiles who were voluntarily undergoing circumcision as adults.

In Galatians 6:13, Paul did not introduce a new subject but is speaking out against the same group he polemicizes in verse 12 and throughout the letter.[21] The Gentile Christians whom Paul referred to, who have received circumcision and are not following the law (Gal. 6:13), are also the subjects of the previous verse: "It is those who want to make a good showing in the flesh that would compel you to be circumcised, and only in order that they may not be persecuted for the cross of Christ" (Gal. 6:12). Both verses assert the self-centred impetus behind the drive for the circumcision of Galatian Gentile Christians: "so that they may not be persecuted" (12); "so that they may boast about your flesh" (13).

Among Paul's main opponents in Galatia, then, are circumcised Gentile Christians who are adding to their numbers new members from the Galatian churches by persuading them to submit to circumcision. Paul explains that his judaizing opponents are trying to persuade the Galatian Gentile Christians to become circumcised so that the judaizers could avoid persecution for "the cross of Christ" (6:12), a term most logically understood as a reference to Christian teachings and lifestyle (Esler 1994: 55). Whether these Gentile Christian persuaders originated from Galatia or from outside of the area is difficult to ascertain. Might they be those Gentile Christians who initially became judaizers in the Antioch area (described in Gal. 2), and then visited communities established by Paul with the purpose of countering his gospel by counselling fellow Gentile Christians to behave as they had? Whether the Christian judaizers originated from outside Galatia or not, it is clear that the problem very much *became* an internal Galatian issue, since some of the Galatian Gentile Christians did succumb to their persuasion and became judaizers. The situation was likely rather complicated. While the primary instigators of judaizing were Gentile Christians (either originally from Galatia, or some other locale such as Antioch), Jewish Christians from outside the Galatian community (i.e., from Jerusalem? Antioch?) might have agitated the Galatians as well (see Richardson 1969: 96; Murphy-O'Connor 1996: 193). Ultimately, of course, "the letter is not addressed to the troublemakers at all but to the Gentile Galatians" who were judaizing, as Lloyd Gaston rightly observes (1987: 81).

Why Did Galatian Christians Judaize?

BARCLAY'S ARGUMENT THAT GENTILE CHRISTIANS found the judaizers' message appealing for sociological reasons addresses some of the aspects that obtained at Galatia but is, ultimately, incomplete. He argues that their conversion to Christianity entailed major cognitive and social readjustment: their relationships with "family, friends, fellow club members, business associates and civic authorities" were no doubt severely disrupted (1988: 59). Barclay postulates that, because they distanced themselves from their pagan roots and at the same time were rejected by the local Jewish community, their social identity was precarious and insecure (1988: 58). According to Barclay, it is understandable that Gentile converts would have found the judaizers' message appealing: "[b]y becoming proselytes the Galatians could hope to identify themselves with the local synagogues and thus hold at least a more understandable and recognizable place in society" (1988: 60).[22] While these points are valid and may explain some of the *social* factors pertaining to the situation Paul addresses in Galatia, Barclay neglects another, more compelling reason why these Gentile Christians succumbed to pressure from Paul's opponents to undergo circumcision: their *theological* insecurities.

Paul's Christian judaizing opponents may have instilled a sense of insecurity in the Galatian Gentiles regarding their acceptability and status within the Christian community. In Galatians 4:17 Paul alludes to how his opponents were behaving towards his Gentile readers: "They make much of you but for no good purpose (ζηλοῦσιν ὑμᾶς οὐ καλῶς); they want to exclude you, so that you may make much of them (ἀλλὰ ἐκκλεῖσαι ὑμᾶς θέλουσιν, ἵνα αὐτοὺς ζηλοῦτε)" (Gal. 4:17). The term ζηλόω can mean "to be deeply concerned about someone, court someone's favor" (Bauer 1979: 338). This allusion suggests that, in Galatia, circumcised Christians of Gentile origin were paying special attention to fellow Gentiles. Perhaps they tried to convince the latter that becoming circumcised *was crucial to being a true Christian and member of the people of God*. At the same time, they may have argued that Gentile Christians who did not accept their teachings about circumcision would be "shut out" or "excluded" from the church (Schlier 1971: 212ff).[23] Paul counters their argument in Galatians 4:21–5:1, where he tries to persuade the Galatian Gentile Christians that they "are children of the promise, like Isaac" (4:28), without having to yield to "a yoke of slavery" (5:1) by keeping the law. As Gaston avers, "Paul's argument is not against circumcision (or Judaism) as such, but for adult Gentiles to circumcise themselves would mean seeking to earn something and thus deny God's grace. Such Ishmael people are not heirs of the promise, for even if they are in a sense children of Abraham, they are not children of Sarah" (1987: 90).

In Galatians 3:6, Paul abruptly introduces the topic of the blessing of Abraham and how people may share in it, a discussion he continues for the next two chapters. The nature of Paul's argument is in the form of a rebuttal and confirms that he was responding to an argument put forth by his opponents. They argued that in order to be admitted to the covenant of Abraham, and to share in God's promised blessings, it was necessary for Gentile men to undergo circumcision. This argument, primarily based on Genesis 12 and 17, would have been hard to resist. Genesis 17:14, for example, explicitly states that: "Any uncircumcised male who is not circumcised in the flesh of his foreskin shall be cut off from his people; he has broken my covenant." The Hebrew scriptures made it very clear that in order to be blessed by God it was necessary to be part of the Jewish people and this for males entailed becoming circumcised. Paul tries to counter this argument by reasoning that it was Abraham's belief that made him acceptable to God, and so too Gentiles can be justified by faith (3:6-9).

Although at first Gentiles in Galatia accepted Paul's teaching about salvation through grace and life in the Spirit, they came to distrust his version by judging it to be incomplete. While they did not reject Paul's version of the gospel outright, they came to believe that he had left out some crucial parts; they apparently felt that his gospel lacked reference to circumcision and other obligations pertaining to the Mosaic law, which the Christian judaizers believed to be the full message taught by Jerusalem Christians.

This distrust could have developed in different ways. It would have been quite natural for Gentile converts to conclude from reading Jewish scripture that circumcision was required of all who desired to be a part of the people of God. Perhaps Paul's discussions about the Jerusalem Jewish Christian community were misunderstood. As Gaston observes, "Paul always speaks of the Jerusalem church in positive terms" (1987: 109), for example, he refers to leaders of the Jerusalem church as "apostles" (Gal. 1:19, 2:8) and "pillars" (Gal. 2:9). This may have inadvertently created within Gentile Christians "a longing to be like the Jewish Christians there, who [were] imagined to be real Jews and Christians at the same time, and who preach[ed] circumcision and the observance of the Law" (Munck 1959: 279).[24]

The fact that some Christians did observe the law might have added to their confusion, so that some Gentile Christians in Galatia may have thought that all Christians in Jerusalem were circumcised and followed the law.[25] Perhaps Paul had deliberately distorted his version of the gospel by dropping the circumcision requirement? Perhaps the Jewish Christians in Jerusalem had the more authoritative gospel? Gal. 5:11 suggests that Paul's Gentile Christian opponents declared that Paul's own teachings buttressed their cause. Here Paul claims "But my friends, why am I still being persecuted if I am still preaching circumcision? In that case the offense of the cross has been removed." This statement implies that Paul's opponents claimed that Paul (at one time or at present) endorsed submission to circumcision (Bruce 1982: 236-37).[26] It is understandable why they might have done so. By arguing that Paul himself endorsed circumcision for Gentiles, his opponents could try to influence Gentiles who had been converted to Christianity by Paul and who may have been stubbornly refusing to be circumcised out of loyalty to Paul. Perhaps his adversaries cited Paul as support for their position by pointing out the fact that Paul himself was circumcised, so "why should he want to hold [them] back from this same mark of distinction; let [them] all be circumcised" (Richardson 1969: 90).

The congregations established by Paul were deeply unsettled by the influence of the judaizing Christians who had "succeeded partly in putting the churches into a state of uncertainty, and partly in winning them over to themselves" (Munck 1959: 89). Christian judaizers may have attempted to persuade the Galatians that simply to believe in Jesus was not enough for them to be a part of the believing community: they had to do more to secure their membership in the community by observing Jewish customs, including circumcision for the men. Their appeal was clearly successful among the Galatian Christians; the urgency with which Paul writes is proof of this.

The Location of the Galatian Churches

BECAUSE THE PLACE NAME "Galatia" is ambiguous, there is uncertainty as to the location of the "Galatian churches" Paul addresses with such vehemence (Gal. 1:2). When Galatia became a Roman province in 25 BCE, it included not only the ethnic district of Galatia, located north of the great inner plateau of Asia Minor where Celtic tribes had settled, but also part of Pontus, Phrygia, Lycaonia, Pisidia, Paphlagonia and Isauria (Magie 1950: 453).[27] The provincial boundaries included Antioch, Iconium, Lystra and Derbe, listed in Acts 13 and 14 as the towns Paul had visited on his first missionary journey. There is uncertainty as to whether Paul's use of the term "Galatia" denoted only the ancient tribal territory—referred to in scholarship as the North Galatia theory, which included the cities of Celtic north Galatia, Ancyra, Pessinus and Tavium—or the provincial area, which would have encompassed the towns Paul visited—referred to as the South Galatia theory.[28]

Unfortunately Paul does not supply an itinerary of his travels, thus one cannot be certain of exactly which churches and areas he visited. Acts does describe a missionary journey of Paul through the southern part of the province during which time churches were established in Lystra, Derbe, Iconium, and Pisidian Antioch, and if "Galatia" can be interpreted in the broader sense, it is possible that these are the churches to which Paul is writing. If the narrower sense is correct—then the churches must have been located in the northern region where the nation of Galatians lived; one can only guess where the churches were or how they came to be established. Acts does not describe any visit by Paul to that area, but this certainly does not mean he never got there, given the fact that Luke reported only what he considered relevant to his purposes. The fact that Paul generally used geographical terms in the Roman sense creates the strong presumption that by "the churches in Galatia" he is referring to churches located anywhere within the province, and therefore the letter may indeed address the towns in the south. Paul's letter was written in Greek; the fact that Greek funerary inscriptions from this time period were rare in the northern territory, "contrasting sharply with the region immediately to the south, confirms the view that the majority of the rural population did not use Greek" (Mitchell 1980: 1058), points in favour of the South Galatia theory.[29]

In Galatia, certain Gentile members of the nascent Christian community were practising a variety of Jewish customs, including circumcision (Gal. 2:3; 5:2-12; 6:12, 15), Sabbath observance (4:10) and various festivals (4:10). The primary source of this pressure, as argued here, was not coming from Jews, nor from Jewish Christians, but from Gentile Christians who had already submitted to circumcision and who were trying to persuade fellow Gentile Christians to conform to their example. Certainly the fact that Gentiles promoted judaizing behaviour to fellow Gentiles increased the potency of their teaching. While the judaizers compelling the Galatian Gentiles might have travelled to Galatia from elsewhere (such as Antioch, for example), their presence in Galatia was felt significantly in the community. They successfully penetrated the churches, producing an internal Galatian struggle that deeply troubled Paul. From his perspective, Christian judaizers compromised their faith in Jesus because they understood judaizing to be necessary in order to attain salvation. In response, Paul denounced this teaching with a characteristic combination of sarcasm and acerbic wit. In so doing, he included some descriptions of Jewish practices that would offend Jews; as I have shown, these descriptions were originally intended to correct the behaviour of Gentiles. Such behaviour, however, did not cease. Indeed, Christian judaizers were an enduring problem for leaders of Christian communities in Asia Minor long after Paul's time.

Christian Judaizing in Syria: Barnabas, the *Didache*, and Pseudo-Clementine Literature

◄◦►

VIDENCE INDICATES that the problem of judaizing in Syria was
not restricted to the earliest members of the Christian community.
In the fall of 386 and 387 CE, John Chrysostom, bishop of Antioch, preached sermons in which he produced some of the most vehement
anti-Jewish rhetoric in Christian history (Wilken 1983). Some of his very
own Christian congregants attended synagogue services and observed certain Jewish rituals including circumcision, dietary laws and rites of purifi-
cation. In response, Chrysostom declared the synagogue to be "not only
a whorehouse and a theatre; it is also a den of thieves and a haunt of wild
animals... not the cave of a wild animal merely, but of an unclean wild animal"; he stated further that: "[t]he Jews have no conception of [spiritual]
things at all, but living for the lower nature, all agog for the here and
now, no better disposed than pigs or goats, they live by the rule of debauch-
ery and inordinate gluttony. Only one thing they understand: to gorge
themselves and to get drunk" (*Against the Jews* 1.3, 4; PG 48, 847, 848).

Is there evidence that judaizing also occurred during the period *between*
Paul's letter to the Galatians and John Chrysostom's sermons? This chapter investigates three early Christian documents from the Syrian region
that range in date from the late first century to the middle of the second
century CE: the *Epistle of Barnabas*, the *Didache,* and the Pseudo-Clementine literature. Each of these indicates that some Gentile Christians continued to be infatuated with Judaism and its rituals, but the authors or
editors of these texts responded in different ways to this. Those of *Barnabas* and the *Didache* warn believers in Christ against those who maintained Jewish customs. These warnings represent an effort on behalf of
ecclesiastical leadership to create a distinct Christian identity, differentiated
from Judaism and its practices. While some of the material expresses a
strong anti-Jewish sentiment and appears to be directed toward Jews, the
debate within them was fundamentally *intra muros* and reveals more
about internal *Christian* conditions and the fluidity of boundaries between
Jews and Christians than about Jewish behaviour. A contrary response is

---

Notes to chapter 4 start on page 161

found in the literature of the Pseudo-Clementines, which expressed explicit encouragement of Torah observance among Gentile Christians and hostility toward Paul's "law-less" gospel. The Christians promoting this position may be Jewish Christian or, perhaps, the judaizers themselves.

The Epistle of Barnabas

THE DATE, PROVENANCE, and authorship of the *Epistle of Barnabas* are matters of continued scholarly debate. The approach to its date usually revolves around the interpretation of evidence pointing to contemporary events within the epistle itself. The process of interpretation, usually fraught with uncertainty due to the arbitrary nature of the task, is further complicated in this case by the strong probability that the author of the *Epistle of Barnabas,* whom we will refer to as Barnabas and whose identity is discussed later, incorporated different sources into his epistle. It is possible, however, to state with confidence that *Barnabas* was written after the destruction of Jerusalem by Titus in 70 CE, since the epistle refers to this event (*Barn.* 16.4); this is the first Christian document, as J.A.T. Robinson observes, to refer explicitly to the destruction of the city of Jerusalem in the past tense (1976: 313). And its *terminus ad quem* must be c. 130 CE, since an author such as Barnabas, who was so interested in disparaging the Jews, would surely have exploited the failed Bar Kochba revolt under Hadrian, had it already occurred (Lightfoot 1890: 505; Paget 1994: 9).

The following passage (*Barn.* 4.4-5) is considered crucial to the investigation of the date of the epistle:

> (4) And the Prophet also says thus: "Ten kingdoms shall reign upon the earth and there shall rise up after them a little king, who shall subdue three of the kings under one" (τρεῖς ὑφ᾽ ἓν τῶν βασιλέων). (5) Daniel says likewise concerning the same: "And I beheld the fourth Beast, wicked and powerful and fiercer than all the beasts of the sea, and that ten horns sprang from it, and out of them a little excrescent horn (μικρὸν κέρας παραφυάδιον), and that it subdued under one three of the great horns."

While only the second quotation is attributed to Daniel, both quotations are from that book (v. 4 is from Dan. 7:24 and v. 5 from Dan. 7:7-8). Neither is an exact rendering of any of the extant Greek texts of Daniel in the Septuagint, Theodotion, nor the surviving papyri. Because it is clear that Barnabas is using a source, many scholars deem the verse irrelevant to the question of date, arguing that it relates to historical circumstances in Daniel's time and does not reveal anything about contemporary events during the time of Barnabas.[1] It does not seem prudent, however, to cast aside all hope of determining the time at which Barnabas wrote simply because he incorporated material from other sources into his writing. Adherents of this position seem to be making the large assumption that the author did not select or in any way alter material to correspond to what he wished to communicate, but that he blindly or mechanically slotted other material into his text. Rather, the evidence suggests that Barnabas did alter his sources, as no extant texts of Daniel contain the words παραφυάδιον (*Barn.* 4.4) or ὑφ᾽ εν (*Barn.* 4.4, 5).[2] As Richardson and Shukster observe, "If we imagine that he was sensitive to the significance of his version, felt free to accept or reject what he found in his sources, and addressed it to some real situation, then it should be possible to determine its date" (1983: 31-32).

Scholars who are of the opinion that Barnabas selected and modified material from other sources so that it reflected his message have attempted to analyze 4:4-5 of the epistle for information pertaining to the *Sitz im Leben* of Barnabas's contemporary situation. This is no easy task, since there are numerous ways to interpret the verses. The references in the prophecy to a "little king" (4.4) and "little excrescent horn" (4.5) are generally understood to refer to the Roman emperor who was in power at the time during which the epistle was composed—a leader of distinctively underwhelming stature who subdues three other leaders.[3]

Richardson and Shukster persuasively identify Nerva, who ruled the Roman empire from 96-98 CE, and brought the reign of the Flavians—Vespasian, Titus, and Domitian—to an end, as the "little king" and "excrescent horn" who was in power when the epistle was written.[4] A coin, dated to 96 CE and minted by Nerva, bears the inscription *fisci Iudaici calumnia sublata*, which should be translated as "the pretence of the Jewish tax is suppressed" (Richardson and Shukster 1983: 44). It is not clear from this inscription how Nerva modified the tax, but any alteration of former policies concerning the Jewish tax probably would have been a welcome relief for Jews. After the defeat of the Jews in 70 CE, Emperor Vespasian implemented a policy that Jews found profoundly humiliating: he applied the Jewish half-shekel temple tax to finance the building of the pagan temple to Jupiter in Rome. Domitian made the collection process more oppressive by implementing a policy of collecting the *fiscus* not only from people who were born Jews but from anyone else who lived like a Jew, and sanctioned public scrutiny of potential contributors (Suetonius, *Domitian* 12; see Smallwood 1976: 376-78; Williams 1990: 199). Richardson and Shukster observe that, directly on occupying the throne, Emperor Nerva sought to distance himself from his harsh predecessor; they argue that the inscription on Nerva's coin may refer to the fact that he somehow made this taxation process less offensive—a move that would have been received wholeheartedly by Jews of the empire. Linking a midrashic tradition in *Genesis Rabbah*, which discusses the reintroduction of the Jewish Temple tax at a time when the Roman government agreed to the rebuilding of the Jerusalem Temple, to the reign of Nerva, Richardson and Shukster suggest that the hope for the restoration of the Temple of Jerusalem flourished while Nerva was emperor, and that it was against this background that Barnabas wrote his epistle (1983: 47ff).

A related passage used to date the *Epistle of Barnabas* is: "Furthermore he says again, 'Lo, they who destroyed this temple shall themselves build it.' That is happening now. For owing to the war it was destroyed by the enemy; at present even the servants of the enemy will build it up again (ὑπηρέται ἀνοικοδομήσουσιν αὐτόν)" (*Barn.* 16.3-4). This passage indicates that the expectation of the restoration of a temple existed when the epistle was written. Hvalvik's interpretation of this verse as "Now the very servants of [the Jews'] enemies will build it again" and his view that this is a reference to Hadrian's building of the Aelia Capitolina are not consistent with the evidence (1996: 21ff).[5] Barnabas adds ὑπηρέται to the Septuagint version of the text of Isaiah 49:17, thereby specifying that it is the *servants* of the enemy who are to rebuild this temple.[6] Since the reference to "enemy" is obviously Rome, it is odd that Barnabas would qualify it unless he had intended to specify that the rebuilders were Romans and others (see Richardson and Shukster 1983: 37). Barnabas, moreover, refers to the *re*building (ἀνοικοδομήσουσιν) of this temple, which makes the most sense if he meant the Jewish Temple in Jerusalem as opposed to the first-time construction of a pagan temple.

The interpretation of the passage is complicated by the question of whether Barnabas referred to a spiritual temple or the actual Jewish Temple in Jerusalem, and by the existence of textual variants in verse 4. This debate has long engaged scholars. Those who argue that Barnabas was referring to a spiritual temple maintain that this interpretation best corresponds with the context of chapter 16 as a whole (Gunther 1976; Kraft 1965: 42ff; Prigent 1961: 71-83). But this is not an accurate understanding of the chapter. The spiritual temple is discussed, but not until verse 6, where there is a specific topic change marked by an emphatic δέ. Prior to this, the topic is the earthly, physical temple. Since verses 1 and 5 both refer to a physical temple, references to a spiritual temple in verses 3 and 4 would be disjointed and odd (Paget 1994: 19).

Another strong argument against understanding the reference to be a spiritual temple is the use of ὑπηρέται (the "servants of the enemy"). If the temple is spiritual, then these "servants" who rebuild it would be Christians—and this is a most unlikely way for Barnabas to refer to Christians (Paget 1994: 19). It makes more sense to suppose that Barnabas was writing at a time when there were expectations that the Jewish Temple in Jerusalem would be rebuilt. He states that those who destroyed the temple (i.e., the Romans) would take part in rebuilding it in the future (ἀνοικοδομήσουσιν). The reference to the "servants of the enemy," then, is best understood to refer to Jews who were involved with the Romans in the rebuilding of the temple (Richardson and Shukster 1983: 37).[7]

Modification of the *fiscus Iudaicus* and the expectation of the rebuilding of the Jewish Temple in Jerusalem would have generated a heightened sense of purpose and optimism among Jews living in Palestine and in the diaspora. No doubt it would also have had a profound impact on Christians. This fresh influx of confidence may have made an already strong and vital Judaism more attractive to some Gentile Christians who may already have been drawn to Jewish practices. The author of the *Epistle of Barnabas* was dealing with a situation where certain members of his Gentile Christian community were, from his perspective, excessively attached to Judaism and to Jewish rites. He writes his epistle, therefore, in order to instil within his readers an understanding of the distinction between Christianity and Judaism, and of the superiority of Christianity.

Provenance and Author

The *Epistle of Barnabas* was clearly written in a geographical area where Judaism was predominant and where Christians came into contact with Jews. The author used Jewish terminology, for example referring to the "new law (καινὸς νόμος) of our Lord Jesus Christ" (*Barn.* 2.6), and was aware of some obscure details of Jewish practices found only in the Mishnah. For example, *Barn.* 7.6 states that two goats "goodly and alike" (καλοὺς καὶ ὁμοίους) were to be given as a burnt offering for sins. Leviticus 16 does not state that the goats were to be alike, but *m. Yoma* 6.1 states that: "the religious requirement concerning them is that the two of them be equivalent in appearance, height, and value." Further, Barnabas discusses the binding of scarlet wool on the head of the scapegoat (*Barn.* 7.8); once again, this detail is not delineated in Leviticus 16 but is found in *m. Yoma* 4.2. Since Barnabas did not draw his information from an understanding of the Hebrew Bible, he must have lived in an area where he had intimate contact with Jews and access to these details.

Other relevant evidence is in Barnabus's statement: "So then, brethren, the long-suffering one foresaw that the people whom he prepared in his beloved should believe in guilelessness, and made all things plain to us beforehand that we should not be shipwrecked by conversion to their law" (ἵνα μὴ προσρησσώμεθα ὡς ἐπήλυτοι τῷ ἐκείνων νόμῳ) (*Barn.* 3.6).[8] Paget notes that this verse "seems…to take seriously the presence of Jews and their possible influence on Christian praxis" (1994: 58; also Hvalvik 1996: 87).[9] Assuming it is possible that some Christians were influenced by the Jewish hope of the rebuilding of the Temple in Jerusalem and became caught up in its possible eschatological implications, they may have wished to be associated with the Jewish community by identifying their covenant with that of the Jews (*Barn.* 4.6; Paget 1994: 68). It seems reasonable to situate the document in a strongly Jewish region and to assume that some among Barnabas's Christian members were attracted to and closely associated with Judaism.

Most scholars argue that the *Epistle of Barnabas* has an Alexandrian provenance (e.g., Barnard, Baur, Daniélou, Harnack, Kraft, Paget). The facts that the earliest witness to the epistle is Clement of Alexandria, and that Barnabas applies allegorical interpretation to the Jewish law, a form of exegesis popular in Alexandria, are evidence to support the Alexandrian origin of the epistle.[10] Barnabas states that "every Syrian and Arab and all the priests of the idols have been circumcised; are then these also within their covenant?—indeed even the Egyptians belong to the circumcision" (*Barn.* 9.6). Some scholars argue that this demonstrates that Barnabas was a resident of Alexandria because he knew that the priests in Egypt were circumcised and he—erroneously—extended what he knew about Egyptian priests to "all the priests of the idols."[11]

This postulated provenance has been challenged recently by scholars who argue that Palestinian or Syrian territory are more appropriate places of origin for the document.[12] Even though the epistle may have been very familiar to Clement of Alexandria, it need not have originated there.[13] Richardson and Shukster point out that "the verse's emphasis on the circumcision of the Syrians and the Arabs at the expense of the Egyptians would seem to suggest Syro-Palestine as the epistle's likeliest place of origin" (1986: 20). In addition, the word "Egyptians" in verse 9:6 might not be genuine to the text (1986: 20).[14] The argument for a Syrian provenance is compelling.[15]

As to the question of who wrote the epistle, ancient witnesses considered Paul's companion Barnabas to be the author (e.g., Clement; *Strom* 2.6.31; 2.7.35; 2.20.116; 5.10.63; Jerome; *Vir. ill.* 6; Origen; *c. Cels.* 1.63). The modern consensus, however, differs. The fact that the epistle does not mention Barnabas anywhere in the text strongly implies that the ascription was secondary (Windisch 1920: 413). The author, whose real name cannot be ascertained, appears to have had a close relationship with the recipients of his letter. He appeals to them on the basis of this close connection: he refers to them as "sons and daughters" (*Barn.* 1.1) and else-where as "brethren" (*Barn.* 2.10; 3.6; 4.14; 5.5; 6.15). He states that he will show them "a few things, not as a teacher (οὐχ ὡς διδάσκαλος) but as one of yourselves" (*Barn.* 1.8; cf. 4.9) and in 4.6 makes a request "as being one of yourselves, and especially as loving you all above my own life." Barnabas wished to prepare his readers early in the epistle for receiv-ing his advice by assuring them of his love for them and stressing that he was one of them. That he did not lack self-confidence is indicated in his proclamation that "no one has heard a more excellent lesson from me, but I know that you are worthy" (*Barn.* 9.9).

Whether the author of the epistle was of Jewish or Gentile origin con-tinues to be debated. The Jewish character of the document reflected in the use of the Two Ways material, the author's familiarity with extra-biblical Jewish traditions (discussed above), and the Jewish exegetical method of *gematria*, among other factors, favours a Jewish origin for the author.[16] On the other hand, Barnabas does not indicate that he has any sense of iden-tity with the Jewish people whatsoever. He refers to historical Israel not as "us" or "we" but as "them" or "they" (*Barn.* 3.6; 4.6; 8.7; 10.12; 13.1, 3; 14.5). He describes the idolatrous behaviour of the Jews in the desert and how Moses, in response, "cast the two tables out of his hands, and *their* covenant was broken" (καὶ σύνετρίβη αὐτῶν ἡ διαθήκη, *Barn.* 4.8, emphasis added). This strongly suggests that *Barnabas* was written by a Gentile Christian. The epistle's acute anti-Judaism is also used as evidence that the author was Gentile, although this interpretation is by no means the sole possibility.[17] According to Gedaliah Alon, Barnabas uses a source that combines extra-biblical material (*halachot* from the *midrash* and *hag-gadah*) with biblical stories and quotes it as if it all came from the Bible (1940/41: 35-37); therefore, Alon argues that Barnabas was a Gentile since the way he uses this material indicates that he lacked proper under-standing of what he was quoting (1940/41: 37).

The evidence allows for strong arguments for either case, but my view is that the author of the epistle was a Gentile who was very familiar with Jewish tradition, probably through daily personal contact with Jews.[18] The origin of some of the recipients of the letter is much more certain. Par-ticular verses—such as 3.6, where Barnabas expresses concern over being "shipwrecked by conversion to their law"; 16.7, which discusses the time "before we believed in God" and how "our heart…was full of idolatry," and the centrality of conversion (chap. 9)—suggest that at least some of the recipients of the epistle—that is, some members of the congregation about whom Barnabas was so concerned—were Gentile Christians (Robin-son 1920: 4; Wilson 1995: 161). Barnabas warns his Gentile Christian readers against adopting Jewish customs regarding fasting, circumcision, food laws and the Sabbath. He attempts to persuade these members that the Jewish law was never meant to be interpreted literally and that the covenant in fact never belonged to the Jews.

Barnabas's Message: The Covenant Is Christian

Barnabas directly addresses what he considers a perturbing attitude held by some members of the community to which he writes (*Barn.* 4.6, 13.1, and 14.1, respectively):

> Take heed to yourselves now, and be not made like some, heaping up your sins and saying that the covenant is both theirs and ours (ἡ διαθήκη ἐκείνων καὶ ἡμῶν).[19] ... Now let us see whether this people or the former people is the heir, and whether the covenant is for us or for them (εἰ ἡ διαθήκη εἰς ἡμᾶς ἢ εἰς ἐκείνους).... But let us see whether the covenant which he swore to the fathers to give to the people—whether he has given it.

Barnabas obviously felt very strongly about how members of his community understood the issue of the covenant since he brings it up in three different places in his letter. His differentiation between Christians and Jews for comparative purposes occurs frequently throughout the epistle, indicated by his contrast of the pronouns "we" and "us" with "they" and "them" (as noted above).[20] The first time he addresses the problem concerning the covenant (in *Barn.* 4.6) indicates that it is a topic of importance to him and is one that has been discussed already among his community. He warns them against following "some" who said that the covenant belongs to the Jews and to the Christians. Is it possible to identify these people?

Stephen Wilson suggests three possibilities: liberal rabbis "who were willing to make room for Christians in the covenant relationship"; Jewish Christians "who in the eyes of the author conceded far too much to, and were prepared to share the covenantal privileges with, the Jews"; and Christian judaizers "committed to the Christian movement but not prepared to abandon Judaism or its ways altogether" (Wilson 1992: 612). There is no indication in the epistle that those promoting such a view are from outside the community; they seem instead to be members of the congregation. This polemical statement (*Barn.* 3:6) provides insight into this issue: "So then, brethren, the long-suffering one foresaw that the people whom He prepared in his beloved should believe in guilelessness, and made all things plain to us beforehand that we should not be shipwrecked by conversion to their law (ἵνα μὴ προσρησσώμεθα ὡς ἐπήλυτοι τῷ ἐκείνων νόμῳ)." There is a textual problem with this verse because the textual witnesses vacillate between ἐπήλυτοι (ms. s) and προσήλυτοι (mss. h, l). The word ἐπήλυτος is not found elsewhere in early Christian literature, nor is it frequently used in Greek literature. It means "newcomer," or those who have "come lately, come after, as followers, imitators" (Bauer 1979: 285). Josephus does not use the term at all, but Philo uses it often to refer to a Gentile convert to Judaism, synonymous with προσήλυτος.[21] If it has the same meaning here in Barnabas, implying conversion, then there is little significant difference between the two textual variants. Lake is right to follow the Codex Sinaiticus, since it is more likely that the Codex Constantinopolitanus reflects a "correction" of the less familiar word (ἐπήλυτος) with one that had become more familiar (προσήλυτος) than the other way around. It is possible, furthermore, that the phrase using ἐπήλυτοι was written deliberately by Barnabas to provoke a comparison between a Gentile "imitating" (or converting to) Jewish law and an alien, or newcomer, in a land that is not his or her own.

In the epistle, then, Barnabas polemicizes against *Gentiles* converting to Jewish law (*Barn.* 3.6), since he would hardly refer to *Jews* converting to the Jewish law.[22] His strong objection to this type of behaviour is reflected in his use of the verb προσρήσσω, "to dash or beat against." This statement can shed light on the context of the letter and the particular circumstances in which Barnabas wrote. Since his community seems to have consisted predominantly of Gentile Christians, and since Barnabas expresses urgent concern about the possible "conversion" of some of his Gentile members to Jewish law, the final option of Christian judaizers for the identity of Barnabas's recipients, as suggested by Wilson, seems to be the most likely. Barnabas was concerned about the difficult consequences of Christian adoption of Jewish law; the criticism of Jewish customs and interpretation of law found in the epistle were written to combat Gentile interest in these customs.[23] Barnabas was afraid that some of his Gentile Christian readers might become persuaded by certain Christian judaizers in the community that the covenant belongs to Jews and Christians equally (also *Barn.* 5.4).[24] From Barnabas's perspective, by holding this view, these people were "heaping up…sins." He states clearly that the covenant "is ours" and goes on to explain that the Jews "lost" the covenant when they "turned to idols" (ἐπιστραφέντες ἐπὶ τὰ εἴδωλα) (*Barn.* 3.7).

The second time he takes up the issue of the covenant, Barnabas raises the central question concerning whether the covenant belongs to the Christians (οὗτος ὁ λαός) or to the Jews (πρῶτος λαός), to us (εἰς ἡμᾶς) or to them (ἢ εἰς ἐκείνους) (*Barn.* 13.1). His answer, of course, is that it belongs to the Christians.[25] In 13.2–3 he employs the biblical story of Rebecca's children Jacob and Esau and how God chose one over the other as an analogy for the relationship between Jews and Christians, with the implication that God

chose the Christians over the Jews, a common theme. In 13.4-6, he employs
the biblical story of Jacob's blessing of Joseph's sons Ephraim and Manasseh and how the younger Ephraim was chosen for the blessing (from Gen.
48:13-20) to argue that the Christians were the blessed chosen people,
not the Jews. Significantly, in his rendition of the story, Barnabas does not
even mention Manasseh, the older son who, in the Septuagint narrative,
is blessed by Jacob with his left hand. The implication is that only the
church ("Ephraim") is blessed, and that the Jews *never were* the chosen
people (Hvalvik 1996: 147-48). Barnabas continues to argue that the Jews
never did possess the covenant. It was given, he declares, "but they were
not worthy to receive it because of their sins" (*Barn.* 14.1). He then goes
on to explain "how we received it" (14.4). The implication of this verse
is that it is Christians who possessed the covenant from *the very beginning*.

Many scholars argue that Barnabas was not writing against Judaism as
a veritable and present enemy.[26] These scholars assert that the debate is an
academic one where Judaism is an abstract entity of no particular relevance
to Christians, and that there is no actual contact made between the two
communities. Windisch, one of the first scholars to employ a source-crit-
ical approach to the *Epistle of Barnabas*, declares that the anti-Judaism in
the epistle belongs to the inherited material incorporated into the epistle
and, therefore, does not represent a polemic by Barnabas against Jews
(1920: 323). Windisch understands the purpose of the epistle to be for the
edification of Barnabas's Christian community (1920: 323). For Wengst,
Barnabas's polemical statements about Jews militate against two positions, one of which he describes as "Normalchristentum" (1971: 100);
this "normal" Christian interpretation—which, according to Wengst is
represented by the statement in Barn. 4.6 about the covenant belonging to
both Jews and Christians—accedes to the temporary validity of the Jewish covenant and law as part of the groundwork for the coming of Jesus,
and was one with which Barnabas disagreed. The second position Barnabas polemicizes against is the Jewish literalist interpretation of scripture
and therefore, for Wengst, his statements about Jews and Judaism were theoretical and did not pertain to actual Jews or Judaism: "sie sind alle vom
eigenen Ansatz des Barnabas in seinem Schriftverständnis zu verstehen"
(Wengst 1971: 101).[27]

Scholars who maintain that the anti-Jewish statements in *Barnabas*
derive more from theological abstractions than from social interaction
tend to perceive post-70 CE Judaism and Christianity as separate movements with sharply defined boundaries, whose adherents rarely, or never,
interacted. Recent studies contradict this understanding and argue that
Jewish and Christian communities frequently intersected.[28] These studies,

and the urgent, personal tone of *Barnabas*, as well as the author's inti-mate knowledge of Jewish rites, repudiate arguments advocating that Barnabas's statements concerning Judaism were merely theoretical. Barn-abas's fixation on scripture in fact attests to his need to address what he perceived as the threatening influence of Judaism and judaizers (Wilson 1995: 137; Hvalvik 1996: 94).[29] The content of the *Epistle of Barnabas*, and the author's focus on such practices most associated with living Judaism as circumcision, food laws, sacrifices, Sabbath, and fasting, fur-ther challenge these arguments.[30]

Kraft contends that the epistle contains anti-cultic, not anti-Jewish, sentiments and even suggests that: "we would do well to dismiss this term (anti-Jewish) altogether from the description of the epistle" (1962: 405). This statement is partially correct. On the one hand Barnabas' response addresses behaviour occurring, as argued earlier, among Gentile Chris-tians within his own community and, therefore, his epistle is not directed toward Jews; in this sense, his statements are *not* anti-Jewish as such. On the other hand, however, many parts of his response to judaizing would be offensive to Jews and, hence, in that sense, may be deemed "anti-Jew-ish." Paget notes that, for example, at 2.9 Barnabas describes Jews "as those who are deceived (πλανωμένους); at 3.6 conversion to 'their law' is equivalent to shipwreck; at 8.1 they are perfect in sin; at 8.7 things are clear to the Christians but obscure to them (see also 10.12); at 9.4 their belief that the command to circumcise was meant literally is attributed to the deception of an evil angel" (1994: 56). Horbury's statement regarding Barnabas's purpose is an accurate assessment of the purpose of the docu-ment: "The overriding necessity is to justify the position of 'us' vis-à-vis 'their' law, and to ward off the peril of assimilation to and absorption in the Jewish community" (1992: 327; also Hvalvik 1996). The Christians to whom Barnabas writes are not sufficiently aware, from his perspective at least, of the distinctions between Christianity and Judaism.

Like the *Epistle of Barnabas*, the *Epistle to Diognetus* is an anonymous document of uncertain date and provenance that directs intense animos-ity toward specific Jewish practices of worship, including Jewish sacrifice, food laws, the Sabbath, circumcision, and Jewish festivals. Diognetus, a Gentile pagan, was *"especially anxious* to hear why the Christians do not worship in the same way as the Jews" (μὴ κατὰ τὰ αὐτὰ Ἰουδαίοις) (*Diogn.* 3.1, emphasis added). The author, seemingly intent on distinguishing Chris-tian practices from Judaism for Diognetus, states that Christians avoid "the general silliness, deceit, fussiness and pride of the Jew" (τῆς μὲν οὖν κοινῆς εἰκαιότητος καὶ ἀπάτης καὶ τῆς Ἰουδαίων πολυπραγμοσύνης καὶ ἀλαζονείας ὡς ὀρθῶς ἀπέχονται Χριστιανοί, 4.6). Marrou argues that the author views the separation between the church and the synagogue to have been accomplished and that this epistle is testimony to the animosity brought about by such a separation. Indeed, notes Marrou, among the anti-Semitic Christian literature "il y a peu de textes qui atteignent ce ton uniformement méprisant et cette violence dans l'insulte" (1965: 114). In my view, however, the bitter, disparaging tone of the *Epistle to Diognetus* suggests that the separation between Jews and Christians was *not*, from the perspective of the author, secure. The author asserts that Jewish "attention to the stars and moon, for the observance of months and days, and for their arbitrary distinctions between the changing seasons ordained by God, making some into feasts, and others into occasions of mourning;—who would regard this as a proof of piety, and not much more of foolishness?" (4.5). Calling their behaviour δεισιδαιμονία (4.1), ἀσεβές (4.3), and χλεύης ἄξιον (4.4), the author assumes that Diognetus does not need to have reiterated to him that Jewish "scruples about food and superstition about the Sabbath, and their pride in circumcision and the sham of their fasting and feast of the new moon (καὶ τὴν τῆς νηστείας καὶ νουμηνίας εἰρωνείαν) are ridiculous and unworthy of any argument" (4.1). It is significant that this anti-Jewish rhetoric was directed toward a *Gentile* audience. The need to ridicule Jewish observance perhaps derives from its being too closely intertwined with Christian behaviour and identity.[31]

As for Barnabas, he found himself face to face with what was for him an alarming possibility: that more members of his Christian community would adopt the view that the covenant belonged to both Jews and Christians. He was already aware of Christian judaizers who claimed this understanding, and he sought to prevent further spread of their influence. In his epistle, he sought to persuade his readers that the covenant was the possession of Christians alone and, more, that the covenant had never belonged to the Jews in the first place.

The Problem of Fasting

In chapter 3 of the epistle, Barnabas uses Isaiah 58:4-10 to criticize the Jews for misunderstanding God's command to fast by interpreting it literally. The prophecy in Isaiah was used at this time to admonish Jews prior to undertaking a fast (*t. Ta'an.* 1.8) and is still read on Yom Kippur (*m. Meg.* 31a). It is found in other Christian writings as a proof-text for explaining why Christians diverged from the Jewish custom of fasting, as in Justin's *Dialogue with Trypho* 15 and Clement (*Paed* 3.90.1ff). The text is used polemically by Barnabas, particularly as he addresses the discussion "to them" (πρὸς αὐτούς, *Barn.* 3.1) and then "to us" (πρὸς ἡμᾶς, *Barn.* 3.3). Clement introduces the same prophecy with περὶ νηστείας (*Paid.* 3.90.1) without the "us" and "them" designations, and consequently lacking the polemical tone; Paget rightly suggests that "the absence of this polemical note in Clement might serve further to back up our polemical reading of the two chapters" of Barnabas (1994: 109).[32]

Horbury astutely observes that "the remarkable prominence of fasting in Barnabas 3 corresponds not to its relatively modest place in the Pentateuchal laws, but to its high importance *in contemporary Jewish custom*" (1992: 325; emphasis added). The observance of regular fasting by Jews is indicated in the New Testament (Mark 2:18; Luke 18:12) and other early Christian literature. For example, the *Didache*—discussed below—confirms Jewish participation in bi-weekly fasts. In that document, Christians are warned, "Let not your fasts be with the hypocrites, for they fast on Mondays and Thursdays, but do you fast on Wednesdays and Fridays" (*Didache* 8.1). This information coheres with later rabbinic regulations that stipulated fasting on those particular days of the week (*m. Taʿan.* 1.6; 2.9 and *m. Meg.* 3.6).

Ptolemy's *Letter to Flora* (c. 160 CE), makes some intriguing comments about the rite of fasting among Christians. Like Barnabas, Ptolemy decries the literal interpretation of the commandment and teaches that it should instead be understood as avoiding corrupt behaviour: "He does not want us to keep a bodily fast, but a spiritual one, in which there is abstention from all iniquity" (33.5.13).[33] Unlike Barnabas, however, Ptolemy admits that members of his community observe fasting and, furthermore, that it can be a *positive action* under specific circumstances:

> Even those of our religion, however, observe the fast of outward appearance, since, when it is done in a reasonable way, it can contribute something even to the soul, *when it is not kept in imitation of certain people* (ὁπότε μήτε διὰ τὴν πρός τινας μίμησιν γίνεται) or because of custom (μήτε διὰ τὸ ἔθος), or because of what day it is (μήτε διὰ τὴν ἡμέραν), as though a day were set [for the] purpose. (emphasis added)

The way this is expressed suggests that, at one point, members of Ptolemy's community *did* fast "in imitation of certain people" since he finds it necessary to explicitly state that that type of fast is ineffective. The "certain people" who are imitated may refer to Jews whose custom it was to fast on specific days. Thus, Ptolemy's instructions to Flora may be that literal fasting could be observed by Christians to the benefit of the soul, but not if it is done in imitation of Jews.[34] Like Ptolemy several years later, Barnabas was aware that some Gentile Christians from his community observed fasting in order to imitate Jews.

Circumcision: An (Un)desirable Seal of Acceptance

Barnabas also discusses the rite of circumcision and how the Jews misinterpreted the commandment of God by interpreting it literally (chap. 9). Circumcision of the foreskin, argues Barnabas, was never meant to occur: he felt that the Jews "erred because an evil angel was misleading them" (ὅτι ἄγγελοᾶς πονηρὸς ἐσόφιζεν αὐτούς, 9.4). Neither Philo, Paul, nor even Marcion present such a radical assertion to attribute the Jewish comprehension of the Torah to an evil angel. Barnabas appears to counter an argument he has heard from members of his own community: "But you will say, surely the people has received circumcision as a seal?" (9.6). Perhaps there were some Gentile Christians who desired to become circumcised because they understood it to represent participation in the covenant of God and, hence, an integral part of being a Christian. Hvalvik (1966: 99) rightly suggests that Jews could argue that

> they—and not the Christians—worshipped God in the right way. And the Christians could easily be accused of neglecting God's requirements....This was the kind of argument that Jews could use over against Christians, a reasoning which could easily impress Gentile Christians who had some knowledge of the Old Testament.

An argument advocating Torah observance as an essential dimension of behaviour for believers in Jesus would be all the more compelling coming from a judaizer. In his epistle, Barnabas warns his readers about not imitating others who stray from proper Christian behaviour (*Barn.* 4.6) and he declares that "a man deserves to perish who has a knowledge of the way of righteousness, but turns aside into the way of darkness" (*Barn.* 5.4), which may also refer to judaizers from *within* the community.

Interestingly, the author of the *Epistle to Diognetus* assumes that his readers are aware of the Jewish "pride in circumcision" (τὴν τῆς περιτομῆς ἀλαζονείαν, 4.1). He also asks: "And what does it deserve but ridicule to be proud of the mutilation of the flesh (τὴν μείωσιν τῆς σαρκὸς) as a proof of election, as if they were, for this reason, especially beloved by God?" (4.4). The phrase τὴν μείωσιν τῆς σαρκὸς is certainly a derogatory way to refer to circumcision, reminding one of Paul's sarcastic remark about circumcision (Gal. 5:12). The author of *Diognetus* clearly seeks to ridicule circumcision; he expresses no appreciation for the meaning it has within Jewish belief and makes no attempt to interpret this ritual as having been replaced as "circumcision of the heart" in Christianity (Brändle 1975: 54ff). Further, he misrepresents the Jewish meaning of circumcision by suggesting that Jews believed they were loved by God as a result of this act.

Barnabas also attempts to negate the desire among Gentile Christians to become circumcised by arguing that circumcision was not a seal of

God's covenant (see Romans 11, Paget 1994: 164-65, Horbury 1992: 329). He claims that, as all Syrians, Arabs, priests of the idols, and "even the Egyptians" undergo circumcision, it was not, therefore, a special sign representing membership in the covenantal community of the Jews.[35] True circumcision, according to Barnabas, was of "hardness of...heart" (9.5). This section of the epistle indicates that Barnabas was aware that some Gentile Christians desired to be circumcised.

The Laws of Kashruth

Barnabas argues that the Jewish food laws were never intended for literal use, but for allegorical instruction regarding correct ethical behaviour (chap. 10). He states that "the ordinance of God is not abstinence from eating, but Moses spoke in the spirit" (Μωϋσῆς δὲ ἐν πνεύματι ἐλάλησεν, 10.2). And he disparages the Jews by suggesting that their incorrect understanding of the law was from a moral deficiency: "Moses received three doctrines concerning food and thus spoke of them in the Spirit; but they received them as really referring to food, owing to the lust of their flesh" (ἐπιθυμίαν τῆς σαρκὸς) (Barn. 10.9). That Barnabas was facing challenges regarding interpretation of the food laws is apparent in the very last verse of chapter 10. There he states: "But how was it possible for them (ἐκείνοις) to understand or comprehend these things? But we (ἡμεῖς δὲ) having a righteous understanding of them announce the commandments as the Lord wished" (10.12). This is a polemical statement, which, in its negative contrast of Jews with Christians, differentiates Christians from Jews.

In light of the author's expression of concern about members of his community being led astray by "conversion to their law" (Barn. 3.6), it seems plausible that there was interest among Christians in applying literally Jewish laws of kashruth to their lives and that this inclination was part of the impetus for his epistle. Barnabas seeks to draw people away from a literal understanding of these laws by providing an innovative interpretation of them. Hvalvik suggests that: "[t]he reason for dealing with these [food] laws is obvious. Together with circumcision and Sabbath observance, the food laws were probably the most significant hallmark of the Jews. It was thus a natural topic for an author fighting against Jewish law observance" (1996: 187-88).

Sabbath Observance

Another issue of significance to Barnabas's community was that of Sabbath observance. His discussion of the Sabbath likely was prompted by his awareness that some Christians in his congregation were practising this custom. Once again he seeks to show how the Jewish interpretation of the commandment is incorrect, this time arguing that God ordered that the Sabbath be sanctified "with pure hands and a pure heart" (15.1) and "[i]f, then, anyone has at present the power to keep holy the day which God made holy by being pure in heart, we are altogether deceived" (ἐν πᾶσιν πεπλανήμεθα, 15.6) because this will only happen when the Lord returns (15.7).

Hvalvik incorrectly argues that, despite the author's reference to the celebration of the eighth day, "he is not arguing that the Sabbath has been replaced by the Lord's day" but instead seeks to demonstrate that God's commandment "relates to another Sabbath than the seventh day of the week, [that is, the] cosmic Sabbath" (1996: 126). While it is correct that Barnabas argues that the weekly Sabbaths, which are "not acceptable" (15.8), have been replaced by an eschatological Sabbath, Barnabas does seem to be trying to dissuade his readers from making the Sabbath (that is, Saturday) their special day. He emphasizes that Christians have their *own day of celebration*, the "eighth day," or Sunday, which honours "the eighth day in which Jesus also rose from the dead" and anticipates the "beginning of another world" (15.9).

In his discussion of the Sabbath, Barnabas seeks to negate the Jewish understanding of what it meant to keep the Sabbath. Why he does this for what I contend is a primarily Gentile Christian readership is his desire to encourage Christians to worship on Sunday instead of Saturday. Barnabas's community may not have been as aware as he was of the distinction between or the significance of the two practices.

The author of the *Epistle of Barnabas* criticizes Jewish interpretation of scripture and Jewish religious practices in order to dissuade members of his community from attraction to Judaism and from observing Jewish customs. In reaction to what he perceived to be excessive attachment to Judaism among his members, Barnabas juxtaposes Christian tradition and interpretation of the law against Jewish customs and interpretation of the law. He does so to instruct his readers about the difference between Christianity and Judaism, and to demonstrate the superiority of Christian behaviour and understanding. He aims to negate the validity of Jewish ritual by taking a radical interpretation of the Jewish law and argues that the Mosaic law was never supposed to be interpreted literally. Jews who lived according to the literal understanding of the law, therefore, were wrong, and Christians who found Jewish customs attractive and practised them, were also wrong.

Barnabas's anti-Judaism suggests that he perceived Judaism to be a threat to his community. He warns his Gentile Christian readers against becoming "shipwrecked by conversion" to Jewish law (3.6). Distressed that some members of his community understand the covenant to belong to both Christians and Jews, and therefore were not differentiating sufficiently between Jewish and Christian behaviour, he warns others against being influenced by these individuals. "Take heed to yourselves," he anxiously advises (*Barn.* 4.6).

The *Epistle of Barnabas* is best understood as a document written against a background of Jewish optimism that the Temple in Jerusalem would be rebuilt. The potential for fulfilling this Jewish longing probably heightened Gentile attraction to Judaism and, as such, provided a context for why some Gentile Christians were inclined to follow Jewish customs. Within the epistle, Barnabas directly criticizes Christians claiming that the covenant belonged to Christians and Jews; there is also indirect evidence that Christians at the time were observing the Jewish Sabbath, following Jewish food laws, undergoing circumcision, and participating in Jewish fasts. Barnabas's theology is a result of the context in which he wrote. He denigrates Jewish religious practices because, as I have demonstrated here, he fears that the Christians whom he addresses in his epistle found Jewish customs too attractive.

The *Didache*

LIKE THE *Epistle of Barnabas*, the *Didache* reflects a deliberate attempt to encourage the practice of Christian rites in contradistinction to Jewish customs. One of the most perplexing documents in early Christian literature, the *Didache* contains a variety of internal inconsistencies. While there is wide agreement that it is a composite text, the question of the development of the document prior to its present form has long been contentious. Early interpreters such as Harnack assumed that the *Didache* was produced by a single author who brought together a number of traditions (1884: 24-63), but this hypothesis is held by only a minority of modern scholars (e.g., Wengst 1984: 18-20). Most interpreters of the text, employing literary critical methods, propose different stages in the development of the text and then distinguish which texts fit into each particular stage.[36] My interest is not in the various rhetorical stages of the text, but in its final form and particularly in the second century CE community that embraced it and found it meaningful.

Features of the *Didache* suggest that the people who used this document in its final form were predominantly Gentile. Like the *Epistle of Barnabas*, it incorporates portions of the so-called "Two Ways" material. The framework of the Two Ways material is derived from the Jewish decalogue; ethical teachings from the decalogue and from Jewish wisdom tradition are fitted into this structure (Audet 1958: 283; Harnack 1884: 64; Jefford 1989: 142-45; Niederwimmer 1989: 116-17). Among the admonitions are instructions not to engage in pederasty, magic, abortion, and infanticide (*Didache* 2.2; 5.1-2). These are best understood to be directed toward Gentiles from pagan backgrounds. The Jerusalem manuscript (*Hierosolymitanus* 54) of the *Didache* bears two successive titles: the first is Διδαχὴ τῶν δώδεκα ἀποστόλων ("The Teaching of the Twelve Apostles") and the second is Διδαχὴ κυρίου διὰ τῶν δώδεκα ἀποστόλων τοῖς ἔθνεσιν ("The Teaching of the Lord through the Twelve Apostles to the Gentiles"). This second title in particular indicates that the tractate was eventually embraced by a group of predominantly Gentile Christians (Draper 1991: 362; Rordorf 1996: 155).

One of the striking characteristics of the document is its inconsistent attitude toward Judaism. On the one hand, the *Didache* in its present form is a very Jewish composition. Chapters 1 to 6, for example, are thoroughly Jewish in style and content. As Kloppenborg has noted (1995: 102; see also Jefford 1989: 91), the *Didache* argues from the decalogue and

> the authority of the decalogue is not in dispute but is simply self-evident, and the author of this early Christian Two Ways document makes use of that authority. The fact that the framer of the document can do this implies that the text is edited and employed in an environment in which the authority of the Torah *can be taken for granted*.[37] (emphasis added)

At the same time, however, in certain parts of the text, Christian rites are placed in explicit juxtaposition with Jewish practices. For example, Christians are encouraged to pray on Wednesdays and Fridays rather than with "the hypocrites" (i.e., the Jews) on Mondays and Thursdays (*Didache* 8.1ff). At these points, the text is combatting Gentile Christian observance of Jewish customs within the church.

Provenance and Date

Egypt and Syria are usually offered as plausible locations for the writing of the *Didache*. Kraft notes that "Christianity in general, and Eastern (including Egypt and Asia Minor) Christianity in particular, retained such more or less conscious vestiges of its Jewish heritage for decades and centuries after the 'victory' of Gentile Christianity" (1965: 77). He favours a place of origin somewhere in Egypt, arguing that, "if Egypt seems somewhat more probable than Syria, it is because the later uses of the *Didache* tradition…and the earliest textual evidence point most strongly to that area" (Kraft 1965: 77). This is not a compelling argument, however, since many manuscripts were preserved in Egypt because of its climate and thus finding a manuscript there does not necessarily indicate the origin of the text. The reference in the text to wheat (bread) scattered on the mountains in the prayer (*Didache* 9:4) evokes imagery from somewhere other than Egyptian wheat flats. A Syrian provenance seems more likely, particularly in light of the literary connections existing between the *Didache* and other Syrian documents; most commentators now opt for it (Audet 1958: 206; Rordorf and Tuilier 1978: 97; Draper 1996) or for Syro-Palestine (Niederwimmer 1977). The *Didache* probably dates to the late first or early second century CE, with parts of it, such as the Two Ways material, probably from an earlier period.[38]

The Two Ways Material

The lightly Christianized Jewish Two Ways material (chaps. 1–6) is also found in the *Epistle of Barnabas* (18–20). Although there are differences in the order in which both texts present this material, there are so many instances where the wording is identical in both documents that many scholars have argued that one document depended on the other.[39] The discovery of the *Manual of Discipline* at Qumran and its publication in 1951 made a significant impact on scholarly perception of the Two Ways material in the *Didache* and *Barnabas*. The "Two Angels" section of the *Manual* (1 QS 3.13–4.26) confirmed the idea that a Jewish document containing the Two Ways material probably circulated prior to and separately from the *Epistle of Barnabas* and the *Didache*; at present most scholars agree that they drew on a common source.

Draper suggests that the *Didache* is best understood as a set of instructions communicated as a community rule that was altered at various times "by trial and error, by erasing words or phrases, by inserting new words or phrases above the line or in the margin, which are later incorporated into the text," not unlike the alterations evident in the manuscript of the *Community Rule* of the Qumran Sect (1991: 349). This scenario allows for multiple authors, contradictions and inconsistencies in the text, a view that seems to fit the *Didache*. At several points, material found in the *Didache* echoes material found in the Gospel of Matthew, prompting much scholarly musing about whether the authors or editors of the *Didache* knew the Gospel of Matthew or shared the same traditions (Jefford 1989; Niederwimmer 1989). Draper has argued persuasively that the *Didache* and the Gospel of Matthew had a dialectic relationship, with both documents evolving together in the same place and significantly influencing one another. He suggests that they drew material from the same traditions, but eventually the Gospel of Matthew incorporated the issues addressed in the community rule, subordinating the rule to the gospel and thereby displacing the *Didache* (Draper 1991: 349).[40]

Using the evidence of the Dead Sea Scrolls, Jean-Paul Audet (1952) argues cogently that the Two Ways material in the first six chapters of the *Didache* was originally a Jewish treatise that had been christianized by the author of the *Didache*. This Jewish treatise, and not the *Didache*, was likely the source for the Two Ways material in the *Epistle of Barnabas* (Flusser 1996: 197). The source that both documents used for the Two Ways material probably was similar to the *Doctrina* and was originally used to instruct new Jewish converts (see Goodspeed 1945). Unlike the *Epistle of Barnabas* and the *Manual of Discipline*, the *Didache* does not set the Two Ways material within an eschatological context (also Kloppenborg 1995: 92).

Other Material Influenced by Judaism

Aside from the Two Ways material, the *Didache* in its final form retains other salient evidence of Jewish influence, such as *Didache* 6.1-3:

> 1) See that no one make you to err from this way of the teaching, for he teaches you without God. 2) For if you can bear the whole yoke of the Lord (ὅλον τὸν ζυγὸν), you will be perfect, but if you can not, do what you can (εἰ δ ᾿οὐ δύνασαι, ὃ δύνῃ, τοῦτο ποίει). 3) And concerning food, bear what you can, but keep strictly from that which is offered to idols, for it is the worship of dead gods.

The instructions in this passage (*Didache* 6.2-3) are generally consistent with Jewish observance of *kashruth*, but with added allowance for leniency. The perfect ones are those who "bear the whole yoke of the Lord" (ὅλον τὸν ζυγὸν) but, if that cannot be done, then they are instructed to "do what you can" (εἰ δ᾿ οὐ δύνασαι, ὃ δύνῃ, τοῦτο ποίει 6.2). The ideal is to "keep strictly from that which is offered to idols, for it is the worship of dead gods...and concerning food, bear what you can" (*Didache* 6.3). Verses 2 and 3 are connected, as Kraft observes, by their "atmosphere of concession" (1965: 161). The ideal was presented first (*Didache* 1, 2a) and then this ideal was adapted to what apparently was more pragmatic. These verses, which are not found in other documents that contain Two Ways material, demarcate two categories of Christians for the *Didache* community: those who attain the ideal, and those who do the best they can. These verses stipulate that the minimal obligations of Gentile Christians toward the Mosaic law are: to do their best to keep the whole law and to do their best to eat food that is kosher—at the very least avoid eating meat that had been offered to idols. The use of "yoke" in association with the law (*Didache* 2a) is found in later Jewish literature. Tractate *Gerim* 1.2, for example, has the following *varia lectio*: "if he (the future proselyte) says, 'I am not worthy to place my neck under the yoke of Him Who spoke and the world came into being, blessed be He,' they receive him forthwith, and if not he is dismissed and goes his way" (Cohen 1971: 603 n.5; also Flusser 1996: 207). In *m. Abot* 3.5, R. Nehunya b. Haqqanehstates: "He that takes upon himself the yoke of the Law (כל המקבל עליו עול תורה) from him shall be taken the yoke of the kingdom and the yoke of worldly care."[41] Draper proceeds to show how the word ζυγός (yoke) refers to the Torah four out of five times in the New Testament; in Matthew (11:29-30), the new "yoke of the Lord" is introduced as a law of Jesus that is much easier to bear than that of the Pharisees (1991: 365).

One section of the *Didache* (7.1 to 8.3) deals with the issues of baptism, fasting, and prayer—three significant practices in the Christian life essential for a new convert to follow. *Didache* 7.1 provides rules for baptism that mirror Jewish practices by stating that baptism is to take place in "running water" (ὕδατι ζῶντι). Within Jewish practices of immersion for purity, the water to be used is מים חיים: *living* or fresh water (Klausner 1939: 157-64; Niederwimmer 1989: 161).[42] The next verses compromise this instruction: "but if you have no running water, baptize in other water, and if you cannot in cold, then in warm" (7.2). Rordorf and Tuilier suggest that this concession was made because of the weather: "The text here appears to evoke the impossibility of using cold water because of the season. In winter it was in fact necessary to heat the baptismal water" (1978: 171, trans. from French). While this is a common-sense suggestion, the concession suggests little concern for appeasing Jewish sensibilities and strictly following Jewish tradition. It may reflect a time of diminishing Jewish membership among whom the *Didache* was written.

The Anti-Jewish Voice

The text in other respects betrays a strong desire to distance Christian practise from Jewish rites. Criticism is addressed to Christians who are manifesting what the leaders of the second century community deem to be excessive involvement in Jewish ritual behaviour. The people addressed by the *Didache* are instructed to fast on Wednesdays and Fridays so as not to fast "with the hypocrites (μετὰ τῶν ὑποκριτῶν), for they fast on Mondays and Thursdays" (*Did.* 8.1). Readers furthermore are prohibited from praying "as the hypocrites" (ὡς οἱ ὑποκριταί, 8.2). These prohibitions imply that "there must be *at least* some perceived chance that what is prohibited may be done, and *at most*, someone has already flagrantly disobeyed [the author]; but perhaps it is a case of action being performed in naive ignorance" (Barclay 1987: 84). The desired outcome from the instructions given in chapter 8 was for members of the *Didache* community to conduct themselves differently from "the hypocrites." Who are the hypocrites that the *Didache* community is being warned not to emulate?

Draper is probably correct when he asserts that "the term simply designates the Jewish opponents of the community" (1985: 279; also Wilson 1995: 225; Niederwimmer 1989: 165–66). Monday and Thursday were the market days in Palestine, when many people would gather in towns and villages; as they would have been able to attend the synagogue, these days were chosen as fasting days (Bradshaw 1981: 19). In the discussion of *Barnabas* 3, I noted that this statement on fasting in the *Didache* corresponds to rabbinic regulations given in the Mishnah (e.g., *m. Taʿan.* 1.6; 2.9, 12a; *m. Meg.* 3.6).

Rordorf and Tuilier insist that the "hypocrites" are Christians who pray as the Jews do: they simply cannot be Jews, for "it would be surprising if a writing like the *Didache*, which owes so much to the Jewish tradition, expressed itself in such a violent manner toward the Jews" (1978: 36–37, trans. from French). It is true that, if the "hypocrites" are not Christians but Jews, a double message is indeed being communicated—but an inconsistent attitude toward Jewish tradition is one of the consistent aspects of the *Didache*. Wilson has pointed out that this text is an example of literature in which "evidence of Jewish influence goes hand in hand with a conscious distancing from, or even hostility toward, Judaism" (1995: 224). Interestingly, the *Didache* Christians are not to behave like Jews, yet the instruction to fast on Mondays and Thursdays is still keeping the Jewish practice of fasting twice a week, and the instruction to pray three times a day is consistent with that Jewish custom.[43] The fact that the *Didache* simply states "Pray thus three times a day" (3.1) without specifying precisely when these prayers were to be offered suggests that those to whom the *Didache* was addressed would have known when to pray because they were aware of the times that Jews traditionally offered their prayers (Bradshaw 1981: 26). Even the "innovated" Lord's Prayer that Christians are instructed to recite (*Did.* 8.2), which is almost identical to the Matthean version, is thoroughly Jewish.[44]

The purpose of the instruction in *Didache* 8.1 is to promote fasting on different days from those used by the Jews, probably because some Christians continued to fast on Mondays and Thursdays with Jews. The ὑπόκριται of 8.1 are Jews, but the instruction not to fast with them is directed to members of the Christian community who were fasting with Jews or who might be tempted to do so. Rordorf and Tuilier, then, were primarily correct when they argue that "chapter 8 of the *Didache* would here be condemning the attitude of certain judaizing Christians (*chrétiens judaisants*) in denouncing in particular the return to Jewish observance in the Christian community" (1978: 37, trans. from French).[45] The text, however, does not describe the behaviour as a "return" to judaizing behaviour, as if these Christians had stopped observing Jewish practices for a time before they took them up again. It may have been the case that some Christian Gentiles had maintained Jewish rites from the very beginning of their Christian experience, without viewing such behaviour as contradictory to their belief in Jesus or their identity as Christians.

Chapter 14 of the *Didache* indicates that there was a need to differentiate between Christian and Jewish practices regarding the day of worship: "On the Lord's Day of the Lord (κυριακὴν δὲ κυρίου) come together, break bread and hold Eucharist, after confessing your transgressions that your offering may be pure" (*Did.* 14.1). The phrase κυριακὴν δὲ κυρίου is peculiar and seems to be redundant. The term κυριακή means "belonging to the Lord" or "the Lord's" and κυρίου means "of the Lord"; so the literal translation of the phrase is "Lord's of the Lord" (Gingrich and Danker 1979: 458). Scholars usually translate the phrase as "on the Lord's Day of the Lord" (Lake 1985: 331) or "on the Lord's own day" (Bauckham 1982: 227) or "the Lord's Day" (Louth 1987: 197). The actual meaning of the phrase is ambiguous: does it refer to Sunday? Does the redundant κυρίου make the term a reference to Easter?

Other ambiguous uses of κυριακή in documents from the late first and early second centuries CE include Ignatius's letter to the Magnesians (9.1) (κατὰ κυριακὴν ζῶντες) and the *Gospel of Peter* 9.35 and 12 (in both cases κυριακή appears without κυρίου). Evidence from the later second century can be more clearly understood to refer to Sunday: for example, the *Acts of Paul* refers to Paul praying "on the Sabbath as the Lord's Day drew near" (ἐπερχομένης τῆς κυριακῆς), which cannot be understood as the annual celebration of Easter (Bauckham 1982: 229).[46] The term ἡμέρα (του) κυρίου refers to the eschatological "Day of the Lord." Likely, κυριακὴν ἡμέρα became established as the Christian term for Sunday as a way to distinguish it from the eschatological Day of the Lord (Bauckham 1982: 225). By the late second century, the word κυριακός came into common use as an alternative to τοῦ κυρίου and eventually κυριακή on its own was used to identify Sunday (Bauckham 1982: 226).[47]

The redundant phrase κυριακὴν δὲ κυρίου in the *Didache* (14.1) serves as a means of emphasis: the Eucharist was to take place on Sunday, not on another day. The author or editor of the *Didache* deemed it necessary to stress this instruction because he was so disturbed by the practice of Christian observance of the Jewish Sabbath (Louth 1987: 199; Stanton 1996: 176). That the keeping of the Sabbath by some Christians was problematic in the late first and/or early second century CE in Syria is indicated in *Barnabus* (15.8-9), where that author attempts to negate the

Jewish understanding of keeping the Sabbath, as argued earlier, to discourage Christians from observing this rite.[48]

In its final form, the *Didache* reflects divergent voices. Jewish influence
is reflected in the Two Ways material and in stipulations for minimal
requirements regarding observance of Torah, including food laws and
instructions concerning baptism in "living water." There are, furthermore,
indications that Jewish influence concerning fasting and prayer continued
within some parts of the Christian community, with some members maintaining attachment to Judaism and these rites. The text attempts to establish a clear demarcation between Christian and Jewish behaviour by
prohibiting imitation of Jewish customs by Christians. This attempt indicates that some Christians of the second century were attracted to and
perhaps practised certain Jewish customs such as prayer, fasting, and Sabbath observance.

The Pseudo-Clementine Literature

THE PSEUDO-CLEMENTINE LITERATURE is a collection of Syrian documents that is dated to the fourth century and, like other documents investigated here, contains earlier traditions. This literature describes the
fictitious story of Clement of Rome's conversion to Christianity, his travels with the apostle Peter to cities along the Syrian coast, and his reunion
with long-lost family members. The writings present an apologetic and
systematic compendium of Christian doctrine and consist of two main
components, the *Homilies* (H) and the *Recognitions* (R) (Strecker 1992:
485).[49]

These two components have so much material in common that it is
believed that they derive from a basic source (G = *Grundschrift*). Similar
to the Q hypothesis, G is a hypothetical document whose contents are
deduced from common material in both H and R. This putative primary
text was probably written in Syria early in the third century (Strecker
1992: 488). In turn, scholars have determined that this basic source
depended on earlier sources, one of which is the so-called *Kerygmata
Petrou* (Κηρύγματα Πέτρου), or "Preachings of Peter" (KP).[50] This is a
hypothetical document understood to be the gospel that was preached by
Peter, and is usually dated to the second century and assigned a Syrian
provenance (Strecker 1981: 219).[51] Strecker reconstructs the *Kerygamata
Petrou* from what he believes are the "introductory writings" to the KP, the
Epistula Petri and the *Contestatio* (Strecker 1981: 137ff; Strecker 1992:
488ff).[52]

Strecker's understanding of these documents was widely accepted for an
extended period of time. Recently scholars have expressed skepticism,

however, regarding whether it is possible to detect independent sources embedded in the Pseudo-Clementines based on stylistic criteria and vocabulary (Lüdemann 1989: 169-70; Jones 1982: 1-33, 63-96; Jones 1995: 1-38). It may not be possible to outline precisely the sources of the Pseudo-Clementine text, but it is possible to detect different themes and attitudes in the material, and this is sufficient for our purposes (see Wilson 1995: 144).[53] Two prominent themes found in this literature are a positive attitude toward Judaism and a negative assessment of Paul.

The KP comprises material in the Pseudo-Clementines that reflects Jewish Christian elements and concerns, among them the Jewish Christian *Contestatio* and the *Epistula Petri*, which are prefixed to the KP.[54] One of the dominant elements in the *Kerygmata* is "the true prophet," who brought divine revelation by manifesting himself in a series of changing characters, including Adam (R.1.47), Moses (H.2.52) and Jesus (H.3.17-19; Strecker 1965: 107). The knowledge brought by the true prophet is characterized as identical with the law of Moses; Moses passed it on to seventy elders, and it is now in the possession of the Pharisees and scribes. These representatives of Judaism have been ineffectual in their teaching of the knowledge, however, necessitating the sending of the true prophet Peter. Paul is presented as the antagonist to the true teaching, the negative syzygy-partner of Peter, and the representative of false female prophecy.[55] His proclamation of the termination of the law is understood to be a false doctrine (H. 11.35.4-6).

The KP reflects a milieu in which there was close association with Judaism and Gnosticism (Strecker 1992: 491). The attitude toward Jewish tradition reflected in this source is positive; Judaism is highly esteemed and is presented as an example to be imitated. As mentioned above, Jesus is understood in this document to be the "true prophet" who earlier had manifested himself in Adam and Moses. Jesus' teachings are consistent with those of Moses in that they uphold the obligations associated with the Mosaic law. One passage seems to reflect a dual-covenant theory, one covenant being revealed by Moses for the Jews and the other by Jesus for the Gentiles; "equally valid and equally valuable, the parallel covenants are efficacious for those who do not hate or oppose the other" (Wilson 1995: 152). Strecker (1981: 164-65, 257) assigns the passage to KP:

> It is therefore the peculiar gift bestowed by God upon the Hebrews, that they believe Moses, and the peculiar gift bestowed upon the Gentiles is that they love Jesus....By which it is certainly declared, that the people of the Hebrews who were instructed out of the law, did not know Him; but the people of the Gentiles have acknowledged Jesus, and venerate him,...But he who is of the Gentiles and who has it of God to believe Moses, ought also to have it of his own purpose to love Jesus also (R. 4.5).[56]

As Wilson notes, the message expresses "a remarkably generous vision of salvation, which places Christianity and Judaism on a par. It is not precisely the same view as that of the judaizers in the *Epistle of Barnabas*, where the author spoke of sharing one covenant rather than allowing for two covenants, but the underlying spirit is the same" (1995: 141). These Pseudo-Clementine verses, in fact, may represent the perspective of judaizers themselves.

Hostility toward Paul, Teacher of the "Lawless" Gospel

Another relevant dimension of this literature is that the writing strongly advocates law observance for Gentiles and is hostile toward Pauline Christianity, which does not require Gentiles to maintain Jewish customs. The Pseudo-Clementine texts express the authors' anger over the fact that his views concerning the Mosaic law have been misrepresented, for the individual named "Simon" (a reference to the apostle Paul)[57] has taught Gentiles that he and Peter agreed that they did not need to be observant. Gager rightly concludes that "the literary materials embedded in the Pseudo-Clementines reveal a stream of Christianity in close contact with contemporaneous Judaism, committed to the observance of the Mosaic commandments for all of its members, and constituted to a significant degree by Gentiles" (1985: 125).

The Pseudo-Clementine literature describes hostile confrontations between the author's perspective (represented by "Peter") and his rival Simon Magus, who is described as a missionary to the Gentiles (H. 2.17.3). Simon Magus is the magician (introduced in the book of Acts 8:9-24) who is condemned by Christian heresiologists as the father of Gnosticism. Most scholars of the Pseudo-Clementine literature agree, however, that later editors added the name "Simon Magus" and that Paul was the original opponent of Peter (Meeks 1972: 178).

At several points in the writing, Peter expresses great distress over the fact that some Gentile Christians do not observe the Mosaic law. He argues passionately against Paul, whom he blames for the behaviour of these Gentile Christians. In his cover letter to James, Peter warns that, "some from among the Gentiles have rejected my lawful preaching and have preferred a lawless and absurd doctrine of the man who is my enemy" (*Ep. of Peter* 2.1). Peter (*Ep. of Peter* 2.4-5) laments how even during his lifetime, certain people attempted

> to distort my words by interpretations of many sorts, as if I taught the dissolution of the law and, although I was of this opinion, did not express it openly. But that may God forbid! For to do such a thing means to act contrary to the law of God which was made known by Moses and was confirmed by our Lord in its everlasting continuance. For he said: "The heavens and the earth will pass away, but one jot or one tittle shall not pass away from the law."

According to this text, Peter believes that Paul deliberately misrepresented his gospel by claiming that Peter does not expect Gentile Christians to observe the Mosaic law. Elsewhere Peter claims that "Simon" preaches "under pretext of the truth, in the name of our Lord, but actually is sowing error" (H. 11.35.5 in Meeks 1972: 181).[58]

Paul's Damascus-road vision of Christ is denigrated by Peter, who declares, "one who puts his trust in a vision or an apparition or dream is in a precarious position, for he does not know what it is he is trusting. For it is possible that it is an evil demon or a deceitful spirit, pretending in the speeches to be what he is not" (H. 17.14.3 in Meeks 1972: 181). Paul was not a true apostle of Jesus, because he did not learn directly from Jesus, but through a vision, which was not reliable. In fact, its source was not God but evil. Peter states, "no one can see the incorporeal power of the Son or even of an angel. But if someone sees a vision, let him understand this to be an evil demon" (H. 17.16.4 in Meeks 1972: 182). A little later he asserts, "the fact that one sees visions and dreams and apparitions by no means assures that he is a religious person" (H. 17.17.5 in Meeks 1972: 182). It is clear from these descriptions that Paul is the intended enemy, particularly in this statement: "So even if our Jesus did appear in a dream to you, making himself known and conversing with you, he did so in anger, speaking to an opponent. That is why he spoke to you through visions and dreams—through revelations which are external" (H. 17.19.1 in Meeks 1972: 182). Peter asks "Simon": "How could he have appeared to you, when your opinions are opposed to his teaching?" (H. 17.19.4 in Meeks 1972: 182). This text expresses the view that the lawless gospel taught by Paul contradicted what Jesus himself taught; that is, Jesus taught law observance to Gentiles.

The teaching by Paul ("Simon") is described as thoroughly false because, as observed earlier, he is a spiritual descendant of the false female prophet, he is "merely a helpmate of the feeble left hand (of God, i.e., the evil one)" (H. 2.15.5 in Meeks 1972: 178). Peter describes the doctrine of the pairs of opposites or syzygies, explaining that "Simon" came first and went to be with the Gentiles, and that he, Peter, "came after him and followed him as the light follows darkness, knowledge ignorance, and healing sickness" (H. 2.17.3 in Meeks 1972: 178). According to Peter (PC, H. 2.17.4, 18.1) people were deceived by "Simon" because they were ignorant of the law of pairs of opposites:

> as the true prophet has said, a false gospel must first come from an impostor and only then, after the destruction of the holy place, can a true gospel be sent forth for the correction of the sects that are to come.... Since now, as has been said, many do not know this conformity of the syzygies with law, they do not know who this Simon, my forerunner, is. For were it known, no

one would believe him. But now, as he remains unknown, confidence is
wrongly placed in him.

It is interesting to note that Peter's "true" gospel is not the original gospel
but is described as emerging subsequent to Paul's gospel. The fact that
Jesus taught before both Peter and Paul seems to be ignored completely.
According to this text, the false gospel (i.e., that taught by Paul) *must first
come* and only afterward can the true gospel—that of Peter—be revealed.
This argument contradicts the other anti-Pauline theme, discussed above,
that laments how Paul came *after* Jesus and Peter and distorted both of
their messages. The latter reflects more accurately the dissemination of
Christianity (i.e., it originated with Jesus, followed by Peter, and finally
Paul). The anti-Pauline theme that describes Paul's document as the first
"false" gospel may be part of a rhetorical strategy. If the doctrine of syzygies dictates that Paul's "false" gospel was preached first, the impact and
success of his teaching is necessarily undermined, since the presence of
Christians who follow his version of the gospel are part of a larger plan.
This suggests that there were an appreciable number of "Pauline" Christians in the area—that is, Gentile Christians who did *not* practise the
law—to elicit a response from the author. Their presence was not necessarily exhaustive, since the existence of even a few Gentile Christians who
were not observing the law may have been enough to prompt "Peter" the
author to respond. From this evidence, it is likely that Christian judaizers
as well as non-observant Christians were present in the area.

The Law-Observant Mission to Gentiles: Historical Progenitors

J. Louis Martyn understands the *Kerygmata Petrou* to be a Jewish–Christian source written "for a community living in effective isolation from the
emerging church of the west" (1985: 311). These people understand themselves to be obedient to the law revealed by Moses and endorsed by Jesus,
including advocating a law-observant mission to Gentiles. Martyn suggests that "we have the probability that our Jewish-Christian authors give
true reflections of second-century Law-observant missions to Gentiles,
carried out independently of the Great Church," and he wonders whether
"the evangelistic efforts portrayed in these second-century documents are
descended from a Law-observant mission pursued by Jewish Christians in
the first century" (Martyn 1985: 312).

To pursue this question, Martyn investigates whether there is a connection between the situation Paul addresses in his letter to the Galatians
(1.13) and the Pseudo-Clementine literature. He suggests—mistakenly, in
my view—that the opposing teachers are "circumcised Jews who preach

circumcision to Gentiles as the act appropriate to the universal good news of God's Law" (Martyn 1985: 316). Martyn asserts that, in Galatians, Paul is responding to Jewish Christian teachers who are attempting to persuade the Gentiles to become circumcised and to follow the law in order to become true "descendants of Abraham" (Gal. 3:7). He notes that the *Ascents of James*—which he considers to be another Jewish-Christian source embedded in the Pseudo-Clementine literature—expresses the view that the "true line of religion extends from Abraham to his descendants [and that] indeed for the author of the *Ascents*, God's blessing of Abraham provides the motivation for the Law-observant mission to Gentiles" (Martyn 1985: 320). Martyn admits that "we cannot be sure that the Teachers in Galatia are historical progenitors of the communities of Christian Jews we see reflected in the second-century sources cited," but he goes on to suggest that "[w]ith a high degree of probability we can say, however, that like the evangelists in those later communities the Teachers pursue their own Law-observant mission among Gentiles" (1985: 323).

Martyn's thesis is intriguing. He is correct to point out that the Christian situation in the first century CE was not simply divided into Jewish Christians who kept the Mosaic law, and Gentile Christians who did not. There is strong evidence that some Gentile Christians combined a commitment to Christianity with adherence, in varying degrees, to Jewish practices. I argue in chapter 3 that the situation in Galatia was even more complex than the one Martyn describes, for not only Jewish Christians but in particular circumcised Gentile Christians were putting pressure on Gentile Christians in Galatia to become circumcised and follow the law. The *Kerygmata Petrou* is a document that urges judaizing behaviour for Gentile Christians and, as such, one can see a connection with the first-century CE phenomenon encountered by Paul in Galatia.

Strecker stresses that "the Jewish Christianity of the *Kerygmata* should be understood in the context of Bauer's hypothesis," in that it had not cut itself off from the "great church" and was not "sectarian" in nature, but likely was "the sole representative of Christianity and the problem of its relationship to the 'great church' had not yet arisen" (Strecker in Bauer 1971: 271). Strecker's point is an important one, and should also be applied to the understanding of Christian judaizing. The observance of Jewish religious rites, for many Gentile Christians in Syria—and in Asia Minor, as argued in the next chapter—was not necessarily in its earlier manifestations a "heretical" view but was understood to be regular Christian behaviour.

Each of the documents examined in this chapter deals with Gentile Christian attraction to and observance of Jewish religious rites and, as such, they are connected to one another. The authors of the *Epistle of Barnabas* and the *Didache discourage* Gentile Christian attachment to Judaism by advocating the practice of Christian religious rites rather than Jewish customs. In contrast, one of the central themes detected in the Pseudo-Clementine literature denounces the law-free gospel of Paul (identified as "Simon") and another explicitly *promotes* judaizing. Thus, Gentiles who adhered to the instructions advocated by this literature would become Christian judaizers.

It is plausible that the Torah-observant Gentile Christians who followed the instructions stipulated in the Pseudo-Clementine literature are precisely the people whom the Syrian authors of the *Epistle of Barnabas* and the *Didache* were struggling against. Barnabas and the author/editor of the *Didache* are aware of Gentiles in their respective communities whose interest in Judaism extended to the practice of a variety of Jewish rituals, such as fasting, circumcision, and Sabbath observance—as well as *kashruth*, in the case of Barnabas. It is precisely this behaviour that the Pseudo-Clementine literature encourages. Reactions of ecclesiastical leaders to judaizing contributed toward the development of a distinctive Christian identity and behaviour, since their criticism of unacceptable Jewish behaviour clarified, for members of their immediate communities and for generations of Christians who subsequently read these texts, what constituted "proper" Christian behaviour.

Gentile Christian attachment to Judaism continued to be a problematic phenomenon in Syrian Christian communities long after Peter, Barnabas, and other Jewish Christians ceased eating with Gentile Christians in Antioch, Syria, and prompted judaizing behaviour in that city during the Pauline period (Gal. 2). In the next chapter, I investigate evidence for Christian judaizing in Asia Minor and, among the documents, discuss the letters of Ignatius of Antioch. The content of two of his letters indicates that Ignatius encountered judaizing in Asia Minor while on his journey from Antioch to Rome during the early second century CE. In light of the evidence for the existence of judaizing in Syria reflected in the *Epistle of Barnabas*, the *Didache*, and the Pseudo-Clementine literature, however, it is possible that Ignatius's confrontation with Christian judaizing in Asia Minor was not his first, but that he was already cognizant of the phenomenon in Syria.

━◆━

CHAPTER 5

Christian Judaizing in Asia Minor: Revelation, Ignatius, and Justin Martyr

◄○►

T HAT SOME GENTILE CHRISTIANS were attracted to Judaism and practised Jewish customs in Asia Minor is indicated clearly in let- ters by Ignatius of Antioch, Syria, during his travels through Asia Minor and in Justin Martyr's *Dialogue with Trypho*. Justin provides one of the most explicit references to Christian judaizing in early church liter- ature, proving that ecclesiastical leaders continued to grapple with the vitality of diaspora Judaism and its attraction for Christians in the mid- dle of the second century CE. The compelling evidence for the existence of the phenomenon in Asia Minor found in the writings of Ignatius and Justin Martyr helps to elucidate two anomalous statements made in the Book of Revelation—another Asia Minor document written approxi- mately twenty years earlier than the date of Ignatius's correspondence. These statements, which are usually understood to be polemics against Jews or Jewish Christian opponents, are better interpreted to be the author's reaction to Christian judaizers. Since it is the earliest of the documents investigated in this chapter, it is with the Book of Revelation that I begin.

The Book of Revelation

IN THE SECOND AND THIRD CHAPTERS of the Book of Revelation are obscure accusations embedded in letters addressed to two churches in Asia Minor: Smyrna and Philadelphia. The author of Revelation accuses his opponents there of falsifying their identification as Jews, for which he calls them members of a "synagogue of Satan" (Rev. 2:9; 3:9). Scholars typically understand these statements to be Christian slander of local Jews, and so have viewed them as evidence that the Christian community rep- resented by the Apocalypse of John was engaged in vigorous conflict with Jews and Judaism toward the end of Emperor Domitian's reign (c. 95 CE).[1] In this chapter I demonstrate that Gentile Christians who were attracted to Judaism and became attached to the synagogue are the target of the accusations in Revelation (2:9 and 3:9) and that, instead of reflecting a

---

Notes to chapter 5 start on page 169

Notes to chapter 5 start on page 169

struggle between Jews and Christians, these verses reflect an internal Christian controversy.

Revelation 2:9 and 3:9

The accusations found in two of the messages to the seven churches of Asia Minor that follow the introduction in the first chapter of the Book of Revelation come prior to the throne vision presented in chapters 4 and 5. The first accusation (Rev. 2:9) is taken from the letter to the church in Smyrna:

> I know your affliction and your poverty, even though you are rich. I know the slander (βλασφημίαν) on the part of those who say that they are Jews and are not (τῶν λεγόντων Ἰουδαίους εἶναι ἑαυτοὺς καὶ οὐκ), but are a synagogue of Satan (συναγωγὴ τοῦ Σατανᾶ). Do not fear what you are about to suffer. Beware, the devil is about to throw some of you into prison so that you may be tested, and for ten days you will have affliction. Be faithful until death, and I will give you the crown of life.

The second (Rev. 3:9) is taken from the letter to the church in Philadelphia:

> I know that you have but little power, and yet you have kept my word and have not denied my name. I will make those of the synagogue of Satan (συναγωγῆς τοῦ Σατανᾶ) who say that they are Jews and are not, but are lying (τῶν λεγόντων ἑαυτοὺς Ἰουδαίους εἶναι, καὶ οὐκ εἰσὶν ἀλλὰ ψεύδονται)—I will make them come and bow down before your feet, and they will learn that I have loved you.

In both letters, the author of Revelation accuses those who "say that they are Jews and are not" of committing "blasphemy" (βλασφημίαν) and lying, and identifies them as members of the "synagogue of Satan" (συναγωγῆς τοῦ Σατανᾶ).[2] This harsh reprimand conveys the author's anger and sense of betrayal by the actions of these people. The identity of "those who say that they are Jews and are not" is believed by most scholars to be a reference to Jews in Smyrna and Philadelphia.

Jewish Persecution of Christians?

Many scholars view Revelation 2:9 as reflecting a situation in which Jews in Smyrna were delivering members of the Christian community into the hands of the Romans.[3] Yarbro Collins (1986: 312-13) asserts:

> In favor of understanding "those who call themselves Jews"as members of the local Jewish community or synagogue in Smyrna is the juxtaposition of the reference to them with the prediction that some Christians in Smyrna will be detained in prison pending trial in the near future. This juxtaposition suggests that the "synagogue of Satan" are instigators of legal action against the persons whom John is addressing.

For Yarbro Collins, it can only be Jews who would induce legal action against Christians. For her, Christian judaizers would not be a threat to other Christians: "No matter how strong the tension between an allegedly judaizing Gentile Christian group and the group loyal to John the prophet, it is unlikely that members of one Christian party would accuse members of another Christian subgroup before local or Roman authorities. The former would be too vulnerable themselves to take such a step" (1986: 313). Those who claim to be Jews and those who are perpetrating the persecution, however, are not necessarily the same people (Wilson 1995: 163). Nor does it make any more sense that *Jews* from either Smyrna or Philadelphia would accuse Christians who imitated the Jewish lifestyle before local or Roman authorities, as they too were dependent on the Romans for their well being and the right to live their own lives according to Jewish law.

Scholars who postulate that Jewish persecution of Christians occurred in Asia Minor rely on the Book of Acts and the *Martyrdom of Polycarp* as evidence for such action (Hemer 1986: 67; Schüssler Fiorenza 1973: 572; Sweet 1990: 85; Yarbro Collins 1986: 313). These scholars hold that the Jews were allied with Rome and would denounce Christians and that, with Jewish co-operation, the Christians of Smyrna were thrown into jail to await trial (Yarbro Collins 1985: 204). Schüssler Fiorenza, for example, argues that: "[a]n example of this bitter hostility of the Jews against the Christians in Asia Minor can be seen in the decisive role that the Jews of Smyrna played in the martyrdom of Polycarp" (1973: 572).[4] A closer look at the material from this period typically used as evidence for the argument that Jews persecuted Christians suggests that more caution needs to be used before drawing conclusions. In this regard, Sanders states that: "the evidence that we do have of any kind of Jewish denunciation of Christians is limited, ambiguous, and inconclusive" (1993: 186).

The evidence from Acts—usually used as proof that such denunciation of Christians occurred—includes the accounts of Jewish accusation of Christian teachers before local authorities (Acts 17:6-8) and the Roman governor (Acts 18:12-17). But there are also accounts of Pagan accusations against Christians; for example, Acts 19:21-40 describes a riot in Ephesus led by the worshippers of Artemis, and Acts 16:19-24 describes the arrest of Paul and Silas in Philippi by the Pagan owners of the exorcised slave girl. These examples suggest that, at the time the author of Acts wrote his narrative, delation was a regular occurrence and anyone might accuse Christians or other vulnerable people for a bit of money. Sanders points out that the schematization of Paul's missionary activities in Acts— whereby Paul goes first to a synagogue, where he is eventually rejected, and

then turns to Gentiles, who accept his message—is of questionable historical accuracy (1993: 181). It fits into Luke's theme of wanting to show
how God's salvation has gone from the Jews to the Gentiles in Christianity. Sanders justifiably concludes that: "[f]rom both Revelation and Luke-
Acts it is possible to glean some evidence about relations between Christians on the one hand and non-Christian Jews on the other. Clearly there
is hostility and name-calling here, but there is in reality very little evidence
of…Jewish denunciation of Christians to Roman and civic authorities"
(1993: 186; also Hare 1967: 163; Simon 1986: 120).

The description of the martyrdom of Polycarp has numerous parallels
to the circumstances surrounding the death of Jesus, rendering its historical value very doubtful. The author, for example, records that Polycarp
"waited to be betrayed as also the Lord had done, that we too might
become his imitators" (*Mart. Pol.* 1.2), and that, similarly to Jesus, he was
betrayed by one of his own (i.e., a house slave [*Mart. Pol.* 6:1]). Further,
he reported that the police captain (εἰρήναρχος) who arrests Polycarp is
called Herod (*Mart. Pol.* 6:2),[5] and that Polycarp makes his entrance into
the city riding an ass (*Mart. Pol.* 8:1). The author states that the Jews cry
out "with one accord"[6] (ὁμοθυμαδόν) for Polycarp to be burned alive at
the stake. As Sanders observes, "Maybe some Jews had something to do
with Polycarp's martyrdom; I could not prove the contrary. But I certainly
do not trust this account, and I have to question the historical acumen of
those who do" (1993: 319 n.95).[7] While the hostile description of Jews in
the *Martyrdom of Polycarp* no doubt reflects the Christian author's perception of the Jews of Sardis as rivals, the portrayal of Jews as inciters of
persecution against Christians ought not to be trusted. While Lieu allows
for the possibility that "rivalry and competition could sometimes lead to
outbreaks of disturbance and that such disturbances would provoke measures which led to or were seen as 'persecution'" between Jews and Christians, she too argues against the broad generalizations about Jews initiat-
ing persecution against Christians, since evidence for it "is hardly to be
found" (1996: 91). The case for Jewish persecution of Christians in the
form of accusations before the Roman authorities is not as strong as some
scholars suggest.

"Those Who Say That They Are Jews and Are Not"

Other scholars argue that the conflict reflected in the Book of Revelation
concerns the spiritual status of Christians and their appropriation of the
Jewish heritage. These scholars maintain that the author of Revelation
challenges the claim by Jews in Smyrna and Philadelphia to Jewish identity because he understands Christians to be the "true" Jews (Borgen 1996;

Cohen 1993; Ramsay 1994; Sanders 1993; Schüssler Fiorenza 1973; Sweet 1990; Thompson 1986; Yarbro Collins 1985; Yarbro Collins 1986).[8] The argument that, in 2:9 and 3:9, the author of Revelation is asserting that Christians are the authentic Jews ('Ιουδαῖοι) does not correspond, however, with the usual way Christians expressed their ownership of Israel's inheritance. In such formulations, the tendency was for early Christian authors to use the term "Israel"—as demonstrated by Justin—and not the term "Jew." The term "Israel" was adopted by Christians more slowly than were other Jewish terms (i.e., "people," "elect," "brethren"). For a long time after these other terms were used by Christians to describe themselves, "Israel" continued to be applied to Jews in their "spiritual" capacity as the exclusive "people of God" (Richardson 1969). The Christian claim to be the true, new people of God occurred gradually over a period of nearly two centuries. The idea is adumbrated in certain early documents, such as some of the Pauline letters (e.g., 1 Cor. 10:32) and the Gospel of Matthew (21:43) and Luke-Acts (e.g., 9:2). With the passage of time and their fading expectation that Jews would accept their message, Christians became bolder in their claims to the legacy of Israel. Such forthrightness is effectively demonstrated in the *Epistle of Barnabas*, as discussed, for example, where the author asserts that the covenant in fact belonged to the Christians, and that it had never been inherited by the Jews. But even there, "Israel" is not equated with Christians or Christianity.[9] The first explicit claim by Christians that they had replaced the Jews as the true people of God occurred in the mid-second century CE, in Justin Martyr's *Dialogue with Trypho*, where he forcefully argues that Christians were the "new Israel" (11.5; Richardson 1969: 9ff).[10] The argument that Revelation 2:9 and 3:9 are in effect assertions that "the Christians were now the true Jews" (Hemer 1986: 67) would be more compelling if these statements had used the term "Israel" rather than "Jew."

The fact that the author instead used the word "Jew" ('Ιουδαῖος) in Revelation 2:9 and 3:9 indicates that the issue at stake is ethnicity rather than spiritual status. The use of the term 'Ιουδαῖος to refer to ethnicity by Epictetus, a contemporary of the author of Revelation, substantiates this understanding of the meaning of the term in Revelation (Arrian, *Diss. of Epictetus* 2.19-21; Stern #254):

> Why, then, do you call yourself a Stoic, why do you deceive the multitude, why do you act the part of a Jew when you are Greek? Do you not see in what sense men are severally called Jew, Syrian, or Egyptian? For example, whenever we see a man facing two ways at once, we are in the habit of saying, "he is not a Jew, he is only acting the part." But when he adopts the attitude of mind of the man who has been baptized and has made his choice,

then he both is a Jew in fact and is also called one. So we also are counter-
feit "Baptists," ostensibly Jews, but in reality something else.

Epictetus, as Cohen notes, is "interested in the correct application of
names, and knows of people who act the part of Jews, are called Jews, but
are not Jews" (1993: 34). According to Epictetus, only when the person
has decided to convert and undergo ritual immersion is that person in fact
a Jew; until then, he is only "acting" the part of a Jew—behaviour that,
unfortunately, Epictetus does not describe, but probably involved maintaining Jewish customs in varying degrees.

The author of Revelation employs the term "Jew" in the same way as
Epictetus does, that is, to refer to Jewish ethnicity. The opponents referred
to in 2:9 and 3:9—identified as part of the "synagogue of Satan" in Smyrna
and Philadelphia—are claiming to be of Jewish ethnic identity but are
not. The most logical and obvious interpretation of John's accusations,
therefore, is that he was referring to Gentiles who falsely claimed to be Jews
and followed a Jewish lifestyle (Gager 1985: 132; Gaston 1986: 42-43;
Wilson 1995: 163).[11]

These Gentiles could have been non-Christian Gentiles, but the hostile
tone of the accusations would make more sense if the judaizers were Christians. In his study on social conflict, Lewis Coser argues that the closer the
ties are between two opposing groups, the more intense is the conflict: "If
individuals witness the breaking away of one with whom they have shared
cares and responsibilities of group life, they are likely to react in a more
violent way against such 'disloyalty' than less involved members" (1956:
69). John's strong condemnation of "those who say that they are Jews
and are not" reveals the deep sense of betrayal and animosity that he feels
towards these fellow Christians who have deviated from what he considers to be acceptable behaviour. The demonic characterization of an opposing group in intramural disagreements is not unusual in Jewish and Christian literature. For example, the Qumran sect condemns Jews who are
not part of their sect to be part of "the congregation of traitors" (CD
1.12) while, in the War Rule, the sons of light fight against "the company
of the sons of darkness, the army of Satan" (CD 1.1). The Thanksgiving
Hymns furthermore state that their opponents are "an assembly of deceit,
and a horde of Satan" (2.22). In a letter to Smyrna, Ignatius warns fellow
Christians, "he who does anything without the knowledge of the bishop
is serving the devil" (Smyrn. 9.1; cf. Collins 1985: 210).

Ignatius's letters to Philadelphia and Magnesia, as I demonstrate below,
provide evidence for the existence of judaizers in the same geographical area
and time period as Revelation. This evidence reinforces the understanding
of these judaizers in Revelation as Christians. The situation reflected in the

Book of Revelation is a conflict among Christians, who, perhaps at one time, were members of the same Christian congregation as the author. Christians who were interested in addressing an eclectic collection of concerns—including Jewish-Christian relations and eschatological events—edited the originally Jewish Sibylline Oracles during the middle of the second century. Oracle 7 makes an intriguing warning about false prophets of the end days "who putting on the shaggy hides of sheep will falsely claim to be Hebrews, which is not their race" (οἳ μὲν δυσάμενοι προβάτων λασιότριχα ῥινὰ Ἑβραῖοι ψεύσονται, ὃ μὴ γένος ἔλλαχον αὐτοί) (Oracle 7, lines 134-35 in Charlesworth 1983: 413; the Greek is from Geffcken 1967). Collins understands the "shaggy hides of sheep" to be a reference to the dress of Hebrew prophets who prophesy falsely (1983: 413). There might be a connection here with the warning in the Gospel of Matthew 7:15: "Beware of false prophets, who come to you in sheep's clothing (ἐν ἐνδύμασιν προβάτων) but inwardly are ravenous wolves." The term 'Hebrews' "may well be used in a spiritual sense or merely be an allusion to Rev. 2:9, 3:9" (Collins 1983: 409). The excerpt from Oracle 7 conveys a sense of immediacy; Gager observes that this passage "clearly indicates a rivalry in which one group is attacked for falsely assuming the name 'Hebrews'" (1972: 94). There are several different possibilities for who the Hebrews are and which groups are involved. This warning might have been made by a Christian of Jewish birth (a Jewish Christian) to Christians of Gentile origin, who were claiming to be Hebrews and possibly members of the "true Israel" (Gager 1972: 95; Geffcken 1902: 34ff). The struggle would also make sense if it occurred between Gentile Christians regarding their own legitimacy or between non-Christian Jewish groups. Wilson speculates whether these passages in the Sibylline Oracles related to Revelation 2:9 and 3:9 in the sense that they refer to the same situation addressed by these verses in Revelation: "that is, does the poet have a particular reason to single out Gentile Judaizers as a threat to his community?" (1995: 104). If verses 133-39 of Oracle 7 are taken at face value, it is possible to understand them to mean Gentiles who are pretending to be Jews. The phrase ὃ μὴ γένος ἔλλαχον αὐτοί can be translated as "which race they did not take themselves" or "which race they did not receive themselves," perhaps indicating that the Hebrew pretenders stopped short of converting to Judaism and truly becoming part of the Hebrew γένος. These people, "by speaking with words," were attempting to "persuade the righteous and those who propitiate God through the heart" (Oracle 7, lines 136-38)—unsuccessfully, according to the author. Perhaps the Hebrew pretenders were trying to persuade others to live like Jews? The Christian author of Oracle 7 might be criticizing Gentile Christians who participated in Jewish practices, likening them to false Israelite priests or prophets. Understanding lines 133-39 as the author's hint at Gentile Christians falsely claiming to be Jews makes as much sense as other interpretations that scholars have offered. Unfortunately, there is insufficient evidence to say more.

Why Might Asia Minor Gentiles Have Judaized?

Eusebius reports that Emperor Domitian (81-96 CE) instituted a time of persecution of Christians and was worse than Nero "in enmity and hostility to God" (*Hist. eccl.* 3.17). Quoting Hegesippus, Eusebius tells the story of Domitian's attempt to get rid of all of the descendants of David by having the grandsons of Jude—said to be the brother of Jesus—brought before him; when he saw that they were lowly farmers with callused, labour-hardened hands, Domitian let them go "and issued orders terminating the persecution of the church" (*Hist. eccl.* 3.20). This story, if accurate, suggests that Christians experienced persecution during Domitian's reign, at the time when the Book of Revelation may have been written.

Pliny the Younger provides further evidence for the ill-treatment of Christians during Domitian's reign. In a letter to Trajan, Pliny reports that he encounters people who had ceased to be Christians "two or more years previously, and some of them even twenty years ago" (*Ep.* 10.96). Twenty years prior—about 113 CE—would place the latter Pliny experience within the reign of Domitian. Persecution may have forced these individuals to stop professing their Christian faith. Perhaps, like Domnus whom Eusebius reported took sanctuary among Jews during a time of persecution in the early third century CE (*Hist. eccl.* 6.12), certain Gentile Christians who feared local persecution took refuge during Domitian's reign by identifying themselves as Jews.[12]

The Jews of Rome and cities in Asia Minor—and Syria, as discussed in chapter 4—enjoyed a number of legal privileges and at times attained social and economic distinction under Roman rule. Judaism had achieved recognition as a *religio licita* in Roman law when, between 49-44 BCE, Julius Caesar prohibited all *collegia* within the empire except for the ones that had existed since antiquity; Judaism was included among the exceptions. This policy was perpetuated by Augustus.[13] Josephus furthermore quotes in *Antiquities* from two important decrees: in the one to Sardis issued by Lucius Antonius, the son of Mark Antony, the Jews are granted the right to build their own place of prayer, to try their own cases, and to obtain approved food (*Ant.* 14.235); the other was issued by the people of Sardis themselves to confirm the right of Jews to gather in their own place of worship, to have judicial authority among themselves, and to have appropriate food brought in by local market officials (*Ant.* 14.259-61).[14] Jews living in Ephesus apparently ate kosher food, worshipped regularly, sent money to Jerusalem, and refused to perform public duties on the Sabbath (*Ant.* 14.226; cf. 14.263-64). Jews in Laodicea in Phrygia observed the Sabbath and other customs (*Ant.* 14.241-42) and in Miletus, Ionia, they kept the Sabbath, tithed their produce and kept other rites as well (*Ant.* 14.245). As Richardson observes, "[l]ocal communities of the Diaspora were able to preserve their way of life against the weight of opinion in many of the cities in which they settled, and they had official sanction for this preservation" (1996: 96).

Stephen Wilson poses an intriguing motivation for Gentile Christians to have decided to judaize: "Could it not be that some Christians in Asia Minor were identifying themselves with the Jews in order to avoid official harassment, given that the Jews had a more stable and established position in the Roman world?" (1995: 163). Wilson's suggestion assumes that judaizing on the part of these Gentile Christians was a calculated decision to seek protection from Roman persecution. Certainly this may be how the author of Revelation perceived the situation. It is impossible to know from the text whether their decision to live like Jews was taken prior to the outbreak of trouble, as a result of contact with Jews and attraction to Jewish customs, or as a result of persecution. Nor is it possible to know whether Gentile Christians would actually attain immunity from Roman hostility through judaizing. The official sanction protecting Jews described above may have been a powerful incentive for Gentile Christians, who perhaps were already inclined toward a Jewish lifestyle, to deepen their attachment to Torah observance during sporadic persecution of Christians by Roman authorities.[15] The perspective of the author of Revelation may have been that certain Gentile Christians called themselves Jews to avoid the difficulties associated with identifying themselves as Christians. His sense of betrayal—and perhaps his fear that further defection by Christians seeking to avoid suffering would ensue—may have impelled him to categorize these defectors as members of the "synagogue of Satan."

If the interpretation of the references in Revelation 2:9 and 3:9 that John is referring to Christian judaizers is correct, then these accusations do not reflect a struggle between Jews and Christians but, rather, a conflict among Christians. The author of the apocalypse expresses hostility toward Gentile Christians who adopt Jewish customs and call themselves Jews, perhaps to avoid persecution. From his perspective, this behaviour is unacceptable, perhaps because he fears the impact it might have on members of his own community, for they too could decide to compromise their convictions.

Ignatius on Christian Judaizers

OTHER LITERARY EVIDENCE FROM ASIA MINOR substantiates this understanding of the accusations in Revelation. A few years after John wrote his seven letters to the churches of Asia Minor, Ignatius wrote seven letters of his own to Asian churches. The two sets of letters share similar concerns, address the same or nearby locations in Asia, and can be used to elucidate the situation both writers faced in Asia Minor (Gaston 1986: 42; *contra* Yarbro Collins 1986: 312). I suggest that the "composite picture" resulting from Ignatius's writing lends credence to the interpretation suggested above for Revelation 2:9 and 3:9, and indicates that Christian judaizing was a persistent phenomenon in Asia Minor in the late first and early second century CE.

Just as Barnabas struggled with Gentile Christian infatuation with Judaism, so too some twenty years later did Ignatius of Antioch. Ignatius's correspondence indicates that he encountered this perturbing phenomenon while travelling through various cities in Asia Minor. Given the evidence for the manifestation of Christian judaizing in Syria, however, it is plausible that his strong reaction reflected in his letters to Magnesia and Philadelphia represents the continuation of an ongoing struggle with judaizing that began earlier in Antioch, Syria. It is impossible to be certain. In this chapter, I show that his letters bear details pertaining to Christian judaizing, but in the Asia Minor communities alone.

Eusebius places the letters of Ignatius in the reign of Trajan (98-117 CE; *Hist. eccl.* 3.36), which seems to be an appropriate date for two reasons. First, in his letters to Christian churches in Asia Minor, Ignatius defends the authority of the bishop; the frequency of requests for obedience to the bishop as well as the urgency of Ignatius's tone indicate that the office of bishop was not yet firmly established there.[16] As such, a relatively early date—such as the one Eusebius offers—for the writing of these letters seems right (Bauer 1971: 70; Schoedel 1993: 289). Second, the context of the letters, with their expression of Ignatius's desire to establish the administrative superiority of one bishop, best corresponds to a time of upheaval: "as long as a harmonious spirit pervades the community, a council of those with similar status can take care of it without difficulty…according to the abilities of each" (Bauer 1971: 62). According to the letters of Pliny, which he wrote to the Emperor Trajan in c. 110-13 CE, Christians in Bithynia experienced a tumultuous and unstable situation, and it is possible that local unrest occurred in other areas of Asia Minor as well.

Asia Minor or Antioch? One Group or Two?

Some scholars believe that Ignatius's letters actually reveal more about the situation of Christian communities in Antioch, Syria, than in Asia Minor. Paul Donahue, for example, argues that Ignatius simply applies his experience in Antioch to Asia Minor since "his responses to various problems are too consistent, too much a part of his own theological outlook, to have arisen on the spot, under such trying conditions" (1978: 81-82; also Bauer 1971: 67; Corwin 1960). On the other hand, Barrett argues that "on the whole, Ignatius gives the impression that he is dealing with a situation that he has encountered on his travels in Asia, rather than with one he has long known and recalled from the days of his settled ministry in Antioch" (1976: 240; also Gaston 1986: 36; Molland 1954).

A combination of each of the views described above best fits the situation: Ignatius addresses the troubles he meets along his journey through Asia Minor, but the opponents he encounters there were not new to him. Given the evidence for judaizing Christians in late first century CE Syria, Ignatius probably confronted them already in Antioch. Statements made in the *Epistle of Barnabas* and the *Didache*, as I postulated earlier, certainly seem to indicate that judaizing among Gentile Christians was deemed very problematic by certain Syrian ecclesiastic leaders; evidence from the Pseudo-Clementine literature demonstrates that judaizing was actually encouraged by other church leaders. At the same time, Ignatius's detailed and vivid descriptions of the circumstances in Asia Minor in *Magnesians* and *Philadelphians* strongly support the view that in these letters, he addresses tangible circumstances he met on his journey through Asia Minor.

Further debate has ensued over whether Ignatius encountered two groups of heretics (docetics and judaizers) or one (docetic judaizers).[17] Molland confidently states that "there can be no doubt…that Ignatius accuses the same persons of Judaism as well as docetism," and indeed the majority of modern scholars seem to agree (Barrett 1976; Gaston 1986; Lightfoot 1989; Wilson 1995: 361 n.96). My view, however, is that, when Ignatius addresses the judaizing Christians in *Magnesians* and *Philadelphians*, his criticism is aimed at judaizing alone. What scholars have understood to be evidence of docetism in these letters is simply Ignatius worrying that the corollary of judaizing will be non-belief in the birth, death and resurrection of Jesus (Schoedel 1993: 303). His letter to the Smyrnaeans contains criticism against docetics and a description of them that distinguishes them from judaizers (*Smyrn.* 5.1):

> There are some who ignorantly deny him, but rather were denied by him, being advocates of death rather than of the truth. There are they whom nei-

ther the prophecies nor the law of Moses persuaded, nor the gospel even until now, nor our own individual sufferings. For what does anyone profit me if he praise me but blaspheme my Lord, and do not confess that he was clothed in flesh?

These docetics are not judaizers, since Ignatius explicitly says that these people have no interest in the Mosaic law. On his journey through Asia Minor, Ignatius probably encountered, or heard about, different types of problematic behaviours and beliefs, among both judaizing Christians and docetic Christians. His letters to the Magnesians and the Philadelphians, which contain evidence of Christian judaizing, are the focus of the following investigation.

Ignatius's Letter to the Magnesians

Ignatius wrote his letter to the church in Magnesia from Smyrna. While he did not visit the city, he did consult with representatives from Magnesia (*Magn.* 15.1); he had already viewed the situation in Philadelphia by the time he wrote to the Magnesians.

Magnesians 8–10 form the core of the letter. Ignatius instructs his readers: "Be not led astray by strange doctrines or by old fables which are profitless. For if we are living until now according to Judaism (εἰ γὰρ μέχρι νῦν κατὰ Ἰουδαϊσμὸν ζῶμεν), we confess that we have not received grace" (*Magn.* 8.1). This is reminiscent of Paul's warning: "You who want to be justified by the law have cut yourselves off from Christ; you have fallen away from grace" (Gal. 5:4). Ignatius's use of the phrase "living until now according to Judaism" can be understood in two different ways: either he is referring to Christians from prior generations, such as Jesus' disciples, who were intimately involved with Judaism; or he is referring to contemporary Christian judaizers who observe Jewish rituals. In the context of this letter as a whole, as well as what we later learn from the letter to the Philadelphians, the latter interpretation seems best. As Wilson suggests (1995: 165), *Magnesians* 8.1 helps to clarify the identity of the group of judaizers:

> It could refer to earlier generations of Christians who had been closely tied to Judaism, but it seems to refer to the Judaizers of Ignatius's day, that is, Gentiles, who formerly (and presently) lived like Jews and expounded Judaism.... Most obviously they would have been former God-fearers or sympathizers, who had been attached to the synagogue, had now joined the church, and had brought with them the predilections of their former existence.

Ignatius's instruction to his readers not to be "led astray by strange doctrines or by old fables which are profitless" (*Magn.* 8.1) is reminiscent of statements made in documents that may be associated with the region of Asia Minor during the early second century CE. Certain provocative verses in the Pastoral letters—New Testament documents dating to the early second century CE—reflect the lively presence of Judaism, along with a distinct sense that it is being promoted among Christians, particularly among Gentiles. For example, the author of 1 Timothy warns his readers "not to occupy themselves with myths and endless genealogies" (1 Tim. 1:4); he also mentions that certain members have "deviated [from] a pure heart, a good conscience, and sincere faith" (1 Tim. 1:5) to engage in "meaningless talk, desiring to be teachers of the law (θέλοντες εἶναι νομοδιδάσκαλοι), without understanding either what they are saying or the things about which they make assertions" (1 Tim. 1:6–7; cf. Titus 3:9). The term νομοδιδάσκαλοι, which occurs elsewhere only in Luke (5:17) and in Acts (5:34), might best be understood as referring to teachers of the Mosaic law, thereby connecting the opponents in this document with Judaism (also see 1 Tim. 1:8–9). It may be significant that the subsequent part of the verse states that these "teachers of the law" (νομοδιδάσκαλοι) do not understand "either what they say or the things about which they make assertions" (1 Tim. 1:7b). The fact that verse 7a states that they desired to be teachers of the law (θέλοντες εἶναι νομοδιδάσκαλοι) may indicate that these individuals had no real claim to that title or function. Perhaps the reference is to Gentiles who cause turmoil among Gentile Christians because they seek to draw interest in the law but, from the author's perspective, are incompetent in their teaching of it.[18]

In his letter to the Magnesians, Ignatius equates "living according to Judaism" with living according to "strange," "old," and "profitless" doctrines (*Magn.* 8.1). By asserting that the prophets "lived according to Jesus Christ," Ignatius denies them even their Jewishness (*Magn.* 8.2):

> For the divine prophets lived according to Jesus Christ. Therefore they were also persecuted, being inspired by his grace, to convince the disobedient that there is one God, who manifested himself through Jesus Christ his son, who is his Word proceeding from silence, who in all respects was well-pleasing to him that sent him.

Ignatius expresses a rather extreme perspective. He essentially "Christianizes" Judaism, and denies that Judaism made any contribution whatsoever toward the implementation of God's plan.

Ignatius implies that one of the Jewish rituals kept by the judaizers of Magnesia was observance of the Sabbath (*Magn.* 9.1):

> If then they who walked in ancient customs came to a new hope, no longer living for the Sabbath, but for the Lord's Day (μηκέτι σαββατίζοντες, ἀλλὰ κατὰ κυριακὴν ζῶντες), on which also our life sprang up through him and

his death,—though some deny him,[19]—and by this mystery we received faith, and for this reason also we suffer, that we may be found disciples of Jesus Christ our only teacher.

Schoedel suggests that Ignatius is referring to the early disciples who became (Jewish) Christians (1985: 123) but, in light of the radical Christianization of the prophets in the previous sentence (*Magn.* 8.2), Ignatius probably is referring to ancient Jews here. Observance of the Sabbath by contemporary Christians is not explicit but is strongly implied (Bauer 1971: 88). According to Ignatius, if the Jews described in the Hebrew scriptures were actually Christians who discontinued the observance of the Sabbath, then why should present-day Christians observe the Sabbath? Paul Trebilco (1991: 28-29) suggests that *Magnesians* 9.1-2

> was probably prompted by pressure from some Christians in favour of Sabbath observance. Whilst many details of these passages are difficult to interpret, it is clear that Ignatius is talking about Christians in Magnesia who were observing Jewish customs. Ignatius does not say that they are converted Jews, and so, if we assume that the situation was comparable to the one at Philadelphia, we can suggest that again it was the uncircumcised who were also Judaizing here.

Jack Sanders has a different understanding of the situation, suggesting that the congregation of the Magnesian church included both Jewish Christians and Gentile Christians and that it was *Jewish* Christians who continued to observe the Sabbath. This attempt by Jewish Christians "to be both Christians and Jews" troubled Gentile Magnesian Christians, who brought the matter to Ignatius's attention. Thus, according to Sanders, it was Gentile Christians who "felt that the Jewish Christians should give up their Jewish ways" (1993: 187). While Jewish Christians might have been present in Magnesia and might have had influence on non-Jewish members of the congregation, I contend that the evidence points toward *Gentile* judaizing as the problematic phenomenon at Magnesia.

Miriam Taylor argues that "Ignatius' anti-Jewish passages are not injunctions against judaizing, but rather illustrative arguments directed at the dissenters to whom Ignatius addresses his main appeal" (1995: 35). The problem, according to Taylor, was docetic heretical Christians, not judaizers, so that, in *Magnesians* 8.1, for example, Ignatius was not warning his readers about judaizing or Judaism, but "is here drawing an illustrative parallel between the 'vain doctrines' of the Docetists, and the way of 'Judaism'" (Taylor 1995: 35). She furthermore asserts that "the reference to worship on the Sabbath is not a warning against 'Sabbatizing,' but once again, an illustrative comment describing the transformative power of Christ's advent" (Taylor 1995: 36). Taylor claims that Ignatius wished, in effect, to warn his readers that doceticism was invalid and false by drawing a parallel between it and Judaism since, as she contends, "all Magnesian Christians would no doubt be familiar with the church's anti-Jewish tradition which held that the 'Jewish' way was abrogated, outdated, and constituted an admission that one was not inspired by the 'grace' of Christ" (Taylor 1995: 35). This rather bold assumption on Taylor's part is contradicted by the cumulative evidence in both Magnesia and Philadelphia that precisely the opposite was so: Christians in these two cities were behaving in ways that indicated that they by no means considered the "Jewish way" to be nullified.

In fact, Ignatius explicitly discourages judaizing. He writes in *Magnesians*: "It is monstrous (ἄτοπόν) to talk of Jesus Christ and to practise Judaism (ἰουδαΐζειν). For Christianity did not base its faith on Judaism, but Judaism on Christianity, and every tongue believing on God was brought together in it" (10.3). Schoedel understands Ignatius's reference to those who based their faith on Christianity to be "the first generation of Jewish Christians" (1985: 126); however, this verse is better understood to be another manifestation of Ignatius's radical Christianization of Jewish history, and an indication that he perceived the prophets to be Christians, rather than Jews (Grant 1966: 64). From a retrospective point of view, Ignatius is completely dening any historical contribution by Judaism by suggesting that Christianity and not Judaism is the foundational faith. Essentially, he is eliminating the need for Judaism, as if deleting it from the divine plan. Significantly, the statement indicates that Christians at Magnesia are practising Judaism (*Magn.* 10.3).

From Ignatius's perspective, then, the problems in Magnesia consisted of a lack of support for the bishop and the holding of separate meetings (*Magn.* 4.1; 7.1-2); more significantly, some Gentile members of the congregation were judaizing (*Magn.* 10.3; 8.1), which might have included keeping the Sabbath instead of, or in addition to, Sunday (*Magn.* 9.1).

Ignatius's Letter to the Philadelphians

Ignatius actually spent some time with the Philadelphian congregation— as indicated in his letter to the Philadelphian church (3.1; 7.1)—and therefore was able to view the situation in that city personally. A verse that is relevant to this discussion of Christian judaizers states: "But if anyone interpret (ἑρμηνεύῃ) Judaism to you do not listen to him; for it is better to hear Christianity from the circumcised than Judaism from the uncircumcised" (*Phld.* 6.1).[20] The reference to hearing "Christianity from the circumcised," probably indicates the presence of Jewish Christians, but the intriguing reference at the end of this statement indicates that there were

Gentiles (i.e., the "uncircumcised") in Philadelphia who "explained" or "interpreted" Judaism. If so, Ignatius declares that Jews who explain Christianity are preferable to Gentiles who discuss Judaism. The fact that these Gentile Christians were apparently approaching people within the congregation and "explaining" Judaism to them suggests that some prose-lytizing was occurring (Lightfoot 1989: 264). To those who are approached by any such person, Ignatius instructs "do not listen to him" (μὴ ἀκούετε αὐτοῦ) (*Phld.* 6.1).

Wilson notes that this sentence indicates that "some (if not all) of the judaizers were Gentile in origin" and that this is the "plain sense" of the statement (1995: 164). Indeed, scholars who do not take this sentence at face value attempt to explain that, instead, Ignatius was referring to a Jewish group which, in an attempt to attract converts, dropped the circum-cision requirement. Consequently, these scholars have offered some rather bizarre explanations as to the identity of these Jews. Schweizer, for exam-ple, suggested that they had come under the influence of Pythagorean ideas (1976: 249), while Hoffmann postulates that they were Marcionites who were being critical of Judaism (1984: 57-63), and Barrett offers the explanation that "there was in Philadelphia a Jewish group, almost cer-tainly unorthodox in its Judaism" and "we cannot expect to be well informed" about such "fringe groups" (1976: 234-35).[21] Donahue makes the odd suggestion that this statement does not mean that the judaizing opponents were not circumcised but that "the law-free gospel does not per-mit distinctions among Christians" (1978: 89).

Schoedel concludes that "no one was actually recommending circum-cision, and the issue had probably been injected into the debate by Ignatius under the influence of Pauline models" (1985: 203). But Schoedel need not offer this explanation, since circumcision is simply not an issue. Nowhere else does Ignatius raise the topic of circumcision, which surely he would have if he was concerned with it. As Wilson asserts, "the terms circumci-sion and uncircumcision in *Phld.* 6.1 are simply a convenient way of refer-ring to Jews and Gentiles" (1995: 164). The same distinction is used in Eph-esians: "you Gentiles by birth, called 'the uncircumcision' by those who are called 'the circumcision'" (2:11) and is also found in *m. Nedarim* (3.11; cf. Marcus 1989).[22]

What Ignatius means by "interpreting" Judaism is not entirely clear: perhaps these Gentiles were promoting the observance of Jewish rites and customs. Ignatius gives some indication of their behaviour when he writes "For I heard some men saying, 'if I find it not in the charters in the Gospel I do not believe (ἐὰν μὴ ἐν τοῖς ἀρχείοις εὕρω ἐν τῷ εὐαγγελίῳ οὐ πιστεύω),' and when I said to them that it is in the Scripture, they answered me, 'that is exactly the question'" (*Phld.* 8.2). Ignatius is describing an argument he had with his opponents involving their dependence on the Hebrew scriptures for direction in what they believe. The statement should be understood as "If I do not find it (the point at issue) in the archives, I do not believe it (because it appears) in the Gospel" (Lightfoot 1989: 271ff; Schoedel 1985: 207). It is generally agreed that the reference to "charters" or "archives" is to the Hebrew scriptures.[23]

The last line—"that is exactly the question"—may indicate that the opponents were not satisfied with Ignatius's attempt to prove his point from the Hebrew scriptures. He therefore appeals to "an even higher authority," Jesus Christ (Schoedel 1985: 208; Grant 1966: 106). Wilson suggests that "from the immediate context it is clear that 'expounding Judaism' did not involve promoting Judaism in general. Rather, the judaizers had a particular view of the scriptures, and were especially inclined to dispute any Christian beliefs that they could not find in them (*Phld.* 8.1-2; 9.1)" (1995: 165). According to Gaston, Ignatius's identification of "their teaching as 'Judaism' probably has to do more with their use of the LXX to support their doctrines than with their Christian worship on the Sabbath. The fact remains that this 'Judaism' is taught by the uncircumcised" (1986: 38). Schoedel notes that Ignatius did not include observance of Jewish customs such as circumcision or the Sabbath in his verbal struggle with his opponents in Philadelphia: "Perhaps, then, all that Ignatius means to say is that his opponents' preoccupation with Scripture prevented them from keeping Christ in the center of the theological stage to his satisfaction" (1985: 209). It seems logical, however, that if these Gentiles relied on Jewish scripture to direct their behaviour, they would have been aware of the ritual obligations of the Mosaic law and might have felt themselves obliged to carry out certain rituals. The ensuing dispute about scripture, therefore, likely involved the promotion of Judaism, specifically in terms of whether Christians should be obliged to keep Jewish customs.

Taylor is right to criticize Paul Donahue's identification of the opponents as Jewish Christians (1995: 33; Donahue 1978). The focus is not hearing Christianity from Jews ("the circumcised"), but hearing Judaism from Gentiles ("the uncircumcised"),[24] as Lightfoot states: "In this case the teachers would be represented, not as Jewish Christians, but as Gentile Christians with strong Judaic tendencies. This seems the most natural interpretation" (1989: 264). For Ignatius, furthermore, those who do not speak of Jesus Christ are "tombstones and sepulchers of the dead" (*Phld.* 6.1). Clearly he does not take lightly the compromising of (his version of) Christianity.

That the judaizers were part of the Christian community in Philadelphia is inferred by Ignatius when he describes how he was almost deceived by the judaizers (*Phld.* 7.1-2).[25] When he cried out that the bishop was to be obeyed, it is possible that his cry was not prompted by "the Spirit" but by his prior knowledge of the situation in the congregation.[26] At any rate, it is clear that the judaizers were at the Christian meeting when he gave his response and that they were part of the Christian congregation (Schoedel 1985: 205; Wilson 1995: 165). The closing of the letter indicates that Philo and Rheus Agathopous, two messengers who likely informed Ignatius that all was well in Antioch (*Phld.* 10.1), were treated badly by some members of the Philadelphian congregation (*Phld.* 11.1); perhaps Ignatius and those who thought like him were not completely accepted by the congregation. Schoedel observes that: "It is now easier to understand why the freshly confident Ignatius must proceed as cautiously as he does in this letter. People in Philadelphia were still on good terms with judaizers and their disapproval of the messengers (and of Ignatius himself) required rebuttal" (1985: 214). Judaizing may have been more troubling to Ignatius than to anyone else in the community; in fact, other members of the Philadelphian congregation may not have viewed such proclivities to be deviant at all.

The situation in Philadelphia, according to Ignatius, was one in which people whom I identify as Gentile Christians were teaching Judaism (*Phld.* 6.1) and were relying too heavily on the Hebrew scriptures (*Phld.* 8.2). It seems furthermore that they held a separate Eucharist service (*Phld.* 4.1) from the one in which Ignatius was involved.[27] The specificity of his comments regarding the situation in Philadelphia reinforces the assertion that Ignatius was dealing with actual circumstances he encountered on his journey through Asia Minor, rather than simply projecting issues he had experienced in Antioch.

On his trip through Asia Minor, Ignatius encounters judaizers in Philadelphia and hears about their existence in Magnesia. He expresses great concern about how this phenomenon has caused and will continue to cause divisiveness within the Christian congregations of these cities. Interestingly, in his struggle against judaizers, Ignatius does not describe the Passion in a way that is hostile to the Jews—unlike Melito of Sardis and other apologists of the second century—and he does not vilify Jews in general. My interpretation is that this apparent contradiction arises because Jews are not causing the problem—Christian judaizers are.

While it is true that Ignatius does not denounce Jews generally, in his own way, he denies the Jewish scriptures and history any intrinsic validity. Just as Marcion, whose possible connection with judaizing is discussed in the next chapter, also does not allow for any contribution to Christianity by Judaism through his presentation of Christianity as completely separate from Judaism, with a different and superior God, different scriptures and different Messiah, Ignatius denies Judaism any worth or contribution *as Judaism* because, for him, Jewish history is Christian history and Jewish prophets are Christian. Such is the extent of his appropriation of things Jewish. In this, Ignatius does not recognize even a limited historical role for Judaism.[28]

Gentile Christians in Asia Minor may have continued with prior practices of Jewish rites adopted when they were God fearers on the periphery of the synagogue: they simply did not change their lifestyle when they became Christians (Wilson 1995: 165; also Munier 1993: 406). Or, perhaps in the setting of a vibrant diaspora Judaism, Gentile Christians became exposed to Judaism through social interaction with Jews.

Justin Martyr's *Dialogue with Trypho*

JUSTIN MARTYR—BORN IN NEAPOLIS (ancient Shechem, modern Nablus) in Samaritan territory in about 100 CE (1 *Apol.* 1.1)—was brought up a Gentile and was not circumcised (*Dial.* 28.2), appears not to have known Hebrew,[29] and was not familiar with the Bible prior to his conversion to Christianity (*Dial.* 2-8). The conversation between Justin and Trypho terminates with Justin indicating that he would soon set sail (*Dial.* 142.2), probably to Rome (Williams 1930: *x*). He was martyred in that city sometime between 162 and 168 CE, when Junius Rusticus was prefect of Rome (Chadwick 1964/65: 278; Harnack 1904: 274-84). Justin wrote the *Dialogue* sometime after the Bar Kochba revolt; he states that Trypho, his Jewish opponent, was in Ephesus because he had fled from the revolt in Judea, and it is in Ephesus that the dialogue supposedly took place (*Dial.* 1.3; 9.3; also Eusebius *Hist. eccl.* 4.18.6). Possible dates for the document range from the mid-130s to c.160 CE.

The *Dialogue with Trypho* describes a conversation between the Christian Justin and the Jewish Trypho. Scholars have debated extensively whether this conversation actually took place and whether Trypho was a historical person. Harnack is of the view that, by the time Justin wrote, there was little or no exchange between Jews and Christians; the *Dialogue,* according to him, then, does not reflect a real polemic against the Jews, since, by the time Justin wrote, the battle had already been won by the Christians (1913: 47-98). Chadwick suggests, on the other hand, that "we are being given an essentially veracious autobiography, even if Justin's memory, looking back some twenty years, is likely to have foreshortened and compressed the story. Like the rest of us, Justin is remembering the past in a way that the present requires" (1964/65: 280; Trakatellis 1986: 297). Barnard calls Trypho "a Hellenistic Jewish layman who combined the cul-

ture and inquiring spirit of the hellenistic world with a knowledge of traditional Jewish exegesis and haggadah. He has no knowledge of the
Hebrew language but knows accurately the Septuagint version of the Old
Testament" (1964: 398). Goodenough, however, considered Trypho to be
"in many respects a straw man, who says the right thing in the right place"
and who never truly challenges Justin or throws him off his argument
(1923: 90).

Whether the dialogue actually occurred and whether Trypho was a real
person is not, for my purposes, a crucial matter. Wilson aptly suggests
that what is more important is "whether Trypho is a plausible representation of at least one strain of Judaism and whether the *Dialogue* gives a
proper sense of the issues and the arguments that would have concerned
Jews and Christians engaged in debate in the mid-second century" (1995:
260). Scholarly consensus holds that the opinions exchanged in the *Dialogue* are realistic, as Justin does appear to be knowledgeable about
Judaism. For example, he describes a phylactery (*Dial.* 46.5), is familiar
with post-biblical details about Jewish rituals on Yom Kippur (*Dial.* 40.4),
and is aware that the Septuagint is read during services in synagogue
(72.3). Justin travelled extensively and so had opportunities to become
familiar with different Jewish communities; Trypho may represent a combination of Judaisms that Justin encountered (MacLennan 1990: 64, n.62).
Using Trypho as a tool, Justin raises issues relevant to the relationship
between Jews and Christians at that time.[30]

The dialogue between Justin and Trypho is set, shortly after the Bar
Kochba revolt, likely in Ephesus.[31] Strabo describes Ephesus as the greatest commercial centre of Asia Minor north of the Taurus range (*Geog.*
14.1.24).[32] The environment in this metropolis was remarkably diverse.
Although the remains of a synagogue are yet to be found in Ephesus itself,
there is archaeological and literary evidence that Jewish communities flourished throughout Asia Minor during the second century CE.[33] Two thou-
sand Jewish families from Babylon were settled in Lydia and Phrygia by
Antiochus III in about 210 BCE. The privileges granted them by Caesar's
lieutenant Dolabella in 44 BCE (*Ant.* 14.225-27) were confirmed by the
civic authorities and by Augustus and his lieutenants (*Ant.* 16.162-68,
172ff) and it is likely that the Jewish community in Ephesus benefitted from
this political protection. MacLennan notes "the Jews had a large community which apparently was not very cordial either to Paul or to Justin.
Throughout the *Dialogue*, Trypho's Jewish companions laugh at Justin
or walk away in amazement and disgust (see *Dial.* 16.4; 9.2; 8.2; 56;
122)" (1990: 70). By the end of the first century, different Jewish groups
called Ephesus home, and various Christian groups were also represented

in the city, including disciples of John the Baptist (Acts 19:1-7) and converts instructed by Paul (Acts 19:8-10; Köster 1995: 133).

Christians Are the "True Israel"

In the dialogue Justin proclaims: "[W]e are the true and spiritual Israelitish nation, and the race of Judah and of Jacob and Isaac and Abraham" (Ἰσραηλιτικὸν γὰρ τὸ ἀληθινὸν, πνευματικὸν, καὶ Ἰούδα γένος καὶ Ἰακὼβ καὶ Ἀβραάμ) (*Dial.* 11.5), and "[W]e shall inherit the Holy Land together with Abraham, receiving our inheritance for a boundless eternity, as being children of Abraham because we have like faith with him" (*Dial.* 119.5; cf. 123.7; 124.1; 135.3). This is the first time in Christian literature that such an explicit claim concerning Christians being the "true Israel" and thereby replacing the Jews was made (Richardson 1969: 9).

Justin's statements explicitly express a view that took time and required a distinctive theological setting to develop. In Christian literature prior to the middle of the second century, the substitution of the Jews by Christians as the people of God is only implied. The tendency is present in the Gospel of Matthew, for example, but as Richardson notes, "this identification is difficult to attain for it is still an *intra muros* struggle. The Christian community is no longer tied to the institutions of Israel, but it shies away from making the rupture complete by transposing titles" (1969: 189). There are likewise traces of the idea of the Christian Church as the "new" or "true" Israel in 1 Peter, Hebrews and Pauline letters, but the complete appropriation of the term "Israel" is not reflected in any of the New Testament documents.

Justin's *Dialogue with Trypho* reflects a very different understanding of the relationship. Expressed for the first time in extant Christian literature is the idea that Gentile believers in Jesus replaced the Jews as the chosen people of God. By the middle of the second century, the hope had waned that Jews would turn to Christianity in large numbers; by their rejection of the Gospel, the Jews relinquished their inheritance and Gentile Christians claimed it. Richardson observes (1969: 204) that:

> As long as the Church was viewed as a community gathered from Gentiles and Jews, it could not readily call itself "Israel." But when it was sharply separated from both, and when it had a theory that Judaism no longer stood in a continuity with Israel *ante Christum*, and when Gentiles not only could take over other titles but in some cases could claim exclusive rights to them, then the Church as an organizational entity could appropriate "Israel."

Christians and the Law

Trypho, in *Dial.* 10.3, expresses surprise that Christians say that they worship God and consider themselves "to be superior to other people" but do not separate themselves "in that you keep neither the feasts nor the sabbaths, nor have circumcision...you yet hope to obtain some good from God, though you do not do His commandments." In one of his harshest responses to Trypho's criticism of Christian non-observance of the Mosaic law, Justin (*Dial.* 16.2) sides with Rome against the Jews:

> For the circumcision according to the flesh, that was from Abraham, was given for a sign, that you should be separated from the other nations and us, and that you alone should suffer the things you are rightly suffering now, and that your lands should be desolate and your cities burned with fire, and that foreigners should eat up the fruits before your face, and none of you go up unto Jerusalem.

Circumcision, says Justin, was commanded of the Jews to set them apart for suffering (also *Dial.* 28.4; 92.2-3; 137.1). He also argues vehemently against the adoption of this practice by Christians: "You, indeed, who are circumcised in your flesh have need of our circumcision, but we, possessing this, have no need of that" (*Dial.* 19.2), since, if circumcision were necessary, God would not have created people prior to Abraham uncircumcised.[34] Justin explains that Christians would be circumcised and would observe the festivals and Sabbaths "if we did not know the reason why it all was enjoined even on you, namely, because of your transgressions and hardness of heart" (*Dial.* 18.2).

Food laws, according to Justin's understanding, were given to the Jews because they tended to forget God: "He charged you too to abstain from certain foods, in order that even in your eating and drinking you may have God before your eyes, since you are prone and apt to depart from the knowledge of Him" (*Dial.* 20.1).[35] And regarding the observance of Shabbat, this too was given as a sign "because of your sins and those of your fathers" (*Dial.* 21.1ff). Elsewhere Justin writes: "In the same way He commanded offerings because of the sins of your people, and because of their idolatries, and not because He was in need of such" (*Dial.* 22.1ff). According to Justin, it was no longer necessary to observe any of the law: "For if before Abraham there was no need of circumcision, and before Moses none of keeping the Sabbath, and of festivals, and of offerings, neither in like manner is there any need now, after the Son of God, Jesus Christ" (*Dial.* 23.3).

Why Talk Torah to Gentiles?

Throughout the *Dialogue*, Justin argues that the Mosaic law was created to address the moral weaknesses of the Jewish people, and that it was created for them alone: other peoples were not obligated to keep these commandments. Claudia Setzer (1994: 146) raises important questions regarding the motivation behind the contents of this document:

> Why did these debates take place? Justin is himself a Gentile and by the time of his writing, Christianity is largely Gentile. Why is he still arguing with Jews about who is the true Israel and whether or not the commandments should be observed? These do not seem to be issues which would interest the Roman government or the gentile populace in their evaluation of Jews.

In response, Setzer offers the following: "The debate may represent simply the search for self-understanding and self-definition. Yet it is possible that Jews and Gentiles are competing for gentile converts" (1994: 146). Although this latter proposal approaches the correct answer, neither of these explanations is completely satisfactory.

A more reasonable motivation for Justin to deal with issues regarding the law is because he was cognizant of the fact that *Gentile Christians* were interested in Torah observance. At the beginning of chapter 46, Trypho asks Justin: "If some even now desire to live in accordance with the precepts of the Mosaic law (βούλωνται φυλάσσοντες τὰ διὰ Μωσέως διαταχθέντα), and yet believe that the crucified Jesus is the Christ of God and that to him it has been given to judge without exception all men, and that his kingdom is eternal, could they also be saved (δύνανται καὶ αὐτοὶ σωθῆναι)?" In his response—which extends into chapter 47—Justin delineates four different types of Christians (of both Jewish and Gentile origin) who follow the law, and discusses whether he deems them to be accepted ("saved") or not:

- Jewish Christians who followed the Law but continue to believe in Jesus and live with Christians without trying to convince them "either to receive circumcision like themselves, or to keep sabbath, or to observe other things of the same kind" are to be accepted (*Dial.* 47.2).
- Jewish Christians who believe in Christ but "in every way compel those who are of Gentile birth and believe on this Christ to live in accordance with the law appointed by Moses, or choose not to have communion with them that have such a life in common" are not accepted (*Dial.* 47.3).
- Gentile Christians "who follow their advice and live under the law, as well as keep their profession in the Christ of God will I suppose, perhaps [or probably] be saved (σωθήσεσθαι ἴσως ὑπολαμβάνω)" (*Dial.* 47.4).

- Former Gentile Christians who "once professed and recognized" Jesus as Messiah but "for some cause or other passed over (μεταβαίνω) into the life under the Law" and deny Jesus "cannot, I declare, in any wise be saved" (*Dial.* 47.4).

Justin's third and fourth responses indicate that he was familiar with the phenomenon of Christian judaizing; that is, he is explicitly aware that some Gentile Christians in his congregation observed Torah. The Gentile Christians practised the law and maintained Christian beliefs, while the former Gentile Christians defected from the Christian church altogether to join the synagogue and live as Jews.[36] Regarding these apostates, Wilson observes that "this is the clearest reference to such a group in early Christian sources" (1995: 166).

It seems clear that Justin is commenting on issues with which he was personally familiar. Trypho's question, which precipitates this discussion, is in the conditional form (ἐὰν δέ τινες), as are the other stipulations within the discussion. Wilson reasonably observes that "the conditional is perfectly normal on the lips of partners in a dialogue, and could still refer to types of Christian known to both" (1995: 166).[37] Skarsaune notes that Justin not only made use of traditional material in his writing but added and expanded these texts and arguments when he deemed it necessary; he suggests that Justin is "very much on his own in the concluding chapters 46ff concerning the observance of the Law by Jewish Christians" (1987: 426).

It is significant that Justin accepts the observance of Mosaic law by Jewish Christians, as long as they do not try to persuade other Christians to do likewise, as well as by Gentile Christians, albeit reluctantly. It seems that he views Gentile Christians who observed Jewish customs as dissidents rather than apostates; that is, he considers them as erratic members of the church but members nonetheless, and deems them worthy of being saved.[38] In his acceptance of Christian judaizers as being legitimately within the Christian fold, Justin demonstrates more tolerance than earlier Christian writers who encountered this phenomenon, such as Ignatius, the author of Revelation, and even Paul himself.

According to Justin, certain Gentile Christians (i.e., the third group in the list) judaize because they have been persuaded (πειθομένους αὐτοῖς) to live under the law (ἐπὶ τὴν ἔννομον πολιτείαν). "But if any of your people, Trypho, profess their belief in Christ, and at the same time force the Christian Gentiles to follow the Law instituted through Moses, or refuse to share in communion with them this same common life, I certainly will also not approve of them" (*Dial.* 47.3). According to this statement, Christians judaize because Jewish Christians convince them to. Perhaps these Jewish Christians threatened that they would not associate with the

Gentiles unless they complied. Unfortunately, Justin is less forthcoming regarding why certain Christian judaizers abandon their faith and "switch over" to Judaism (i.e., the fourth group). He simply says that they do so "for some cause or other (ᾗτινιοῦν αἰτίᾳ)" (*Dial.* 47.4).

Justin is obviously frustrated by continued law observance by Gentile Christians; to impede the spread of the phenomenon, he declares that he does not approve of Jewish Christians who attempt to influence Gentile Christians "to be circumcised like themselves, or to keep the Sabbath, or to perform any other similar acts" (*Dial.* 47.1).[39] This declaration indicates that circumcision and Sabbath observance were among the Jewish rituals maintained by Gentile Christians in Justin's area. These two rites are frequently mentioned in connection with Gentile Christians in other Christian documents from Asia Minor, such as Paul's letter to the Galatians, Ignatius's letter to Magnesia, and the letter to the Colossians.[40] It is furthermore interesting to note, as Wilson observes, that Justin is "noticeably harsher in his judgment of those who propagate Jewish observance than of those Gentiles who succumb" (1995: 166).

Justin describes a mixed community of Jewish and Gentile Christians with these variations:

- Christians (Justin does not specify whether they are of Gentile or Jewish origin) who refused fellowship with law-observant Jewish Christians;
- law-observant Jewish Christians who were putting pressure on Gentile Christians to maintain some Jewish rituals;
- some law-observant Jewish Christians (perhaps from the previous group) who refused fellowship with Gentile Christians;
- Jewish Christians who did not observe the law;
- Gentiles who became Christians, began observing the law and eventually rejected Jesus as Messiah;
- Gentile Christians who observed the law (i.e., Christian judaizers); and
- Gentile Christians who did not observe the law.

This description affords a valuable glance into the constituencies of an early Christian community. Justin was personally familiar with a wide spectrum of conduct manifested by Christians of both Jewish and Gentile origin that he categorizes according to their acceptability for salvation. He is aware that some of them—Gentiles who became Christians, described above—became so enmeshed in Jewish practices that they eventually abandoned their faith in Christ, thereby straying beyond the limits of the Christian community altogether. These latter individuals, whom he declares could not "in any wise be saved" (*Dial.* 47.4), succumbed completely to Jewish ways. Perhaps this departure is precisely what other Christian

leaders in both Asia Minor and Syria feared and fought with such feroc-
ity: that Gentiles who had faith in Jesus but began to observe Jewish customs would eventually abandon their belief in Christ and become Jewish
converts.

The Audience of the Dialogue

The portrayal of the relationship between Jews and Christians that emerges
from Justin's *Dialogue with Trypho* is complex and multi-dimensional.
On the one hand, Justin presents his Jewish partner in the debate as polite,
gentle and open-minded; on the other hand, he frequently mentions the
Jews cursing Jesus and believers in Jesus, and persecuting Christians. He
takes the radical step of explicitly claiming the title "Israel," the chosen people of God, for Christians alone, and even appropriates Jewish scripture
because, in his view, Jews do not understand it. He argues against Jewish
ritual and attributes the bestowal of the law by God on the Jews to their
moral decrepitude. Yet there remains within Justin hope for the salvation
of the Jews, as he does not completely abandon them to a horrible fate; for
example, "I hope that some one of you can be found to belong to [the seed]
which...is left over unto eternal salvation" (*Dial.* 32.2; also 14.8; 35.8;
38.2; 39.2; 44.1; 102.7; 108.7). Most importantly for my purposes, Justin
not only acknowledges that sometimes Gentile Christians succumbed to
persuasion from fellow Jewish Christians to follow Jewish law, but he
accepts Christian judaizers as legitimate members of the ecclesiastical community.

A strong and vibrant Jewish presence existed in the Roman Empire,
particularly in Asia Minor. Justin was faced with explaining the relationship between Christianity and Judaism to a Gentile audience that was
familiar with and attracted to Judaism. In *Dial.* 23.3, Justin addresses
Trypho "and those who wish to be proselytes (καὶ τοῖς βουλομένοις
προσηλύτοις γενέσθαι)," saying "[a]bide as you have been born (μείνατε
ὡς γεγένησθε)."⁴¹ This was the message Justin wished to communicate to
the Gentile Christian readers of his *Dialogue* who were attracted to
Judaism: "Stay as you are. Do not become circumcised, do not observe the
Sabbath, or other rites of the law."⁴²

In his *Dialogue with Trypho*, Justin describes a dichotomous Christian
community containing Christians of Jewish and Gentile origin both observing parts of the Mosaic law. While he accepts Christian judaizers as part
of the legitimate ecclesiastical community, he denies the salvation of those
Gentile Christians who begin to maintain certain Jewish customs and
eventually abandon their faith. For these Gentiles, Christianity is a transitional, temporary state between paganism and Judaism. Justin directs

most of his animosity and judgment toward *Jewish Christians* who, through their threats of ceasing to associate with non-judaizing Gentile Christians, compel Gentile Christians to observe Jewish practices such as circumcision and the Sabbath. He disapproves of this process and wishes to prevent its occurrence. To try to curtail their influence, Justin denies the salvation of such Jewish Christians.

Interestingly, Justin does not deny the salvation of Christian judaizers who maintain their faith in Jesus. By grudgingly accepting them as members of the Christian congregation, Justin was being more tolerant than several other early Christian writers who deal with this phenomenon in Asia Minor. His tolerance likely was prompted by a self-serving purpose: by accepting Christian judaizers within the Church, Justin sought to prevent their Christian identity from being merely transitory. If welcomed within the Christian congregation, perhaps they would not become proselytes to Judaism.

Gentile Christian interest in Judaism angered the authors of these texts, prompting them to denigrate Jews and Judaism, a reaction that has contributed significantly to anti-Jewish attitudes among members of the early Christian Church. The Book of Revelation reflects a situation where Gentiles live like Jews. Ignatius encounters Christian judaizers who wish to adhere to certain Jewish customs and ways of thinking while maintaining membership in the church. Christian judaizing was such an urgent and troubling concern for Justin Martyr that Gentile Christians with this proclivity are apparently the primary readers toward whom the *Dialogue with Trypho* is directed. His aspiration for Gentile Christians was that they would remain as they were and not become judaizers. If they did succumb in some measure to the persuasion of the Jewish Christians, Justin accepted them as legitimate members of the Christian church as long as they retained their faith in Christ.

The Asia Minor documents discussed here each contain statements that directly connect Christians with Judaism or Jewish behaviour. In Revelation 2:9 and 3:9, Christians are accused of falsely identifying themselves as Jews and are called a "synagogue of Satan"; in *Philadelphians* 6.1, Ignatius indicates that he had been hearing "Judaism from the uncircumcised"; and, in his *Dialogue with Trypho*, Justin describes how certain Gentile Christian members of his congregation "lived under the Law" (47.4). Each of these authors was responding to the existence of Christian judaizing within his respective community.

◄○►

CHAPTER 6

Marcion and Melito: More Evidence of Christian Judaizing in Asia Minor?

◄○►

G IVEN THE PREPONDERANCE OF EVIDENCE I have presented for the existence of Christian judaizing as a problematic phenomenon for church leaders in Asia Minor in the second century CE, this hermeneutic may be used to explore teachings promoted by two other Christian leaders associated with the Asia Minor region, Marcion and Melito. Wilson (1995) has proposed that each of these leaders' attitudes toward Jews and Judaism was shaped, at least in part, by the fact that they were responding to the attraction to Judaism by their own Christian members, a position that I believe has much to commend it. Marcion's teachings assert the separation of Judaism and Christianity in terms of deity, scriptures, and Messiah; while his views can be understood in other ways, reconsidering his attitude toward Judaism in light of the existence of Christian judaizing provides new insights into the historical situation to which he may have been responding. Melito, Bishop of Sardis, expresses scathing anti-Jewish polemic in his *Paschal Homily* (*Peri Pascha*). His criticism may have been provoked not by Jewish action but by Gentile Christians who were interested in Judaism within his own Quartodeciman congregation. While the evidence on which these proposals are based is implicit rather than explicit, lending a tentativeness to this part of the analysis, my intent here is to contribute to the ongoing discussion of the issues.

Marcion

UNFORTUNATELY, NONE OF MARCION'S own writings is extant and the only information we have about him is derived from his critics who rejected Marcion's teachings outright. Rather than cast aside these sources, however, interested scholars can approach this material with a measure of suspicion.[1] Marcion's opponents report that he was born and raised in Sinope, a port city on the Black Sea in the province of Pontus in Asia Minor (Epiphanius, *Panarion* 42.1.3), and he left Sinope for Rome about 130-140 CE. Precisely why he left is uncertain: one story suggests that he had

---

Notes to chapter 6 start on page 174

departed the Christian community in Sinope after a quarrel with his father, a local bishop; another rumour disseminated by his adversaries was that he had been forced out of the city after seducing a young woman. Aside from this narrative, no charges of immorality were made against Marcion or his followers; instead, the evidence portrays him and his followers as leading moral, chaste lives of disciplined ascetics (R.S. Wilson 1933: 73; S.G. Wilson 1995: 212). Marcion arrived in Rome a wealthy ship owner or merchant seaman (*naucleros*; cf. Tertullian *adv. Marc.* 1.18; 3.6; 5.1; May 1987/88: 136-37).[2] He became involved in the flourishing Christian community at Rome and reportedly made a considerable financial donation to the church. In about 144 CE, he attempted unsuccessfully to convince the Roman churches to accept his interpretation of the Christian gospel, and his donation was returned. After this, he came into contact with Cerdo, the gnostic teacher, who became a major influence on his life (Irenaeus *Haer.* 1.27. 1-3; Tertullian *Marc.* 1.2; 1.22; 3.21; 4.17; Wilson 1995: 208-211). From this point, until his death in approximately 160 CE, Marcion engaged in establishing a thriving movement that espoused his particular teachings. Among his numerous adherents were many who were willing to suffer martyrdom—which was probably the way Marcion himself died (Eusebius, *Eccles. hist.* 5.16).

Some scholars have speculated that Marcion was of Jewish origin. Harnack asserts that Marcion's understanding of the messianic prophecies correspond to a Jewish perspective, and that "[o]ne detects nothing of the Hellenistic spirit in him, the Jewish expositions of the Old Testament are well known to him, and his entire attitude toward the Old Testament and Judaism can best be understood as one of resentment." He proposes that Marcion was born to parents who had converted to Judaism and that, after he converted to Christianity, Marcion resentfully disparaged his former faith (Harnack 1990 [1921]: 15). Hoffmann likewise postulates that Marcion was "a convert from the Jewish community in Pontus" (1984: 29). There is little evidence, however, to substantiate this suggestion. Surely if it were correct that Marcion converted from Judaism to Christianity, then his critics Tertullian, Epiphanius, or Irenaeus would not have overlooked mentioning this in their writing.

Marcion's Teachings: Separate Deities, Scriptures, and Messiahs

Marcion taught that there were two gods: the deity who created the universe and was the God of the Jews, and the deity whom Jesus introduced for the first time to the world, a higher God who was the God of the Christians. Tertullian explains that Marcion "had an unhealthy interest in the problem of evil—the origin of it—and his perceptions were numbed by the very excess of his curiosity" (*adv. Marc.* 1.2). Indeed, it seems that in his struggle to understand how a good God could have introduced evil into his creation, Marcion concluded that the creator of the world was an inferior deity who was a malevolent judge and prone to petty outbursts, rather than a loving God. This was the God of the Jews and author of the Hebrew scriptures. The other God, introduced to the world for the first time through Jesus, was very different: this was a kind, peaceful and thoroughly good deity (cf. Tertullian, *adv. Marc.* 1.2; 1.6).

Marcion taught not only separation of Jewish and Christian gods, but also separation of Jewish and Christian scriptures: according to Tertullian, Marcion's *Antitheses* "are designed to show the conflict and disagreement of the Gospel and the law, so that from the diversity of principles between those two documents they may argue further for a diversity of gods" (*adv. Marc.* 1.19). Marcion distinguished between two gods as a way to give "a rationale for the failure of the lesser God—for mankind in general and the Jews specifically—to recognize the redeemer…the Creator is fickle and cruel in his dealings with mankind; but he is not explicitly culpable, being ignorant of the higher revelation" (Hoffmann 1984: 203).[3] In fact, Tertullian states that "it is precisely this separation of Law and Gospel which has suggested a god of the Gospel, other than and in opposition to the God of the Law" (*adv. Marc.* 1.19), and that "the whole of the work he has done, including the prefixing of his *Antitheses*, he directs to the one purpose of setting up opposition between the Old Testament and the New, and thereby putting his Christ in separation from the Creator, as belonging to another god, and having no connection with the law and the prophets" (*adv. Marc.* 4.6).

For Marcionites, Paul's letters, Luke's Gospel (altered to reflect the "true Gospel"), and Marcion's *Antitheses* became the replacement for the rejected Hebrew scriptures. Marcion thereby created the first canon of scriptures, an action that prompted the orthodox church to differentiate between spurious and sacred scriptures, resulting in the construction of its own canon. R.J. Wilson notes that Marcion "found the orthodox church catholic in its syncretism and its universal mission, but with no authoritative book and no central, catholic doctrine. The reaction against Marcion gave it both" (1980 [1933]: 178). It is ironic that Marcion's opposition to the church of the second century challenged the church to develop the very tools it would need in order to triumph over Marcionism; "it is one of the curiosities of history that his work has established that which he thought to reject" (R.J. Wilson 1980 [1933]: 178).

In Marcion's view, Jesus gave his disciples the true gospel, but they had so distorted it that its true meaning was lost until Paul received his revelation. Paul was the only one who understood Jesus' message correctly and, although his writings had been corrupted through interpolation, Marcion was able to restore the original texts (Grant 1984: 208). He selected Paul's epistle to the Galatians to be the first document in his collection—not a surprising choice, since, of the entire Pauline corpus, Galatians is the letter that directs the most hostility against Jewish law and against Christians who wish to observe its precepts.[4] From Marcion's perspective, in his letter to the Galatians, Paul asserts his position and authority over the Jewish Christian apostles who had distorted the Gospel (e.g., Gal. 1:1, 12, 16, 17, 19; 2:6, 11).

Marcion apparently argued that the Jews in fact were not mistaken when they did not accept Jesus as Messiah, for Jesus was not their Messiah. According to Tertullian, Marcion's contention was that Jesus was not the Messiah of the Jews because "they would beyond doubt have recognized him and have treated him with all religious devotion if he had been their own" (adv. Marc. 3.6).[5] The Jews were to await another Messiah, "another Christ who is destined by God the Creator to come at some time still future for the reestablishment of the Jewish kingdom. Between these he sets up a great and absolute opposition, such as that between justice and kindness, between law and gospel, between Judaism and Christianity" (adv. Marc. 4.6). This may have been the way in which Marcion grappled with the reason why the Jews did not accept Jesus as Messiah, yet continued to thrive. S.G. Wilson observes that Marcion's proposal so effectively addresses this issue that "[f]ar from being surprised at the appearance of Marcion, we should perhaps be surprised that his enthusiastic and fairly numerous supporters were alone in coming to the same conclusion" (1995: 220).

Like Ignatius, who sought the dissociation of Christianity from Judaism (Magn. 10.3; cf. also 8.1, 9.1 and Phld. 6.1, 8.2, 9.2), Marcion appears to have fought strongly against a close association of Christianity with Judaism, as evident in the various changes he makes to the texts that he used. For example, he deletes from Galatians chapter 3 verses 6-9 and 15-25, which discuss the close relationship between Christians and Abraham; Tertullian notes that "it becomes evident how much … the heretic's diligence has erased the reference, I mean, to Abraham, in which the apostle affirms that we are by faith the sons of Abraham, and in accordance with that reference he here also has marked us off as sons of faith" (adv. Marc. 5.3). Hoffmann (1984: 151) aptly proposes that from Marcion's perspective:

> The mission of Paul was the prototype of his own attempt to preserve the message of Jesus concerning the unknown God from corruption by latter-

day "judaizers": bishops who had not yet been weaned from the law and continued to appeal to the OT as if it still counted for something; who spoke "with authority" of "a new law in Jesus Christ"; gave thanks "for the knowledge of the past"; and declared that "even Moses had spoken through the Spirit."

Marcion understood himself to be engaged in the same struggle that had been undertaken by Paul: to proclaim the true version of the Gospel of Jesus in an environment where the Christian message had been distorted by too close a connection with Judaism. Marcion's vehement rejection of any type of association with Jewish elements in his teachings may have been motivated by something immediately relevant to his own life situation: Christian attraction to Judaism.

One piece of evidence may point to Marcion's concern with Jewish ritual—more precisely, with Christian practice of Jewish ritual. It is reported that Marcion instructed his followers to fast on Saturday, the "time of rest for the God of the Jews ... lest we do what befits the God of the Jews" (Epiphanius, *Panarion* 42.3.4). Fasting was not an activity in which Jews engaged as part of Sabbath observance, so why did Marcion initiate this action among his fellow Christians? Perhaps he intended to convey the message to these Christians that they were not to observe the Sabbath as a day of rest in imitation of the Jews. As already observed, maintenance of the Sabbath did occur in some Asia Minor Christian congregations (e.g., Ignatius, *Magn.* 9.1), so this proposal ought not to be dismissed out of hand.

The plausibility that Marcion was reacting to Gentile interest in Judaism, and perhaps Christian judaizing, is enhanced by the existence of evidence indicating that Jewish and Christian communities in his home province of Pontus were not isolated from one another in the first century CE. In fact, the relationship between Jews and Christians in Marcion's region may well have been interactive and friendly (see Wilson 1995: 218). Marcion began to teach in Rome, and not Pontus; by the time he moved to Rome, however, he was a man in his late thirties or early forties with his formative years presumedly spent in Pontus. The environment in that province and the nature of the state of Jewish/Christian relations is relevant, therefore, as a possible influence on his life.

The New Testament document 1 Peter provides some insight into the province of Pontus. The letter, probably written in the late first century CE, is addressed to Christians of Gentile and Jewish origin (1 Peter 1:14, 18; 4:3) in the areas of Pontus, Galatia, Cappodocia, Asia and Bithynia (1:1). As it contains frequent usage of and allusion to the Hebrew scriptures and Jewish terminology, likely readers considered these writings authoritative and may already have had some exposure to them (e.g.,Van Unnik 1963: 764). There are approximately forty-six quotations and allusions, including nine explicit quotations, thirteen to fifteen allusions, and twenty implicit allusions, with most of the references drawn from the Septuagint (Schutter 1989: 35-43).[6] Ernest Best observes that 1 Peter incorporates more scriptural quotations and allusions than Paul does in his letters (1977: 47). Certain scholars have found this aspect of the document to be puzzling. W.L. Schutter, for example, states that "most addressees do not seem to have been Jews or proselytes" but Gentiles; he then expresses confusion over why so many Scripture references were used for a letter directed to "non-Jews" (1989: 9). One logical elucidation is the possibility that at least some of the readers were former God-fearers who were exposed to teachings on the Hebrew scriptures when they attended synagogue or mixed with Jews (Von Soden 1893: 111-12; Van Unnik 1963: 764; Van Unnik 1956-57: 81). Some of the recipients also might have been former converts to Judaism (Van Unnik 1963: 765).[7] The preponderance of evidence for pagan attraction to Judaism—as discussed in chapter 2—and, more specifically, for Gentile Christian attraction to Judaism in Asia Minor—as discussed in chapter 5—ought to dispel scholarly puzzlement regarding such texts as 1 Peter.

One of Marcion's contemporaries provides further evidence for Gentile exposure to Judaism in Pontus. Aquila, the translator of the Hebrew scriptures into Greek, was a Gentile who, according to tradition, was a relative of the Emperor Hadrian by marriage and converted to Christianity. Aquila is proof of the drawing power of Judaism: he eventually became a Jewish proselyte.[8]

Although Marcion began his teaching in Rome, he grew up in Asia Minor. There, as I have demonstrated, Gentile Christians continued to be infatuated with Judaism in the second century CE, as evident in Revelation, Ignatius, and Justin Martyr's *Dialogue with Trypho*. Perhaps, like other ecclesiastical leaders familiar with this situation in Asia Minor, Marcion was in part motivated in his teachings by an awareness of Christian attraction to Judaism, and a desire to diminish this attraction.

Melito's ΠΕΡΙ ΠΑΣΧΑ (*Peri Pascha*)

MELITO LIVED ABOUT 120-185 CE, during the reign of Emperor Marcus Aurelius (161-180 CE). Eusebius describes him as a champion of the Quartodeciman view who was a celibate ascetic and one of the luminaries of the church "who lived entirely in the Holy Spirit, and who lies in Sardis waiting for the visitation from heaven when he shall rise from the dead" (*Hist. eccl.* 5.24). He was a talented and prolific writer: according to Jerome, Tertullian called Melito an "elegant and most eloquent spirit" (*elegans et declamatorium ingenium,* Jerome, *De Viris Ilustribus* 24), and Eusebius provides a long list of his works (*Hist. eccl.* 4.25). Most of Melito's writing has been lost, except for a fragment from his *Apology,* which was addressed to the emperor, and the *Peri Pascha.*

There is no direct evidence for judaizers in any of Melito's extant writings. Certain aspects of his attitude toward Judaism evident in his *Peri Pascha* may be better understood, however, by the recognition of the existence of Gentile Christians attracted to Judaism at the time he was writing. Given that Christian judaizing was attested in Asia Minor, it is plausible that the phenomenon existed in the city of Sardis, where Melito was bishop.

Melito was a member of the Quartodeciman movement, which, by the late second century CE, had numerous adherents throughout Asia Minor. Quartodecimans celebrated Easter on the same date as the Jewish Passover (i.e., fourteenth of Nissan). Their manner of observance was Jewish in nature: they held a *Seder* in the same way as the Jews, and their leaders were familiar with the Jewish customs of Passover (Werner 1966: 200).[9] In contrast to churches in Asia Minor, Roman congregations and churches in the western part of the empire celebrated Easter one week after the Passover on Sunday, the day of the resurrection of Jesus. This difference in practice generated much contention among the proponents of each view (Eusebius, *Hist. Eccl.* 4.23-24).

The City of Sardis

Melito's *Peri Pascha* was probably written in Sardis, Asia Minor (*contra* Hall 1979: xix), where a Jewish community had a long history with deep roots. The earliest reference to a Jewish connection with the city may be in Obadiah 20, which refers to "Sepharad" as a place where exiled Jews sought refuge. An early Lydian-Aramaic inscription at Sardis, possibly dated to the fifth century BCE, bears the Aramaic form of the name of Sardis as "Sepharad" (ספרד, Hemer 1986: 135). Josephus reports that Antiochus III transplanted two hundred Jewish families from Babylon to Phrygia and Lydia, whose capital was Sardis, to keep peace in the area c.210 BCE: Antiochus instructed that the Jews should "use their own laws. And when you have brought them to the places mentioned, you shall give each of them a place to build a home and land to cultivate and plant with vines" (*Ant.* 12.147-53).

Josephus presents a series of documents from the Roman government that deal with requests for privileges on behalf of Jewish communities in Asia Minor. Three of these pertain to the city of Sardis.[10] One is a letter from Lucius Antonius, son of Marcus, to "the magistrates, council and people of Sardis," which reveals that the Jews of Sardis have had "from the earliest times ... an association (σύνοδος) of their own, in accordance with their native laws and a place (τόπος) of their own, in which they decide their affairs and controversies with one another"; the letter confirms that these privileges are to be maintained (Josephus, *Ant.* 14.235). A decree "of the people of Sardis" which appears to be later than Antonius's letter, confirms the right of the Jews to "come together (συνάγωνται), have a communal life (πολιτεύωνται), and adjudicate suits among themselves; it also affirmed that a place (τόπος) be given them in which they may gather together with their wives and children and offer their ancestral prayers and sacrifices to God" and further instructs that special measures are to be taken to import food appropriate for the Jewish diet (Josephus, *Ant.* 14.259-61). A letter from proconsul Gaius Norbanus Flaccus, addressed to the magistrates and council of Sardis, states that the collection of the Jewish Temple tax "in accordance with their ancestral custom" is to continue undisturbed and interference is forbidden, no matter how large the sum (Josephus, *Ant.* 16.171). These three documents indicate that Jews lived according to their own laws and customs, adjudicated their own affairs, and had their own designated place to meet; the latter may mean that they had their own building or simply that they gathered in an appointed place (see Richardson 1996: 90-109). They probably had their own market where imported kosher food could be sold, and they were able to collect the temple tax without restraint.

In the period between these first century BCE documents and the third century CE, less evidence about the Jewish community at Sardis is available. A major earthquake ripped through the area in 17 CE, an event that Pliny describes as the greatest disaster in human memory (*Natural History* 2.86.200).[11] Hemer notes that the city's recovery appears to have been rapid, for in 26 CE Sardis was one of the eleven Asian cities competing for the attainment of an imperial temple (1986: 134). By the third century CE, the city appears to have regained most of its former splendour. Remarkable evidence attests to the existence of a prominent, wealthy Jewish community in Sardis. The largest excavated synagogue in the world, dating to the third and fourth centuries CE, was discovered in the heart of ancient Sardis (Kraabel 1971; Crawford 1996). In about the second half of the third century, the synagogue was created from part of the southeast section of an important civic building that housed a Roman bath and gymnasium

(Seager 1983: 168; Crawford 1996: 40). Its placement as part of a significant civic complex in the centre of the city is evidence that the Jewish
community held an accepted and respected position in this mostly Gentile
metropolis.

Excavated multi-coloured mosaics attesting to the considerable wealth
of the community date to as early as the middle of the third century CE (Trebilco 1991: 42). More than eighty inscriptions concerning gifts of interior decorations and furnishings found inside the synagogue are mostly in
Greek; they indicate that several of the Jewish congregants were of high
social status: at least eight were members of the city council (βουλευταί),
three were goldsmiths, one was a marble sculptor, and one was a gem cut-
ter (Trebilco 1991: 43-51; Noakes 1975: 245). The synagogue itself was
never converted into a church but continued to function as a Jewish centre until the whole city was destroyed in the early seventh century CE.[12]

While most of the archaeological and epigraphical evidence attesting to
the circumstances of Jews living in Sardis dates to a period rather later than
the one was in which Melito was writing, cautious extrapolation can be
postulated forward from Josephus's decrees and backward from the excavated synagogue for the second century CE. Co-emperor Lucius Verus,
who ruled with Marcus Aurelius from 161-169 CE, visited Sardis in 166
CE,[13] and, to commemorate the visit, the city erected a statue of Verus in
the gymnasium in 166. An early fragment of a Hebrew inscription that
reads "Beros" (i.e., "Verus"), might represent an honorific inscription for
the co-emperor, perhaps indicative that the Jewish community also wished
to honour him (Seager 1983: 171). This gesture, if indeed it was undertaken, would suggest that the Jewish community possessed an independent presence in Sardis in the second century CE, as well as in the third and
fourth.

The Christian church at Sardis received one of the seven letters of the
Book of Revelation, wherein it is challenged to "wake up, and strengthen
what remains and is on the point of death, for I have not found your
works perfect in the sight of my God" (Rev. 3:1-6). As I have demonstrated, the author of Revelation may have been warning Christians in
the late first century away from Jewish customs. Archaeological evidence
from the fourth century suggests that the large Jewish and Christian communities of the city lived and worked side by side in a tolerant environment:
in about 400 CE, a colonnade with twenty-seven shops and residences was
built contiguous to the synagogue, and objects discovered in these areas
indicate that six shops belonged to Christians and ten to Jews (Crawford
1990; Crawford 1996: 40).[14] Christian/Jewish relations in the period
between the late first century CE when Revelation was written and the

fourth century CE archaeological evidence remain somewhat obscure. According to a fragment from Melito's *Apology* to the emperor Marcus Aurelius recorded in Eusebius, Christians were undergoing some form of persecution (*Hist. eccl.* 4.26).[15] Melito's *Peri Pascha* may be able to shed some light on the relationship between Jews and Christians in the late second century CE.

The Peri Pascha *and Melito's View of Jews and Judaism*

In 1936, Campbell Bonner pieced together fragments from a codex in the British Museum and the library at the University of Michigan and found that, together, they formulated the previously lost work by Melito called *On the Passion* (Hall 1979: xvii).[16] Eusebius provides valuable but enigmatic information regarding this document; for example, he states that Melito wrote two books on the Pascha (τὰ περὶ τοῦ πάσχα δύο), but the work that Bonner reconstructed is undivided and seems to be complete (*Hist. eccl.* 4.26).[17] Elsewhere Eusebius quotes allegedly from the beginning of the *Peri Pascha* (4.26), but his words are not to be found in the extant version of the work Bonner has identified. Despite these uncertainties, S.G. Hall reflects the scholarly consensus when he concludes "while the exact relation of the homily to the two books *On the Pascha* reported by Eusebius remains uncertain, the difficulties are not substantial enough to call in question the authenticity of the homily" (1979: xxi).

In the *Peri Pascha*, Melito expounds his views on Jews and Judaism in a decidedly unsubtle manner. At the beginning of the homily (sections 1-45), Melito discusses the story behind the Jewish Passover and describes the events of the exodus using highly dramatic narration.[18] He probes the "strange mystery" of how Israel was protected from the destruction that befell Egypt and presents for the first time the concept of "preliminary sketch" (προκεντήματος), which he uses throughout this first part of the homily in order to communicate his view of the relationship between Judaism and Christianity: "What is said and done is nothing, beloved, without a comparison and preliminary sketch" (ll. 217-18). A "preliminary sketch," according to Melito, gives rise to the "future thing" (μέλλοντος) which will be "taller in height, and stronger in power," that is, an improvement on the preliminary sketch (ll. 227-31).[19] This expression reflects Melito's view of the relationship between Judaism and Christianity. Judaism served a purpose for a time, but it was a mere foreshadowing of the superior religion yet to come. Once Christianity emerged, Judaism lost its value because it no longer served a function. Melito states this clearly: "But when that of which it is the model arises, that which once bore the image of the future thing is itself destroyed as growing useless having yielded to what is truly real the image of it; and what once was precious becomes worthless when what is truly precious has been revealed" (ll. 235-40).

Melito explains that Judaism, which served a valuable function in the past, has no current value because its service has been rendered void. He observes that Judaism, in a divinely ordered *former* time, made a notable contribution: "For to each belongs a proper season: a proper time for the model, a proper time for the material, a proper time for the reality" (ll. 241-44). Once reality (i.e., Christianity) emerged and the work was completed, however, the preliminary sketch was no longer necessary—nor was it desired. For Melito, Christianity was the "future thing" (μέλλοντος), the "reality" (ἀλήθεια), the "work" (ἔργος) that came, and Judaism was its "preliminary sketch" (προκεντήματος) and "model" (τύπος): "You complete the work; you want that alone, you love that alone, because in it alone you see the pattern and the material and the reality" (ll. 251-55). Melito's assessment of Judaism was not entirely negative, but his positive comments pertain only to Israel's past. Israel's present, in his view, was futile and hopeless.[20]

Christianity Replaces Judaism

For Melito, as expressed in the *Peri Pascha*, Christianity and Christians alone were loved by God at that time: the honoured position which once had belonged to the Jews was now appropriated by the church. Melito explains how and why this change took place (ll. 266-73):

> The model then was precious before the reality, and the parable was marvelous before the interpretation; that is, the people was precious before the church arose, and the law was marvelous before the gospel was elucidated. But when the church arose and the gospel took precedence, the model was made void, conceding its power to the reality, and law was fulfilled, conceding its power to the gospel.

This declaration encapsulates Melito's view of the relationship between Judaism and Christianity: Judaism and its law were defunct, replaced by the church and the gospel. The Jewish people no longer held a special position before God. If any uncertainty remained, Melito dispels it unequivocally with characteristic severity: "the people was made void (ὁ λαὸς ἐκενώθη)[21] when the church arose (τῆς ἐκκλησίας ἀνασταθείσης)" (l. 278). The implication is that Christians had secured the position formerly held by the Jews. This may have been a way of dealing with the continued existence of an attractive Judaism.

Melito concludes his discussion of the Jewish Passover by declaring that it, too, had been replaced: "Once, the slaying of the sheep was precious, but it is worthless now (νῦν δὲ ἄτιμος) because of the salvation of the Lord" (ll. 280-81). The death and blood of the lamb were no longer of value, for Jesus was now the Passover lamb and his death constituted the only valid Passover (ll. 282-300). Melito provides a false etymology for the word πάσχα—that it comes from the Greek word meaning to suffer (παθεῖν) and suffering (πάσχειν)—in order to forge a connection between the Passover and the suffering of Jesus.[22] According to Melito, then, the Jews no longer legitimately celebrated Passover—the Christians did.

Melito Charges the Jews with Deicide

In the *Peri Pascha*, Melito expresses the view that the Jews were responsible for every aspect of Jesus' crucifixion: they prepared "sharp nails" (ἥλους ὀξεῖς) and the false witnesses (*Pascha* l. 555); they fed him vinegar and gall (ὄξος καί μάστιγας) (l. 557); and they brought "forth scourges for his body and thorns for his head" (ll. 559-60). Finally, Melito tells them: "you killed your Lord at the great feast" (l. 565). From Melito's perspective, the tragedy is compounded by the fact that the Jews killed "the Lord," their very creator: he addresses the Jews, telling them that they caused suffering to their "Sovereign, who formed [them], who made [them], who honoured [them], who called [them] 'Israel'"(ll. 584-88). It was Jesus who had guided them "from Adam to Noah, from Noah to Abraham, from Abraham to Isaac and Jacob and the twelve patriarchs," into Egypt and out, and who had established them in their land, and then sent them prophets and set up their kings (ll. 608-24). Melito proclaims "It is he that you killed" (l. 631). The Jews killed "him whom the gentiles (τὰ ἔθνη) worshipped and the uncircumcised (ἀκρόβυστοι) admired and foreigners (ἀλλόφυλοι) glorified" (ll. 673-75).

Melito claims that "even Pilate washed his hands" (l. 676). This perspective is consistent with the apologetic tendency, evident already in the gospels, to exonerate Pilate—and, therefore, the Roman government—and blame the Jews.[23] This positive portrayal of Pilate was meant to represent a positive attitude toward Rome, one which is also evident in Melito's *Apology* to Marcus Aurelius, where he implies that the success of the Roman Empire was a natural outgrowth of the infiltration of Christianity into the Empire (Eusebius, *Hist. eccl.* 4.26).

Melito is the first Christian writer unambiguously to accuse the Jews of deicide (*Pascha* ll. 711-16; see Werner 1966: 191-210):[24]

He who hung the earth is hanging;
he who fixed the heavens has been fixed;
he who fastened the universe has been fastened to a tree;

the Sovereign has been insulted;
the God has been murdered;
the King of Israel has been put to death by an Israelite right hand.

Melito's virulent polemic against the Jews does not distinguish between Jews of Jesus' time and those living during his own time, nor does he make a distinction between the leaders of the Jews and the rest of the Jewish people, as is found in the gospels, for example. For Melito, the term "Israel" refers to all Jews without distinction—thereby making his denunciation all the more destructive.[25]

Were Gentile Judaizers Present?

What compelled Melito to strike out against the Jews in such an acrimonious manner? A plausible answer can be found by elucidating the context in which Melito wrote and the circumstances that he had faced as a Christian leader living in Asia Minor in the middle of the second century. A.T. Kraabel, based on the evidence from the locale and size of the excavated synagogue two centuries later, at one time argued that Melito's bitter attack responded to the fact that the Jews were in a wealthier, more prestigious position than the fledgling Christians whom he represented in Sardis (1971: 83ff). By this account, the *Peri Pascha* expressed Melito's frustration at lacking the same power his Jewish opponents had. Kraabel (1971: 84) suggests that

> [i]t is likely that some of the Sardis Christians in Melito's time were converted Jews or descendants of converted Jews, and that the relationship of Christianity to Judaism was a perennial issue. The Jews' attitude might have been one of hostility toward 'apostates' or one of openness; either way, in the face of such a large and powerful Jewish community Melito felt forced to adopt the stance demonstrated in the *Peri Pascha*.[26]

Noakes likewise draws a contrast between the "well established" Jewish communities in Asia Minor with the "unpopular minority" of Christians and suggests that "the intensity of Melito's polemic against Israel surely testifies to the antagonism between the Jewish and Christian communities in Sardis" (1975: 246). Robert Wilken also argues that "Jews had their own building; the Christians had none," and that the Christians in Sardis "lived in the shadow of the large and influential Jewish community" (1976: 56).

Wilson asserts that evidence may exist to reflect the mutual hostility between the Jewish community and the Christian community in Sardis that was the result of the socio-political scenario described by Kraabel (1971). Wilson observes that Melito's excursion to Jerusalem to find out information about the Jewish Bible is rather peculiar, since consulting the Jewish community at Sardis would have saved him a laborious trip. Even though diaspora communities primarily used the Septuagint for worship, Wilson postulates that the information Melito sought regarding the number and arrangement of the books of the Hebrew scriptures would likely have been available from the Jews in Sardis; the fact that Melito decided to travel so far might indicate the existence of an intense mutual animosity between Christians and Jews in Sardis "which discouraged the informal exchange of information" and is expressed so forthrightly by Melito in the *Peri Pascha* (1995: 253). Wilson understands the cause of Melito's hostility to be strife existing between Christians and Jews in Sardis. Lieu (1996: 228) rightly suggests that

> it would be wrong to project from the strength of Melito's polemic the strength of the Jewish community at the time, as has frequently happened. It is only scholarly imagination which makes Melito's major motivation the Jewish community of Sardis, vibrant, self-confident and influential, while the Christians struggled with poverty of numbers, poor self-image and insecurity. Yet recognition of the interweaving elements which contributed to the passion of the *Peri Pascha* should not make us simply remove the 'synagogue' from the map altogether.

I contend that Melito inveighs against the Jews to create distance between Jewish and Christian communities that were *too closely intertwined.*

Melito may have journeyed to Palestine because the Sardis Jews did not have the answers Melito sought regarding the Hebrew Bible. Eusebius, the only source for information pertaining to Melito's trip, allegedly quotes from one of Melito's letters to "his brother in Christ," Onesimus, who had "repeatedly asked for extracts from the Law and the Prophets regarding the Saviour and the whole of our faith, and...also wished to learn the precise facts about the ancient books, particularly their number and order" (*Hist. eccl.* 26.7). In this letter, Melito states that he was "most anxious to do this...so when I visited the east and arrived at the place where it all happened and the truth was proclaimed, I obtained precise information about the Old Testament books" (Eusebius, *Hist. eccl.* 26.7). The letter indicates that Melito took a trip to Palestine probably for other reasons and, while he was there, found information about the scriptures for his friend. The Jews of Sardis did not necessarily withhold information from Melito out of animosity toward Christians; it is likely that the only scriptures with which these Jews would have been personally familiar was the Septuagint. When Rabbi Meir visited Asia Minor in the middle of the second century CE, there was not a single copy of the *Megillah* (the Book of Esther) in Hebrew to be found and, as a result, he had to write it out from memory (*Megillah* 18b; see Feldman 1993: 72). It is plausible, therefore, that the Jews of Sardis were not certain themselves about the order of the books in Hebrew, and Melito had to go elsewhere for such information.[27]

This journey to the east raises intriguing questions. Why did Melito undertake such a trip? It is intriguing that he made this journey, but I do not think we can answer this question with any certainty. Melito describes his friend Onesimus, who presumably was of Gentile origin, as a devoted Christian, striving "with might and main to win eternal salvation" (Eusebius, *Hist. eccl.* 26.7). Was Onesimus a member of Melito's congregation in Sardis? Why was Onesimus interested in the ancient books in the first place, when he would have had easy access to the order of the books in the Septuagint? Were there others like him, who were interested in learning about the Hebrew Jewish Scriptures? Unfortunately, the limited information available regarding the circumstances of Melito's journey precludes answering such questions with certainty.

Some scholars readily extrapolate backward from the third and fourth century archaeological evidence that points to the prominent position of the Jewish community to apply it to Melito's second-century circumstances. However, they neglect the archaeological evidence from that same time period that indicates that Christians and Jews intermingled along the street beside the synagogue and seemed to have had very good commercial relations. If the one circumstance (i.e., that Jews were in a prominent position) is assumed to have been accurate for the second century CE, perhaps the other should also be applied (i.e., that Jews and Christians got along). Perhaps the relations between Jews and Christians were such that, sometimes, the boundaries of religious practice and belief between them were crossed. Lieu rightly opines that: "Melito neither worked in a social and theological vacuum, nor was a single-issue thinker. With him, as with the whole development of anti-Jewish polemic, a number of forces come together, and the interplay of these personal, social and theological factors has helped produce the vehemence of his attack" (1996: 230). Certainly, as she suggests, some of the fervour was due to his rhetorical style, and some of it was prompted by theological issues. Perhaps one of the forces that Melito sought to combat with the *Peri Pascha* was the attraction of his own congregation members toward Judaism.

Wilson rightly suggests that, while some of the Christians in Sardis may have been converts from Judaism, "there may also have been traffic in the other direction" (1995: 253). This movement may have manifested itself in the form of Christian judaizing or, even more disturbing to a leader of a church, perhaps the outright conversion of Gentile Christians to Judaism. Perhaps the anti-Jewish polemic that Melito expounds in his homily was prompted not by Jews, but by Gentile Christians within his own community, who—like Onesimus—were interested in Judaism.

As Quartodecimans, the Gentile Christians of Melito's congregation in Sardis were already in the habit of fusing their Christian practices with Jewish customs once every year at Passover; adopting additional Jewish rites might have seemed quite natural to them. Melito's attempt to establish boundaries between Jews and Christians could be in reaction to an environment where Christians were exposed and attracted to Judaism. The manner in which he juxtaposes positive assessments of the behaviour of Gentiles with negative evaluations of the behaviour of "Israel" might have been an attempt to discourage Gentile Christians from adopting Jewish customs by denigrating the Jews and discrediting Judaism.

Marcion and Melito both fought against what they perceived to be objectionable linking of Christianity with its parent religion. This is evident in the Marcionite teachings that imposed a radical separation between the Jewish and Christian gods, scriptures, and messiahs; Marcion hoped, apparently, that this program's propagation would be hastened by certain textual alterations eliminating expression of close connection, for example, between believers in Jesus and Abraham (Gal. 3: 6-9, 15-25). From Melito's perspective, Judaism had served a purpose for a time but had been a mere foreshadowing of the superior religion, Christianity. Once Christianity had emerged, Melito declared, Judaism and its Torah had lost all value: it was Christianity and Christians alone who would be loved by God, appropriating the honoured position that had once belonged to the Jews.

Given the nature of their teachings and the preponderance of evidence I presented in chapter 5 for the existence of Christian judaizing as a problematic phenomenon for church leaders in Asia Minor in the second century CE, it is possible that Marcion and Melito were responding in part to the presence of Christian judaizers in their midst. As an alternative interpretation of the historical context of their views, this hypothesis is at least worthy of consideration.

◄〇►

CHAPTER 7

Conclusion: Christian Judaizing and the Forging of a Distinct Christian Identity

◄◦►

THIS STUDY DEMONSTRATES the plausible contention that Christian leaders in the period between c. 50 and 160 CE were responding to Gentile Christian attraction to Judaism and such rites as circumcision, Sabbath observance, or following dietary laws. These Gentile Christians combined a commitment to Christianity with adherence, in varying degrees, to Jewish practices, but apparently did not view such behaviour as incompatible with their Christian faith. From the perspective expressed in the writings of certain ecclesiastical leaders, judaizers dangerously blurred the boundaries between nascent Christianity and well-established Judaism. They were "playing a Jewish game," one that was hardly frivolous but, rather, represented a serious threat to the developing sense of Christian identity. As such, within attempts to suppress this phenomenon, Christian judaizers became the target of anti-Jewish rhetoric in various early Christian writings. This discourse, then, represented part of an *internal* debate among Christians, rather than, as many scholars have characterized it, between Christians and Jews.

Pre-Constantinian evidence for Christian judaizing is *not* lacking in ecclesiastical documents, the authors of which were deeply troubled by Christian judaizing in some Asia Minor and Syrian cities during the first two centuries of the Common Era. John Chrysostom, the fourth-century preacher often understood to be the quintessential combatant of judaizing within a Christian community, in fact stands as a rather *late* example of an ecclesiastical leader grappling with Christian judaizers. This factor demonstrates the endurance of the effect of judaizing on Jewish/Christian relations in Antioch, Syria, during the post-Constantinian period.

Why Christians Judaized

A WIDE VARIETY OF JEWISH CUSTOMS are raised for discussion in the literature surveyed, including circumcision, Sabbath observance, *kashruth* (food laws), synagogue attendance, fasting, new moon celebrations, fes-

---

Notes to chapter 7 start on page 178

117

tival gatherings, and prayer. The first three are most frequently discussed by the authors noted here—three rites that most effectively served to distinguish Jews from non-Jews.[1] I have suggested that these practices were attacked by these authors because they were being practised by members of their own congregations. From the literature surveyed I have elucidated a variety of factors that may have motivated Gentile Christians to judaize, none of which is mutually exclusive of others. In some cases—for example, the situation reflected in Galatians, and in Ignatius's letters—their own reading of the Septuagint may have persuaded individual Christians that, to belong to the people of God, they needed to observe the Mosaic law. Those church congregations that were influenced by Paul may have been motivated by Paul's speaking highly of Jewish Christians and Jerusalem when he alluded to Hebrew scripture; this may have generated judaizing behaviour among Gentile Christians in churches founded by Paul. Some Gentiles may have brought an interest in Judaism and adherence to Jewish customs with them when they became Christians, then simply voluntarily continued to live in the same manner they had prior to their conversion to Christianity.

Certain Gentile Christians received encouragement and pressure to judaize from fellow Gentile Christians already engaged in judaizing behaviour—as was likely the case in Galatians, in Ignatius's letters to the Philadelphians and the Magnesians, and in the *Epistle of Barnabas*. They also were likely influenced by Jewish Christians, as reflected in Galatians, the *Didache*, in Justin Martyr's *Dialogue with Trypho*, the *Kerygmata Petrou* in the Pseudo-Clementine literature, and in Colossians. Other Gentile Christians perceived Judaism and/or the synagogue to possess security and confidence greater than that found within their Christian churches, and hence may have been motivated by feelings of insecurity and fear; this situation may be reflected in the Book of Revelation and, perhaps, in the *Epistle of Barnabas*. In Revelation, for example, letters sent to Smyrna and Philadelphia express hostility toward Gentile Christians who were in some fashion living like Jews—"pretending" to be Jews, perhaps to avoid persecution by local Roman authorities.

Assuming that judaizing was indeed occurring, there is no substantive evidence that Jews were the instigators of such behaviour among Christians. Rather, as stated above, this study contends that fellow Gentile Christians more likely were the primary aggressors—as, for example, in Galatia and, possibly, in Philadelphia. In other cases—such as the *Didache* and, possibly, in Colossae—Jewish Christians were the propagating party. Sometimes both Jewish and Gentile Christians were involved—as in Galatia. I suggest that it was unlikely that Jewish Christians followed a policy of aggressive missionizing learned as Jews, for, as discussed earlier, there is no evidence in extant sources from antiquity for a standard missionary policy among Jews, although individuals may have proselytized at certain times.[2] On the other hand, Jews, a minority in the cities throughout the Diaspora in which they dwelled, apparently did not discourage Gentiles who developed a benevolent interest in their own deity. Indeed, as discussed earlier, Jews made room in their Asia Minor and Syrian synagogues—as well as in their Jerusalem Temple—for sympathetic pagans to participate in Jewish ways and worship.

With respect to the types of Jewish customs observed by Christian judaizers, there is no striking contrast among the documents from Syria and Asia Minor, which suggests that this phenomenon manifested itself in a similar fashion in both areas. There is, however, a difference in the tone of the polemic directed against judaizing. One possible explanation for the contrast in tone between the Syrian and Asia Minor documents is Syria's geographical proximity to Judea.[3] Jews living in the Roman province of Syria were closer to the centre of Judaism and the Jerusalem Temple, the primary institution and focus of Jewish worship until its destruction in 70 CE. These factors may have contributed to a more prominent Jewish presence within Christian communities in Syria than in the more distant Jewish Diaspora in Asia Minor. In addition to geographical considerations, Gentile attraction to Judaism had a long history in the city of Antioch, Syria, as has been discussed in chapter 4.[4] In Syria, Christians may have integrated more deeply a Jewish approach in worship and ritual and, consequently, ecclesiastical leaders there may have been less able to promote Christian customs in non-Jewish ways and with non-Jewish terminology than in Asia Minor.

In his letter to the Galatians, Paul describes how Peter, Barnabas, and Jewish Christians influenced by James compelled Gentile Christians in Syria to judaize ('Ιουδαΐζειν) by withholding table fellowship from them (Gal. 2:14). Thus, this text, directed toward Christian congregations in Asia Minor, comprises the earliest extant evidence of Christian judaizing in Syria—in fact, the earliest recorded evidence (i.e., 40-50 CE) of *any* Gentile Christian judaizing behaviour. This link suggests that the practice might have begun in Syria and spread from there into the Jewish Diaspora, eventually reaching the Galatian region of Asia Minor. The genesis of Christian judaizing can be located, then, in the cradle of the nascent Christian movement where there was a strong Jewish presence.

The powerful hold of Judaism in Syria is amply reflected in the documents examined here that originate from that region. The authors/editors of the *Epistle to Barnabas* and the *Didache* sought to discourage judaizing behaviour among their readers by juxtaposing Christian rites alongside Jewish customs and by asserting that the former are superior, while purposely making derogatory observations about the latter. Despite their attempts to differentiate Christianity from Judaism, the Syrian texts nonetheless bear decisively Jewish undertones. Barnabas aims to negate the validity of Jewish ritual by advancing the radical interpretation that Mosaic law was never supposed to be interpreted literally; for example, he discusses the rite of circumcision and how the Jews misinterpreted the divine commandment. Circumcision of the flesh, argues Barnabas, was never meant to be: the Jews "erred because an evil angel was misleading them" (ὅτι ἄγγελος πονηρὸς ἐσόφιζεν αὐτούς) (*Barn.* 9.4). Significantly, however, Barnabas seems to understand that, for his Christian community, the Mosaic law is an integral part of their self-identity. He does not state that the law is evil but, rather, that the Jewish *interpretation* of it was inspired by evil. He does not demand that his congregation members utterly ignore or forget Torah, but counsels that they view it differently.

The author of the *Didache* attempts to establish a clear delineation between Christian and Jewish behaviour by prohibiting imitation of Jewish practice by Christians. Nevertheless, the document betrays its Jewish roots in its use of the Two Ways material (chap. 1-6), particularly in its stipulations of minimal requirements regarding Torah observance, including avoidance of idolatrous food (*Did.* 6.3), baptism in "living water" (*Did.* 7.1), and prayer "three times a day" (*Did.* 8.3). The Pseudo-Clementine literature differs from all of the material analyzed in this study in explicitly *encouraging*—rather than discouraging—the adoption of Jewish customs by Gentile Christians and, in the process, denigrating Paul's "lawless gospel" (e.g., H.11.35.5; H.2.15.5; H.17.17.5). Moreover, a type of dual-covenant theme is present, which treats Christianity and Judaism as equals, a view that may reflect the perspective of judaizers themselves (R.4.5). Thus, even though their authors attempt to establish boundaries between Jews and Christians, these Syrian documents speak with a strongly Jewish voice.

The Asia Minor material examined here is somewhat different from the Syrian documents in reflecting less integration of Jewish elements. Generally, Jewish practices were denigrated in order to promote Christian customs, without a concomitant use of Jewish tradition to express Christian rites (such as, e.g., *Did.* 8.1-2, *contra* Ignatius, *Magn.* 8.1; 9.1). In the material from Asia Minor Christian authors, a more forceful attempt is made to dismiss Jewish law and history completely rather than simply to undermine its worth by more subtle argumentation. The Asia Minor material reveals an ecclesiastical leadership that is more confident and independent of Judaism, particularly in those texts (e.g., by Justin, Marcion, and perhaps those by Melito) that date to a period later than that of the Syrian documents. Ignatius, for example, brazenly Christianizes Jewish history by asserting that the prophets "lived according to Jesus Christ" (*Magn.* 8.2).[5] Indeed, he describes the Israelites or Jews in the Hebrew scriptures as having been, in actual fact, Christians who eventually discontinued the observance of the Sabbath: "[t]hey who walked in ancient customs came to a new hope, no longer living for the Sabbath, but for the Lord's Day (μηκέτι σαββατίζοντες, ἀλλὰ κατὰ κυριακὴν ζῶντες)" (*Magn.* 9.1). Ignatius denies Judaism any contribution toward the implementation of God's plan, and simultaneously eliminates the basis of validity for Gentile Christian observance of Jewish rituals.

Justin Martyr's *Dialogue with Trypho* propounds his view of Christianity as a fully separate entity from Judaism. By the middle of the second century, the Christian hope had waned that Jews would turn to their new movement in significant numbers: by their rejection of the Gospel, the Jews relinquished an inheritance to which Gentile Christians instead laid claim. Expressed by Justin—for the first time in extant Christian literature—is the idea that Gentile believers in Jesus had replaced the Jews as the chosen people of God: "For we are the true and spiritual Israelitish nation, and the race of Judah and of Jacob and Isaac and Abraham (Ἰσραηλιτικὸν γὰρ τὸ ἀληθινὸν, πνευματικὸν, καὶ Ἰούδα γένος καὶ Ἰακὼβ καὶ Ἀβραάμ)" (*Dial.* 11.5). Throughout the *Dialogue*, Justin argues that the Mosaic law was created to address the moral weaknesses of the Jewish people, and that it was for them alone: other peoples were not obligated to keep these commandments. According to Justin, then, observance of the law had never been necessary, and in his time it was even less so: "For if before Abraham there was no need of circumcision, and before Moses none of keeping the Sabbath, and of festivals, and of offerings, neither in like manner is there any need now, after the Son of God, Jesus Christ" (*Dial.* 23.3).

Justin provides the most explicit evidence available for the presence of Christian judaizers in his community, stating that some Gentile Christians were following the advice of Jewish Christians and living under the law. As long as they continue to profess the Christ of God, Justin avers they probably would be saved (*Dial.* 47.4); however, those who "passed over (μεταβαίνω) into the life under the Law" and denied Jesus, would not (*Dial.* 47.4). Justin, then, is the first early Christian writer to describe Christian judaizing explicitly: he exhibits more tolerance than other early Christian writers in Asia Minor, and is the first to accept them—albeit grudgingly—as legitimate members of his congregation.

Justin gives unambiguous expression to a fear shared by other ecclesiastical leaders: that Christian judaizers' might abandon their faith and become proselytes to Judaism. His tolerance of Christian judaizing was almost certainly prompted by a desire to forestall certain Christians, perhaps known to him, from replacing church adherence with synagogue attendance. If they were welcomed within the Christian community, he reasoned, perhaps they would not desert the fold.[6]

The case for Marcion and Melito to have been addressing Christian judaizing in their works is, admittedly, speculative but plausible. In line with Ignatius's quest for a complete dissociation of Christianity from Judaism (*Magn.* 10.3; also 8.1, 9.1 and *Phld.* 6.1, 8.2, 9.2), both Marcion and Melito sought to impose a radical delineation between Christianity and Judaism. Marcion, born and raised in the Asia Minor city of Sinope, taught that Jews and Christians had separate gods, scriptures, and messiahs. For Melito, Bishop of Sardis, the Jewish people no longer held any special position before God. In his late-second-century *Peri Pascha*, he declares "[t]he people was made void (ὁ λαὸς ἐκενώθη) when the church arose (τῆς ἐκκλησίας ἀνασταθείσης)" (l. 278). Christians had secured the position formerly held by the Jews, according to Melito, and the degree of separation between Judaism and Christianity was such that Jews were accused of nothing less than deicide. Not only were they opponents of Christians, they were enemies of God.

How Did Christian Judaizers Identify Themselves?

DID THE EARLY GENTILE CHRISTIANS who observed the Sabbath or Jewish food laws consider themselves to be Christians behaving as if Jewish? Did they, rather, consider themselves to be fully Jewish, or perhaps a Christian/Jewish hybrid? Given the incomplete evidence available, it is simply not possible to know for certain what the Gentile Christian judaizers thought or how they viewed themselves. Their voices are silent in the texts. Most of the evidence about judaizing comes from church leaders who opposed Gentile Christian involvement in judaizing behaviour and felt that it undermined Christian identity.

My reading of the documents has convinced me that, for the most part, Christian judaizers did not understand themselves to be straying outside the boundaries of one community and into another. From evidence in the Pseudo-Clementine literature, Galatians, the *Epistle of Barnabas*, the letters of Ignatius, and Justin's *Dialogue with Trypho*, it would appear that, in its early stages, Christian judaizing was encouraged by Jewish Christians and other Christian judaizers as constituting a normal part of being a Christian. In its earliest years, judaizing did not challenge the self-identity of Christians because Christianity was still perceived to be part of Judaism. Just as Jewish Christians initially were still considered by Jews to be within Judaism, so too were early Christian judaizers considered to be within Christianity. Paul, the first Christian leader to denounce judaizers, did not perceive the situation in Galatia to be one of "Christians" behaving "Jewishly." His view of the trouble at Galatia was that the behaviour of judaizing Christians betrayed a lack of trust in Jesus as the dying, rising, and soon-to-return saviour; as such, Galatian Gentile Christians, by being persuaded by "a different Gospel" (ἕτερον εὐαγγέλιον, Gal. 1: 6,7), were participating in a misguided movement that was, at bottom, one not unrelated to his own.

By contrast, ecclesiastical leaders subsequent to Paul came to understand Christian judaizing behaviour to be blurring the boundary between the Jewish and Christian communities. This perception developed gradually and, by all accounts, it affected the leaders rather than the laity.[7] As such, it fell to the leaders of the Christian churches to instil a clear differentiation between Judaism and Christianity in the minds of their congregants. It was they who were to create the indicators that determined Christian identity—that is, what sort of lifestyle and behaviour were considered properly Christian—largely through their reaction to judaizing. Possible explanations for Christian leaders to have viewed Christian judaizing as a threat include: Jewish rejection of Jesus as an important figure in their self-understanding; the continued vibrancy of Judaism; and the Bar Kochba revolt. Certain Gentile Christians may have been perplexed by the fact that, despite the rejection of Jesus by Jews, Judaism continued to flourish. The Bar Kochba revolt in 132-135 CE, with its unabashedly messianic dimension and its devastating consequences for the Jewish people, may have made Christian leaders desirous of dissociating their movement from Jews and, consequently, less tolerant of those Christians who observed Jewish customs. Due to these developments, adherents to Christianity may have felt threatened by those within their own community who maintained a lifestyle similar to that of the Jews.

One fear Christian leaders may have felt, on observing Christian judaizing, may have been that Gentiles who had faith in Jesus but had begun, or continued, to observe Jewish customs would eventually abandon their belief in Christ and become full Jewish converts. This was not an unfounded fear, for, as noted, Justin Martyr was aware of precisely this phenomenon. In his *Dialogue with Trypho*, he describes a diverse congregation comprising Christians of Jewish and Gentile origin, both observing parts of the Mosaic law (47.2-4). While he accepted Christian judaizers as part of the legitimate ecclesiastical community, Justin denied the salva-

tion of those Gentile Christians who strayed too far and ultimately abandoned their Christian faith. Justin inveighed against these Gentiles, for
whom Christianity was merely a transitional state between paganism and
Judaism.

The Effect of Christian Judaizing
on Jewish/Christian Relations

THROUGH EXPLORATIONS OF A VARIETY of first and second century CE
Christian documents containing criticism of Jews, Judaism, and specific
Jewish religious rites, this study has advanced the position that Christian
judaizing is a heretofore neglected phenomenon along the continuum of
Jewish–Christian relations in antiquity.

Critical statements in the documents explored here, which were ostensibly directed toward Jews, in their original context were often directed
instead toward Gentile Christians who lived like Jews. Ignatius's letters
reflect a supersessionary attitude toward Judaism and an attempt to nul-
lify attraction to Jewish customs.[8] He "Christianizes" Jewish history by
asserting that the prophets "lived according to Jesus Christ" (*Magn.* 8:2)
and that Christianity was the foundation for Judaism (*Magn.* 10:3). In so
doing, he casts Jewish ritual observances as derivative and, hence, largely
meaningless. As I have contended, such Christian supersessionary claims
may actually have been *prompted* by such judaizing. In several of the documents studied—for example, the *Epistle of Barnabas*, the *Didache*,
Ignatius's letter to the Magnesians, Justin's *Dialogue with Trypho*, Marcion's writings, and Melito's *Peri Pascha*—the authors assert the superiority of Christian interpretation of the law or of Christian rites over corresponding Jewish understandings and practices. This was a strategy for
both differentiating between Judaism and Christianity as belief systems and
demonstrating that Jewish ritual practices were absolutely passé.

An understanding of Christian judaizing enriches perceptions of the
complexity of Jewish/Christian relations in the first and second centuries
CE and elucidates the broader issue of the "parting of the ways" of Judaism
and Christianity. Contrary to the conclusions reached by other scholars,
I assert that there is ample textual evidence to demonstrate that the boundaries between nascent Christianity and Judaism remained fluid well beyond
the period of Paul, who is sometimes incorrectly perceived as having successfully established a distinct Gentile Christian identity exclusive of
Judaism. I have demonstrated that, well into the second century CE, there
were Gentile Christians who did not distinguish differences between Christianity and Judaism. For them, the "parting of the ways" was not appar-

ent. Hence, they required instruction for how to behave. The reaction of ecclesiastical leaders toward this Gentile Christian judaizing—as expressed in the documents discussed in this study—contributed toward shaping what constituted acceptable Christian behaviour and was a driving force in the forging of a Christian identity distinct and separate from Judaism.

—◄o►—

Scholarly Perceptions of Jewish-Christian Relations in Antiquity

◄○►

I F THIS SURVEY OF SCHOLARSHIP were to focus only on scholars specifically dealing with the phenomenon of Christian judaizers, it would be a short review indeed. Evidence for Gentile Christians' voluntarily observing certain Jewish customs in antiquity has not received serious attention from New Testament scholars until recently. This review has two objectives. The first is to highlight some of the changes in biblical scholarship regarding scholarly perceptions of Jewish-Christian relations in antiquity, changes that precipitated the recognition of lively and close interaction between Christians and Jews in the first two centuries of the Common Era. The second is to situate these changes within the political and social contexts in which the scholars under discussion wrote.

In order to understand the shifts in early Christian scholarship which facilitated the recognition among New Testament scholars of Christian judaizers as one of many various Christian groups, I discuss several topics pertaining to the nature of the history of Jewish-Christian relations and highlight scholarly paradigms and prejudices. For example, I survey a number of different scholarly positions from before and after the Second Word War regarding how much contact existed between Christianity and Judaism—especially between Gentile Christianity and Jewish Christianity—and whether Jews actively proselytized among Gentiles (particularly Gentile Christians).[1] These issues are relevant to the present study because for a long time scholars interpreted evidence of Gentile participation in Judaism as proof of aggressive Jewish missionizing rather than indicative of a genuine interest in Jewish customs on the part of Gentiles. Such a view was predicated in large part on their perception of Judaism as moribund and unattractive. Another topic that is considered concomitantly is whether early Christian documents, including the New Testament, contained anti-Jewish or anti-Semitic sentiment, and against whom these sentiments would have been directed (Jews? Jewish Christians? Christian judaizers?), or whether such rhetoric was simply a means of establishing Christian self-identity and did not necessarily target any one group associated with Judaism.

Notes to Appendix start on page 178

The Rapid De-Judaization of Christianity

THE IDEA THAT GENTILE CHRISTIANS in antiquity might be interested in Judaism was far from the minds of most European New Testament scholars of the late-nineteenth and early-twentieth centuries. In fact, scholars of this period argue that quite the opposite occurred. Imbued with deep-seated animosity toward Jews, their portrayal of Judaism in antiquity is of a legalistic, unattractive religion quickly rejected by Christians. Jewish Christianity is seen as a movement rapidly repudiated by "orthodox" Gentile ecclesiastical leaders. Jews are described as actively pursuing potential converts, albeit not very successfully. Jewish failure to convert non-Jews is presented as conclusive proof that Judaism was not the "true" religion.

During the early 1800s, the status of the Jews in Europe was changing as they sought political emancipation. In their attempt to integrate culturally, economically and politically into modern life, they met with a great deal of resistance. European intellectuals regarded the Jewish communities of Europe as morally corrupt, degenerate and hostile to anyone outside their own communities. Rabbinic precepts were viewed as strange and uncivilized, and it was felt that these laws reinforced Jewish separation from the rest of society and caused them to bear animosity towards non-Jews. Even those who supported Jewish aspirations did not hold Jews in high regard; for example, Christian-Wilhelm Von Dohm (1751–1820), a Prussian official who was active in Enlightenment circles of Berlin, states in an essay arguing for the granting of equal rights for Jews, "Let us concede that the Jews may be more morally corrupt than other nations…that their religious prejudice is more antisocial and clannish" (Dohm 1957 [1781]: 29).

By the late 1800s, the status of German Jews was as yet unstable and continued to be the subject of heated political debate. Former socialist Wilhelm Marr, who is credited with originating the term "anti-Semitism," comments (1879: 46, cited in Poliakov 1985: 17–18) on how Jewish financial investors emerged from the collapse of 1873 in a better fiscal situation than non-Jewish speculators:

> They do not deserve any reproach. They have struggled for 1,800 years against the Western world. They have beaten it and subjugated it. We are the losers and it is natural that the winners should shout *Vae victis*. We are so Judaized that we are beyond salvation and a brutal anti-Semitic explosion can only postpone the collapse of our Judaized society, but not prevent it. You will not be able to stop the great mission of Semitism. Jewish Caesarism, I am deeply convinced, is only a question of time.

Interestingly, Marr associates the notion of Jewish domination of German society with a "*mission* of Semitism." Pretending to address the Jews on

behalf of the German people, Marr declares, "It is the distress of an enslaved people that speaks through my pen, of a people weeping under
your yoke as you had wept under ours, but which, with the passage of time,
you have put around our neck....You are the masters; we are the serfs. *Finis
Germaniae*" (1879: 50 in Poliakov 1985: 18). Poliakov notes that "[e]ven
an association against anti-Semitism, organized in 1891 with the participation of personalities such as the mayor of Berlin Funk von Dessau,
Theodor Mommsen, the biologist Rudolf Virchow, and even Gustav Frey-
tag the author of the perfidious *Soll und Haben*, stated that its major goal
was the reform of political practices and not the defense of the Jews"
(1985: 25).

Certain biblical scholars used data from the emerging discipline of
archaeology as ammunition in their denigration of the Hebrew Bible. For
example, Assyriologist Friedrich Delitzsch caused a stir with his *Babel
oder Bibel* (1902), where he argues not only that the Mosaic tradition
was derived from Mesopotamia but that the latter culture was superior to
the former. The book was met with protestations from orthodox theologians "and rabbis spoke of the 'higher anti-Semitism' of higher biblical criticism" (Poliakov 1985: 26).

Adolf von Harnack

Adolf von Harnack's scholarship reflects the strong anti-Jewish sentiment
typical of German philosophers and liberal biblical theologians of the late
nineteenth century. He and other Lutheran scholars, such as Wellhausen
and Schürer, "not only systematically depreciated the Judaism of the Diaspora, but went so far as occasionally to mark with a special sign the works
of their Jewish colleagues in their bibliographies" (Poliakov 1985: 26).[2] The
majority of contemporaneous New Testament theologians assumed that
a progressive de-Judaization occurred as Christianity developed and as
increasing numbers of Gentiles joined the movement during the first centuries of the Common Era. I argue here that Harnack portrayed in a negative way Jewish missionaries, contrasting them with the more successful
Christian missionaries who followed their lead, and argued that by the
middle of the second century CE Christianity and Judaism were not influenced by one another.

Harnack was very much a man of his time. His seminal work, *Die Mission und Ausbreitung des Christentums in den ersten drei Jahrhunderten*,
first published in 1902 (and translated into English in 1908), has had a
profound influence on histories of early Christianity since the turn of the
century. In the tradition of *praeparatio evangelica*, found frequently in
Christian historiography, Harnack argues that the development of Judaism

prepared the Roman Empire for Christianity. In his view, pre-Christian Judaism contributed to the eventual triumph of Christianity by founding religious communities, spreading knowledge of the Old Testament, influencing general habits of private worship, making a persuasive case for belief in monotheism, and engaging in proselytism of its religious ideas as a duty of faithful adherents (Harnack 1908: 15).

Harnack states that in the early centuries of the common era "[t]he adhesion of Greeks and Romans to Judaism ranged over the entire gamut of possible degrees, from the superstitious adoption of certain rites up to complete identification," adding that "'God-fearing' pagans" were the majority, with actual converts "comparatively few in number" (1908: 12). From Harnack's perspective, any evidence of Gentile interest in Jewish customs or observance of Jewish ritual was brought about through forceful Jewish proselytism, or pressure from Jewish Christians, not from Gentile initiative: "[t]he keenness of Jewish propaganda throughout the empire during the first century…is also clear from the introduction of the Jewish week and Sabbath throughout the empire" (1908: 12 n.2).[3] Shaye Cohen rightly points out that Harnack's presentation of Judaism as an active missionary religion is based more on his theological conceptions than on solid evidence. In Harnack's view, "Judaism is Christianity *manqué*. It tried to conquer the world, but, hobbled by its ethnocentrism and (later) its ritualism, was doomed to failure" (Cohen 1991: 168). According to Harnack, Christianity succeeded where Judaism failed.

Harnack admits that "[i]t is not quite clear how the Gentile mission arose," but goes on to suggest confidently that it was a gradual development whose "ground had been prepared already, by the inner condition of Judaism, i.e., *by the process of decomposition within Judaism* which made for universalism, as well as by the graduated system of the proselytes" (1908: 48, emphasis added). In Harnack's view, it was at Antioch in Syria that the Gentile Christian mission began in earnest (1908: 50). He expresses surprise that "there is no word of any opposition between Jewish and Gentile Christians at Antioch," and he assumes that "the local Jewish Christians, scattered and cosmopolitan as they were, must have joined the new community of Christians, who were free from the law, without more ado" (1908: 53 n.1).

As Harnack describes it, Gentile converts to Christianity did not struggle with questions about whether to observe the Mosiac law: the "Gentile Christian churches of Syria and Cilicia did not observe the law," for most of these "cosmopolitan converts [understood that] all the ceremonial part of the law was to be allegorically interpreted and understood in some moral sense" (1908A: 54). He adds that "[t]he post-apostolic literature shows with particular clearness that this was the popular view taken by the Gentile Christians" (1908: 54 n.4).[4]

From Harnack's perspective, Christianity and Judaism were separate, opposing movements, with impenetrable boundaries, particularly after 70 CE (1908: 18). By the second century CE, Gentile Christian churches predominated and were "exposed to the double fire of local Jews and pagans," however "they had no relations with the Jewish Christians" (1908: 113 n.2). Indeed, by 180 CE the Catholic church had placed Jewish Christians "upon her roll of heretics" (1908: 63). Harnack writes that Jewish Christians, whom he called "Ebionites," existed beyond the fourth century, in "districts along the Jordan and the Dead Sea" but they were, in his view, entirely inconsequential and made no impact on Gentile Christian churches (1908: 104). He suggests that they "probably dragged out a wretched existence. The Gentile Christian bishops (even those of Palestine) and teachers rarely noticed them" (1908: 104).

Harnack closely adhered to Albrecht Ritschl's analysis of early Christian groups.[5] Ritchl's viewpoint opposed the thesis promoted by F.C. Baur and the so-called Tübingen School. Baur, who applied Hegelian principles to the study of early Christianity, argued that Paul was opposed by Jewish Christian adherents of Peter in Galatia, Corinth and Philippi. These opponents or "judaizers," as he (incorrectly) called them, sought to impose circumcision and Torah observance on all Gentile converts to Christianity (Baur 1866-67). Although Baur's representation of early Christianity as two monolithic groups—Jewish Christians and Pauline Christians—expressing contrary views engaged in struggle with one another was rejected rather early as an oversimplification, his designation of Paul's opponents as Jewish Christian "judaizers" was largely accepted and remains to this day the dominant understanding of the term "judaizer."

Harnack agreed with Ritschl's argument that distinguished between two different groups of Jewish Christians: rigid, extreme judaizers and temperate Jewish Christians. The first group was devoted to strict observance of Jewish law and avoidance of contact with Gentile Christians; this group vigorously opposed and persecuted Paul: "to crush him was their aim" (1908: 61). The other group, to which Peter and the other apostles belonged, had interaction with Gentile Christians and held a more flexible and moderate view; they agreed that Gentile Christians were to "abstain from flesh offered to idols, from tasting blood and things strangled, and from fornication" (1908: 61). Because of their interaction with Gentile Christians, "this Jewish Christianity did away with itself" (Harnack 1908: 61). In the end, of course, "[n]either party count[ed] in the subsequent history of the church, owing to their numerical weakness" (1908: 62).[6]

This latter group of Jewish Christians was awkwardly caught in the
middle and its members "were always falling between two fires, for the
Jews persecuted them with bitter hatred, while the Gentile church cen-
sured them as heretics—i.e., as non-Christians" (Harnack 1908: 63–64).[7]
Harnack declares that the "Gentile church stripped [Judaism] of everything; she took away its sacred book; herself but a transformation of
Judaism, she cut off all connection with the parent religion," a move that
he calls a terrible "injustice" to Judaism (1908: 69). On the other hand,
in a statement that Cohen rightly observes is "certainly not history" (1991:
165), Harnack maintains (1908: 69–70) that

> viewed from a higher standpoint, the facts acquire a different complexion.
> By their rejection of Jesus, the Jewish people disowned their calling and
> dealt the death-blow to their own existence; their place was taken by Chris-
> tians as the new People, who appropriated the whole tradition of Judaism,
> giving a fresh interpretation to any unserviceable materials in it, or else
> allowing them to drop.…All that Gentile Christianity did was to complete
> a process which had in fact commenced long ago within Judaism itself, viz.,
> the process by which the Jewish religion was being inwardly emancipated
> and transformed into a religion for the world [*die Entschränkung der jüdis-
> chen Religion und ihre Transformation zur Weltreligion*].

Harnack understands the relationship between Paul and Jewish Christians to be one of opposition: many of the opponents Paul encountered on
his missionary journeys were Jewish Christians trying to "win Gentiles to
their own form of Christianity" (1908: 61). This hostile reaction from
both Jews and Jewish Christians is not surprising; according to Harnack,
these opponents "hampered every step of Paul's work among the Gentiles…as a rule, whenever bloody persecutions are afoot in later days, the
Jews are either in the background or the foreground" (1908: 58).

In Harnack's view, by the end of the first century the Gentile church had
virtually "cut off all connection with the parent religion," and by approximately 140 CE, "the transition of Christianity to the 'Gentiles,' with its
emancipation from Judaism, was complete.…After the fall of Jerusalem
there was no longer any Jewish counter-mission, apart from a few local
efforts; on the contrary, Christians established themselves in the strongholds
hitherto held by Jewish propaganda and Jewish proselytes" (1908: 69–70).
He notes that "[a]ttempts of the Jews to seduce Christians into apostasy
are mentioned in literature, but not very often."[8] In his *Lehrbuch der Dogmengeschichte* he states that as the church began to use the Old Testament as a source of rules and regulations, there were accusations of
judaizing (1908: 291). Harnack admits that some Christians were attracted
to Judaism, mentioning Domnus, referred to by Eusebius (*Hist. eccl.* 6.21)

as "a man who at the time of the persecution had fallen away from faith in Christ" to Jewish worship (1908: 70). Harnack also notes that Celsus "knows Christians who desire to live as Jews according to Mosaic law" (Celsus, *On the True Doctrine*, 5.61 in Harnack 1908: 298) and that Epiphanius (*Panarion* 14.15), suggests that Aquila was a Christian who later converted to Judaism. Without either discussion or specific evidence, he states that Chrysostom fought against "the heretics" in Antioch (1908: 134).

Harnack's views concerning Judaism and the expansion of early Christianity correspond to contemporaneous liberal Protestant German historicism (White 1985-86: 99; Kümmel 1972: 178). His liberal leaning is reflected in his admission that Jesus expected to return imminently but that "the real content of Jesus' thought [was] faith alone in the present inwardness of God's kingdom" and in his assumption that "the disciples at a very early time abandoned Jesus' way of thinking in favor of a mere hope for the future" (Kümmel 1972: 178). Harnack approached the New Testament with a critical mindset but was concurrently influenced by his theological views. Harnack, who opposed the emerging "History of Religions" school, viewed Christianity as isolated from its religious and historical environment, and located its essence in the teachings of Jesus, which he believed were preserved in their genuine form in the synoptic gospels (Kümmel 1972: 178).[9]

While he recognized that the simple categories "Gentile Christianity" and "Jewish Christianity" did not sufficiently address the complicated situation that existed, Harnack fell short of discussing aspects of that complexity. His theological presupposition that Christianity superseded Judaism thwarted any serious recognition on his part of continued contact between Gentile Christianity and Judaism, whether in the form of Jewish customs or Jewish practitioners.

Walter Bauer's Challenge

WALTER BAUER'S *Rechtgläubigkeit und Ketzerei im ältesten Christentum* (1934, trans. 1971) is significant for New Testament scholars because of the revolutionary approach Bauer proposes for understanding early church history. In particular, his understanding of extant Christian literary evidence is important for this study of judaizing Christians. Bauer's hypothesis undercuts the traditional view of how Christianity developed, creating a new paradigm through which future research would reflect more nuanced and accurate descriptions of nascent Christianity.

Bauer challenges the traditional point of view that orthodoxy preceded heresy as the "purest" or most "genuine" form of Christianity, while heresies were a later deviation (1971: xxiii). He refutes the notion that Jesus revealed "pure" doctrine to his disciples, who faithfully preserved it. According to the conventional ecclesiastical view, after the death of the disciples, "obstacles" arose that caused true believers "to abandon the pure doctrine" and become heretics (1971: xxiii). Bauer argues that diversity in Christian doctrine and practice existed before unity, and that the establishment of ecclesiastical orthodoxy was a gradual process. Furthermore, the texts that have survived from antiquity express what became known as the "orthodox" point of view because it is this point of view that eventually triumphed, defeating other, differing views. These defeated views, which attest to the diversity of early Christianity, were suppressed and eventually became known as heresies.

Based on the vehemence with which the "heretical" views were attacked, Bauer argues that they were initially more popular than those that eventually became the mainstream view: "for a long time after the close of the post-apostolic age the sum total of consciously orthodox and anti-heretical Christians was numerically inferior to that of the 'heretics'" (1971: 231). He suggests that in certain geographic regions some of these so-called heresies originally "were the only form of the new religion—that is, for those regions they were simply 'Christianity'" (1971: xxii). He goes on to suggest that it is possible that the adherents of these "heresies" "looked down with hatred and scorn on the orthodox, who for them were the false believers" (Bauer 1971: xxii). The New Testament reflects the struggle ecclesiastical leaders had with heresies. Bauer's thesis highlights the fact that canonical texts do not express a doctrinal consensus but preserve a spectrum of theological perspectives, ranging from Paul's views to those held by the Jewish Christian author of the Epistle of James. Moreover, a few of these expressions, such as Paul's letters and the Gospel of John, were identified—for a time at least—as heresies from the ecclesiastical perspective (1971: 224-28; 205-12).

One of the most significant and influential aspects of Bauer's approach to understanding the slow formation of ecclesiastical orthodoxy is his emphasis not only on how the developmental process changed diachronically but also on how the process differed from one geographical area to the next: "What constitutes 'truth' in one generation can be out of date in the next—through progress, but also through retrogression into an earlier position. The actual situation in this region may not obtain in that one, and indeed, may never have had general currency" (Bauer 1971: xxii). He pursues this point by surveying evidence for the development of Christianity in several major geographical regions: Edessa, Egypt, Asia Minor, Macedonia, Crete, and Rome, demonstrating that the emergence and manifestations of early Christianity varied from one region to another. The implications of Bauer's study have had extensive impact on the understanding of the development of early Christianity, as reflected in subsequent studies that focus on understanding the local context of textual evidence.[10]

With *Orthodoxy and Heresy in Earliest Christianity,* Bauer disengages from the traditional understanding of how the early church developed and introduces a radically different reading of that history. By putting aside preconceived ideas regarding heresies, he argues that the heresies of the second century were not deviations from a unified faith, but representatives of the diversity that once characterized first century Christianity. Bauer brings to light the reality that many extant Christian texts represent the voices within Christianity that eventually gained the upper hand in the struggle for dominance.[11] As such, these texts do not represent all of the voices in this struggle. They reflect the views endorsed by the "winners," reinforcing their perspective on how the development of Christianity occurred. Bauer strongly advocates that in order to understand the diversity and vitality of nascent Christianity, historians ought to allow the muted or suppressed voices of alleged heretics, which had been part of the variegated Christian movement, to be heard (1971: xxi). His thesis represents a significant contribution to understanding the development of Christianity—one from which modern scholarship can benefit.

Revision of Bauer's View

Although Walter Bauer argued against the ecclesiastical version of church history and advocated for the existence of diversity in Christian doctrine and practice before unity, he did not apply his thesis to the phenomenon of Jewish Christianity. Instead, he endorsed the ecclesiastical view that Jewish Christians were heretics very early in the development of Christianity. This view may be symptomatic, perhaps, of the political and social atmosphere in Europe when Bauer was writing his monograph (the early 1930s). Bauer avers that "Because of their inability to relate to a development that took place on hellenized gentile soil, the Judaists soon became a heresy, rejected with conviction by the gentile Christians" (1971: 236).

The task of addressing the weakness in Bauer's understanding of Jewish Christianity was taken up by Georg Strecker in his 1964 appendix to *Orthodoxy and Heresy in Earliest Christianity* entitled "The Problem of Jewish Christianity." He takes issue with Bauer's contention that Jewish Christianity soon became a heresy, advising that this understanding of the development of Jewish Christianity is misconceived and needs to be amended: "[n]ot only is there 'significant diversity' within the gentile Christian situation, but the same holds true for Jewish Christianity" (Strecker in Bauer 1971: 285).[12]

Expressing surprise that Walter Bauer does not refer to the phenomenon of Jewish Christianity to strengthen his thesis that the traditional understanding of ecclesiastical history is incorrect, Strecker points out that "it is not the gentile Christian 'ecclesiastical doctrine' that represents what is primary, but rather a Jewish Christian theology" (in Bauer 1971: 241). He argues that, by the end of the second century and beginning of the third century CE, "the western church had already forced Jewish Christianity into a fixed heresiological pattern" (Strecker in Bauer 1971: 284). This pattern, which served the purposes of ecclesiastical orthodoxy, incorrectly presents Jewish Christianity as a self-contained heresy which was uniform in practice and structure and "does not do justice to the complex situation existing within legalistic Jewish Christianity" (Strecker in Bauer 1971: 285).[13]

In his refutation of Bauer's view of Jewish Christianity, Strecker emphasizes the protean nature of the relationship between Judaism and Christianity to a greater degree than does Bauer. He notes the mutual development and effect of Jewish Christianity and Gentile Christianity, and how their relationship was extremely complex (Strecker in Bauer 1971: 243):

> [h]ellenistic Jewish Christianity does not represent a closed unity, but the transition from Jewish Christianity to gentile Christianity is fluid, as is shown on the one hand by the adoption of gentile Christian forms by Jewish Christians and on the other by the Judaizing of Christians from the gentile sphere. The latter process is not only to be assumed for the earliest period—as a result of the direct effects of the Jewish synagogue upon the development of gentile Christianity—but is also attested for the later period.

Significantly, Strecker acknowledges the existence of "Judaizing of Christians from the gentile sphere" both in the incipient stages of the development of Christianity as well as in the "later period," though he does not specify which time periods he means.

Many of the points Strecker makes in relation to Bauer's work pertaining to Jewish Christianity can be applied effectively to the phenomenon of Christian judaizing. In my view, Bauer does not sufficiently address the diversity existing within the history of the development of Gentile Christianity, particularly as it pertains to the relationship of Gentile Christians to Judaism. The following notion, for example, suggests that Gentile Christians were repulsed by Jewish Christianity: "As long as Jewish Christianity existed, gentile Christians who came into contact with it were offended by what they regarded as a judaizing perversion of the Christian heritage"

(Strecker in Bauer 1971: 201); this notion needs to be revised. Bauer's perspective here is similar to Harnack's assumptions regarding the relationship—or lack thereof!—between Jewish Christianity and Gentile Christians.

In Bauer's view, Jewish ways were neither tempting nor attractive to Gentile Christians: "[b]ecause of their inability to relate to a development that took place on hellenized gentile soil, the Judaists soon became a heresy, rejected with conviction by the gentile Christians" (1971: 236). Bauer sees the destruction of the Temple in 70 CE as the cause of the cessation of Gentile observance of the Mosaic law: "the catastrophe in Palestine forever erased the demand that the gentile Christians of the diaspora should be circumcised and should to some extent observe the ceremonial law" (1971: 87). The scholarly description of the development of Gentile Christianity as a systematic process of rejection of Judaism needs to be recognized as a point of view artificially imposed by ecclesiastical orthodoxy.

Strecker rightly criticizes Bauer for giving the impression that Jewish Christianity had been quickly considered a heretical movement, rather than having been an authentic and widespread expression of early Christianity. Although Bauer introduced a paradigm for viewing church history that affirms the existence of diverse Christian groups, his perspective on the attitude of Gentile Christians toward the Mosaic law inadequately reflects the variety of attitudes existent during the first two centuries.

Just as Strecker applies Bauer's thesis to Jewish Christianity, so too does Gentile Christianity need to be seen in the context of Bauer's thesis in order for the complexity and fluidity in the relationship between Gentile Christianity and Judaism to be acknowledged. The rigid split between Gentile and Jewish Christians, as well as the impression advocated by Harnack and Bauer that Gentile Christians uniformly rejected all Jewish elements, are inaccurate and in need of scholarly reassessment.

The Effects of the Second World War

JAMES PARKES, WRITING IN THE 1930s through the 1960s, stands out as one of the earliest scholars of Jewish-Christian relations who called for a reassessment of the Christian attitude toward Judaism. His work drew attention to the lively interaction between Jews and Christians and the ways in which Christian teachings contributed toward anti-Semitism (Parkes 1985; 1969; 1963; 1960). Parkes delineates two presuppositions on which the traditional attitude of Christian scholarship was built: the understanding that continuous spiritual degeneration within Judaism occurred between the return from the Babylonian exile and the appearance of Christ; and the presumption that "post-Christian Judaism is without independent spiritual dynamic or vitality," as implied by the coining of such terms as "Spät-Judentum," "bas-Judaisme," and "Late Judaism," all of which denote Judaism as passé (Parkes 1969: 6). Parkes realized that this interpretation of Judaism was "demonstrably false"; the work of Parkes and his British colleagues G.F. Moore and A. Lukyn Williams, argues against the traditional image of Judaism as weak, legalistic and altogether unappealing (1969: 7).[14]

After the Second World War and the horror of the Holocaust, New Testament scholars began to examine the history of Jewish-Christian relations with heightened sensitivity about the contribution of anti-Jewish teachings in the church to the Nazi attempt to destroy European Jewry. Since the middle of the 1960s, with the implementation of Vatican II, this issue has become the focus of introspective discussion and has led to a more nuanced understanding of the relationship between Christianity and Judaism in antiquity.[15]

Two of the most striking aspects of early Christian scholarship since the Holocaust is the effort taken to understand the Jewish environment in which the nascent Christian community emerged, and to recognize the importance and influence of Judaism in ways that past scholars such as Harnack never did.[16] Increasingly, New Testament scholars, following Parkes' lead, have become aware that the unattractive image of Judaism was conceived from the standpoint of Christian theological presuppositions, and that the relationship between the church and the synagogue in antiquity requires renewed consideration.

Through the process of reconstructing the Jewish matrix of early Christianity, New Testament scholars have elucidated first and second century Jewish beliefs and practices, and have highlighted the vitality and dynamism of Judaism during that period. The monograph that perhaps most exemplifies this modern change of perspective is E.P. Sanders' *Paul and Palestinian Judaism* (1977). Among his six objectives for the book, Sanders states that he seeks to "destroy the view of Rabbinic Judaism which is still prevalent in much, perhaps most, New Testament scholarship" (1977: xii). He unveils the manner in which Christian scholars—particularly such German scholars as Weber, Schürer, Bousset, Billerbeck, and Bultmann— have described Judaism anachronistically using terms borrowed from Reformation rhetoric, thereby portraying rabbinic Judaism as espousing the same type of doctrines of which Luther accused Rome.[17]

As Sanders himself emphasizes, his study is a continuation of a path begun fifty years earlier by George Foot Moore; in his article "Christian Writers on Judaism," Moore asserts in the opening line that "Christian

interest in Jewish literature has always been apologetic or polemic rather
than historical" (1921: 197). Moore suggests that in anti-Judaic apologies, such as Justin's *Dialogue with Trypho*, "the Jewish disputant is a
man of straw"; further, he points out that Justin and other authors of
Christian apologies "did not write to convert Jews but to edify Christians,
possibly also to convince Gentiles wavering between the rival propaganda
of the synagogue and the church" (1921: 198).[18] Moore critiques various
eighteenth and nineteenth century scholars for their misconceived understanding and depiction of Judaism, advocating instead for the need for a
profound revision of how scholars view Judaism.[19] His directive, however, went largely unheeded by subsequent scholars.

Marcel Simon: Judaism as a Rival

MARCEL SIMON'S PIVOTAL TREATMENT of Jewish-Christian relations from
135-425 CE was in *Verus Israel: Étude sur les relations entre chrétiens et
juifs dans l'empire romain*, first published in 1948 (trans. 1986). There,
Simon rejects the traditional view that Judaism during the period of Christianity's expansion was ineffectual, insular, and unattractive to outsiders;
instead, he argues that Judaism not only survived this period but was "a
real, active, and often successful competitor with Christianity"—and it
was this rivalry that caused the friction between the two communities
(1986: 385). His theory profoundly altered the perception of how Jews and
Christians interacted in antiquity; it has had an enduring effect on early
Christian scholarship.

According to Simon, Jews and Christians were like "brothers...ranged
in enmity against each other in battle over an inheritance" and this
"explains the sharpness of the conflict, the violence of the hatred" (1986:
xiii). Significantly, he acknowledges the existence of a continuum of sentiment and interaction among Jews and Christians. Simon suggests that a
rancorous attitude may have been held by the orthodox members of Christianity and Judaism toward one another, but that other groups within
each community maintained active contact and had more positive views
of one another (1986: xiv).

Simon identifies judaizing as an important phenomenon within Jewish-Christian relations, one that demonstrates the impact of Judaism on
Christianity, and one that has been ignored by historians treating this
period. He states (1986: 239) that

> [w]ithin the early Catholic Church itself there were a number of believers
> who, though they were not in the strict sense of the word heretical and did
> not form themselves into independent bodies, nevertheless took it upon

themselves to keep some of the Mosaic rules. The importance and size of this minority varied from one area to another. As far as our information goes, such Christians were distinguished by no doctrinal peculiarities whatever.... The conciliary canons and the writings of the fathers call such people "Judaizers," and condemn them. This is surely a second form of Jewish Christianity, more difficult by nature to pin down and define than the preceding form. The fact that it was not an organized and coherent body has insured that the majority of the manuals of Church history and of the history of doctrine pass over it in silence. It nevertheless represents an important manifestation of the impact of Judaism on early Christianity. Indeed, when we consider how widespread it was, we ought perhaps to judge it the most important manifestation of all. The historian has no right to ignore it.

In his discussion of judaizing, Simon asks an important question concerning at whom anti-Jewish rhetoric was aimed: "[W]as the anti-Jewish literature intended to convert the Jews, or to prevent Christians being converted by them?" (1986: 144). He notes that John Chrysostom's sermons, which were full of virulent anti-Jewish rhetoric, were not directed at Jews but at judaizing Christians; that is, they were for "internal consumption" within the Christian community (Simon 1986: 145).[20]

Like Harnack, Simon is persuaded that non-Jewish attraction to Judaism was the result of active Jewish proselytism, which he perceives to be vigorous and persistent. He maintains that "[t]he observance of Jewish ritual by gentiles implies as its precondition an effort on the part of the dispersed Jews to make themselves felt in the gentile world" and that, by the fourth and fifth centuries CE when Jewish missionaries became less militant, "the attractive power of Judaism declined" (1986: 367). For Simon, the success of Christian competition, and not the two disasters for the Jews in 70 and 135 CE, caused the eventual "withdrawal of Hellenistic Judaism" and the "slackening of missionary effort" on the part of Jews (1986: 370). As an act of self-preservation and in reaction to Christians' proclamation that the Law was invalid, Simon suggests that the Jews rigorously began to impose Law observance, thereby reinforcing "the meshes of its protecting barrier" (1986: 374). This imposition, according to Simon, made "proselytism extremely difficult" (1986: 375).[21] He avers that Judaism's emphasis on ritual observance "expressed a rigorous particularism" that led to its defeat by Christianity in their rivalry over converts (1986: 379).

A measure of Christian triumphalistic sentiments reminiscent of earlier scholarship (e.g., Harnack) is detectable in some of Simon's statements regarding the "retrenchment" of Judaism, which he suggests occurred toward the end of the fourth century CE: "The poverty of its doctrine, the absence of the mystical element, the burden of ritual observances, all these go a long way to explain why Judaism was not long able to sustain its appeal to the gentiles in competition with the Christians" (Simon 1986: 379). In many respects, Simon's depiction of a competitive, robust Judaism corrects earlier portrayals that were heavily influenced by the theological prejudice of Christian historiographers. In other ways, particularly in his descriptions of the ultimate "success" of Christianity over "particularistic" (i.e., legalistic) Judaism, traces of prior prejudice are still present.

Johannes Munck: Setting the Foundation

ONE OF THE EARLIEST SCHOLARS to seriously consider the idea that some early Gentile Christians were attracted to Judaism and Jewish customs is Danish scholar Johannes Munck. His book, *Paulus und die Heilsgeschichte*, originally published in 1954, was translated into English in 1959 under the title *Paul and the Salvation of Mankind*. Munck makes a significant contribution toward a new understanding of the relationship between the church and the synagogue in the first century CE. He argues that Paul's opponents were not Jewish Christians, but Gentile Christians who wished to maintain certain Jewish customs because they thought that they had to in order to be true Christians. He suggests that this phenomenon resulted from two factors. Paul's positive teachings about Jewish Christianity and Jerusalem made some Gentile Christians insecure about their status compared with that of Jewish Christians. And Gentile Christians—in particular those who formerly had been interested in Judaism—read the Septuagint on their own without Paul's guidance and became convinced that it was necessary to follow the Law to receive God's promises. Munck's work is foundational to recent scholarship on Christian judaizers by Lloyd Gaston, John Gager, and myself in this book.

Munck argues vigorously against the point of view of the Tübingen School, led by F.C. Baur, regarding Paul and his relationship with the Jerusalem church. According to this view, there was opposition between Paul and the Jewish Christian church and between Gentile and Jewish Christians. Munck retorts that: "[t]he picture of Paul therefore becomes the picture of a lonely apostle, giving all his strength in the unparalleled effort of calling into life church after church of newly converted Gentiles, but losing those churches at once to the judaizing emissaries from Jerusalem who follow hard on his heels" (Munck 1959: 70). Paul's letter to the Galatians is used by advocates of the Tübingen view as the main source of proof for the existent animosity between Gentile and Jewish Christians.

Munck draws on Galatians to present a very different picture of Paul's relationship with the Jerusalem church. He argues that Paul's struggles with the Galatian Christians have nothing to do with Jewish Christianity (Munck 1959: 87). He postulates that, instead, the judaizing opponents in Galatians are not Jewish Christian emissaries from the Jerusalem church, whose purpose was to impose Jewish obligations on Gentile Christians; rather, the judaizers are *Gentile* Christians "agitating for Judaism among the Gentile Christian Galatians" (Munck 1959: 89).[22] Munck states (1959: 124) that these Gentile Christians

> demand from their erroneous point of view that all the Gentiles who are received into the Church shall be circumcised and conform to the Law...they are not content, as Peter is, to take part peacefully in the life of the church. No, they raise a storm by refusing to accept the authority of the apostle to the Gentiles, putting the distant leaders of the Jerusalem church in his place, and wanting to have those leaders' Jewish practices accepted in all the Pauline churches, so that the Gentile Christians may thereby become true Christians.

The Christian judaizers, for Munck, do not view Paul's teachings about salvation to be complete, and therefore demand that his gospel be supplemented by instructions to observe Jewish customs (1959: 124). According to Munck, their argument was sufficiently compelling to unsettle deeply the congregations that Paul established, "partly in putting the churches into a state of uncertainty, and partly in winning them over to themselves" (1959: 89).[23] Munck suggests that Christian judaizing stemmed from a Gentile Christian sense of insecurity and inferiority regarding their salvation and status, particularly compared with Christians of Jewish origin. He contends that "[i]t was difficult for those Gentile Christians within the Church of Jews and Gentiles not to belong to Israel, but to be 'of sinful nations' (ἐξ ἐθνῶν ἁμαρτωλοί). In their opinion indeed the Law justified (Gal. 5:4; cf. 3:2, 5, 11, 21), and the point was that they should have both Christ and the Law (Gal. 5:2-4; cf. 3:12)" (1959: 127-28). For Munck, the Christian judaizer "wants to be just as good as the Jewish Christian, whom he imagines in his ignorance to be at once Jew and Christian" (1959: 128).

Munck argues that Gentile Christians did not judaize as the result of pressure from Jewish Christians. A better explanation lies with the teachings of Paul, and with the Jewish Scriptures. Munck contends that Paul's missionary activities generated the judaizing phenomenon, for "it is not till Christianity goes to the Gentiles and asks for faith in the Gospel that the question arises" about Gentile admission to the church (1959: 130). What Paul had taught them about Jewish Christians and Israel initiated the judaizing tendency among Gentile Christians.[24] As Paul spoke with "sympathy and understanding" about Jerusalem and the churches in Judea,

Munck argues, "[t]hus the Gentile Christian churches had a sympathetic picture of the whole Jewish Christian world" (1959: 131). Gentile Christians converted under Paul would have learned from him to value and respect Jewish Christians and Jerusalem. As Munck suggests, "these two lines along which Paul taught his Gentile Christian churches—to think lovingly of the Jewish Christians and the earliest disciples, and lovingly of God's chosen people...are an important presupposition for the judaizing movement" (1959: 131). For Gentile Christians, Jerusalem became the standard of true Christianity and Munck states that "the cause is to be found in what Paul has reported about the original church and Jerusalem's importance in the past, present and future, and also in the idealization of the Jerusalem of that time on the basis of the Old Testament presentation of Jerusalem and Palestine" (1959: 134).

In addition Munck notes that Pauline churches used the Septuagint "and here there are many utterances that make it appear as if God cared only for the physical Israel, and left other nations to their own devices" (1959: 132); the Gentile Christians could have discovered when they read the Old Testament that "only Israel, and not the Gentiles, had the title to God's salvation" (1959: 132). Or, Munck postulates, if they did not question their inheritance of everything promised to Israel, from their reading of Jewish scriptures, perhaps they comprehended that, in order to be truly counted among the people of God, they needed to be circumcised and observe Mosaic Law (1959: 132). Munck notes that while Paul was with the Gentile Christian communities, he taught them clearly and convincingly about the salvation of the Gentiles, but that when Paul left them, they remained alone with the scriptures and began to doubt his words (1959: 132). Munck wonders how the memory and influence of Paul's teaching during his brief visit with them could endure the "constantly repeated witness" of the texts that they scrutinized "through the Jewish spectacles to which they had become accustomed through their former attendance at the synagogue" (1959: 132).[25]

Munck believes that judaizing was a phenomenon that existed only during the time of the apostles, for "[c]ertainly the Judaizers' demands of circumcision and observance of the Law are not put forward after the time of the apostles; but Jewish piety repeatedly finds expression within the Church, playing a large part even in sub-apostolic times" (1959: 134). He furthermore suggests that the judaizing movement, as a "Gentile Christian heresy [was] possible only in the Pauline churches" (1959: 134).[26] While Munck offers a multitude of insightful comments about judaizing Christians, his views about the duration and geographical location of the judaizing phenomenon are uncharacteristically dubious. This study demonstrates that the existence of Christian judaizing extended well beyond apostolic times in the geographical regions of Syria and Asia Minor, not just in the Galatian Christian communities.

Rosemary Ruether: Christian Anti-Judaism

PERHAPS AS A MEANS OF EXPIATION of guilt for the distorted depiction of Jews and Judaism in previous New Testament scholarship, some Christian scholars in recent decades have focused on statements critical of Jews and Judaism in New Testament texts and have declared this literature to be thoroughly permeated by anti-Semitism. A. Roy Eckardt, for example, states that "[a]ll the learned exegesis in the world cannot negate the truth that there are elements not only of anti-Judaism but of antisemitism in the New Testament" (1967: 126). Certain early Christian scholars link anti-Jewish teachings and criticism perpetrated by Christian literature from the first and second centuries CE to modern day anti-Semitism. Franklin Littell, for example, sees a "red thread" tying Justin Martyr and Chrysostom to Auschwitz and Treblinka, stating that "Christendom was impregnated with hatred of the Jews" that led to the Nazi actions against the Jews (1975: 1, 49).

In *Faith and Fratricide* (1974), Catholic theologian Rosemary Ruether argues that the source of anti-Semitism in Christian civilization is Christian theological anti-Judaism. In her view, the universality of the Christian claim that Jesus is the Savior of humankind means that other religions, including Judaism, are not legitimate. From Ruether's perspective, Paul was opposed to the Torah, and to Judaism generally: "Paul's position was unquestionably that of anti-Judaism.... [t]he polemic against 'the Jews' in Paul, as in the New Testament generally, is a rejection of Judaism, i.e., 'the Jews' as a religious community. Judaism for Paul is not only *not* an ongoing covenant of salvation where men continue to be related in true worship of God: it *never* was such a community of faith and grace" (Ruether 1974: 104).

In order to rid Christianity of anti-Judaism, Ruether recommends nothing short of a complete reconstruction of Christian theology, particularly christology. She suggests reading the Jesus tradition, including the resurrection, "in a paradigmatic and proleptic way" to thereby prevent the Church from "making the absolutistic claims about itself which are belied by its own history" (Ruether 1974: 250).

In Ruether's view, the phenomenon of judaizing Christians belongs to the fourth century, when it was "a new development in the relationship of Christians to the synagogue" (1974: 170). These Christians, who were "not necessarily of Jewish background," were in Ruether's view "attracted to Jewish rites and traditions, while remaining within the mainstream Church, which now had become the official imperial religion" (1974: 170). For Ruether, they did not attend synagogue in order to try to persuade Jews to convert to Christianity: they recognized it as the source of their Christian customs (1974: 170). For these Christians, Ruether postulates, the synagogue was more appealing than the church: "[t]he clapping and good fellowship of the synagogue appear to have contrasted favorably with the growing pomp and long rhetorical sermons of the Church" (1974: 171). Ruether states that the judaizing movement was "a sincere, if eclectic, emotional attraction which continued the identification of Christian traditions with their Jewish foundations" (1974: 171).

Ruether's view that christology is at the core of anti-Judaism has been challenged by certain scholars who argue that the causes of anti-Judaism are far more complicated. These scholars argue, similarly to Marcel Simon, that a vibrant, attractive Judaism was another causal factor, as was the perdurance of Gentile Christian attachment to Judaism and Jewish ritual observance. Indeed, this book advocates that Gentile Christians who were attracted to Judaism provoked strong anti-Jewish reactions by ecclesiastical leaders who, through their criticism of Jews and Jewish customs, sought to dissuade members of their congregation from such behaviour.

Recent Scholarship on Christian Judaizing

AN ALTERNATIVE SCHOLARLY RESPONSE to the Holocaust has been to reassess the post-Reformation traditional understanding of Paul and his teachings, a response perhaps motivated by the desire to find a way for modern Jews and Christians to undertake an ecumenical dialogue. The traditional Protestant view depicts Paul as a Jewish apostate who rejected Jewish legalism and denied the validity of the Mosaic law and Jewish covenant, but who advocated instead salvation by grace through faith rather than through works and thereby excluded Jews from membership in the house of God. In *Paul among Jews and Gentiles and Other Essays*, Krister Stendahl criticizes this view of Paul, pointing out that "we all, in the West, and especially in the tradition of the Reformation, cannot help reading Paul through the experience of persons like Luther or Calvin" (1976: 12). Stendahl maintains this as the main reason for misunderstanding Paul as anti-Jewish and asserts that, in fact, Paul was a "very happy and successful Jew, one who can, even when he thinks about it from his Christian perspective, say in his Epistle to the Philippians: '...as to the righteousness under the law [I was] blameless'" (Phil. 3:6 in Stendahl 1976: 12).

In the past four decades, scholars have paid abundant attention and interest to Paul's *positive* words about the destiny of the Jews. Chapters 9-11 in his Letter to the Romans have been a primary focus, where he asks: "[H]as God rejected his people? By no means!" (Rom. 11:1), and declares that "all Israel will be saved" (Rom. 11:26).[27] As both Jewish and Christian scholars have reconsidered Paul's views of Israel and how he sought to achieve his goal of bringing Gentiles to God through Jesus, they have expressed a more positive evaluation of Paul's view of Judaism.[28] They emphasize that Paul's mission was among Gentiles, not Jews, and therefore his letters with the antinomian directives targeted Gentile Christians, not people of Jewish birth (Stendahl 1976; Gaston 1987).

Lloyd Gaston

In his *Paul and the Torah* (1987), Lloyd Gaston builds on the ideas of Krister Stendahl and, in certain respects, those of Johannes Munck. Gaston has argued that, in order to understand accurately Paul's polemic against Judaism, one must recognitize the existence of Christian judaizers in the communities to which he wrote. According to Gaston, Paul was not antinomian, nor was he anti-Jewish. For Gaston, Paul believed that Gentiles achieved salvation through faith in Christ, while Jews attained righteousness by faithfully observing the Law (sometimes referred to as the "dual covenants view").[29] Paul understood Jesus to be a fulfilment of God's promises to the Gentiles, not to the Jews. Gaston argues that in Paul's letters (particularly the one to the Galatians), he inveighs strongly against the necessity of Gentile observance of the Mosaic law as a means to attain righteousness, and faults fellow Jews for not accepting Gentiles as equal participants in the covenant with God through faith in Christ (Gaston 1987).

According to Gaston, Paul's criticism of Judaism derives not from Paul's opposition to the Torah as such but because he is counteracting the inclination of some of his Gentile Christian converts to live like Jews by observing certain Jewish customs, since they have come to understand that this behaviour was necessary to attain salvation. Just as John Chrysostom in the fourth century CE intended to dissuade Christians from attending synagogue services and keeping certain Jewish customs through his vilification of Jews and Jewish customs, so too were Paul's antinomistic and pejorative comments regarding ritual observance such as circumcision intended to target the problem of Christian judaizing.

Gaston contends that Paul's identity as an apostle to the Gentiles should be taken more seriously; similarly to Munck, he emphasizes that Paul's concern is with Gentile Christians and their issues (1987: 23-25). Ignorance of this fact has led ecclesiastical leaders and scholars to the incorrect assumption that Paul addressed Jews in his letters, and that he polemicized against Jews and Judaism. Significantly, Gaston points out that many of the increasingly virulent anti-Jewish themes found in Christian documents in later centuries were laid down in first and second century Christian literature: "[a]t least some of this development, however, must be understood as a misunderstanding by later generations of the polemic of earlier generations. At least some statements which were later understood to refer to Judaism or to Jews or to Jewish Christians *were originally made to correct beliefs and practices of Gentile Christians*" (1986: 33, emphasis added). In other words, what has been interpreted both by ecclesiastical leaders in antiquity and by modern scholars as a conflict between Jews and Christians was in fact a controversy solely among Christians. Some of the references to "judaizing" and some of the negative comments about Judaism and Jewish customs in Christian literature have unwittingly become the cause of vilification of Jews.[30]

John Gager

In *The Origins of Anti-Semitism* (1985), John Gager applies Gaston's theory of the existence of Christian judaizers in his argument against the consensus view that assumed that Greco-Roman society was thoroughly permeated with anti-Semitism, and that Gentile converts to Christianity incorporated this anti-Semitic perspective in their new faith. Gager understands Christian judaizers to be discrepant Gentiles in Roman society who were interested in Judaism; because of the negative response that these judaizers received from leaders of Christian communities, they became targets of anti-Jewish statements in Christian literature from the first two centuries of the Common Era.[31]

Like Munck, Gager speculates about what motivated Gentile Christians to judaize, suggesting that, prior to becoming Christians, many Gentile converts to Christianity were attracted to Judaism; these individuals might simply have continued to live as they had been living, incorporating their adopted Jewish customs into their lives as Christians (Gager 1985: 112).[32] Focusing on a theme emphasized by Marcel Simon (1986), Gager asserts that judaizing among Gentile Christians prompted anti-Jewish reactions among ecclesiastical leaders (1985: 118).[33] As such, he sees Christian judaizing and Christian anti-Judaism as "intricately intertwined though antithetical elements in that process" (1985: 114). The contemporaneous reaction to judaizing Christians was strong, as Gager states, "[f]or some...the very existence of judaizing Christians was tantamount to a denial of Christianity, or rather of Gentile Christianity," and those who behaved in this way were labelled as heretics (1985: 188).[34]

According to Gager, "Judaizing Christians were a common feature of the Christian landscape from the very beginning," especially in Syria and Asia Minor (1985: 132). Only when Christians began to identify their movement as something other than Jewish, surmizes Gager, did Christian judaizing emerge "for the first time in a clear light" (1985: 114). The persistence of judaizing behaviour well into the second century CE and beyond continued to stoke the fires of anti-Jewish rhetoric "[l]ong after the intense ideological conflicts of the early decades" (1985: 118).

By taking seriously evidence indicating that some Gentile Christians maintained close ties with Judaism despite the reactions of ecclesiastical leaders, Gaston and Gager break with the deeply entrenched consensus over the rapid de-judaization of Gentile Christianity. They provide a more nuanced paradigm for understanding the interaction, development and relationships of Judaism and Christianity in antiquity. This paradigm takes into account historical and literary data previously ignored or misinterpreted by New Testament scholars, and rejects the theory that Judaism had isolated itself from the wider Greco-Roman environment during the emergence of Christianity.[35]

N.T. Wright

The arguments proposed by Gager and Gaston regarding judaizing and anti-Judaism in early Christian literature, however, have not escaped criticism. N.T. Wright strongly objects to many of the points proposed by Gager and Gaston, particularly to those pertaining to the "dual covenant" aspect of their hypothesis. This aspect of the Gager/Gaston arguments is not the focus of the present study; nevertheless, Wright's criticism of this issue is a means of ascertaining his perspective on Paul. In a monograph in which he advocates that a "humble, paradoxical mission of Christians to Jews is still mandatory and appropriate" (1993: 255), Wright's perspective on Paul is laden with theological assumptions. He frequently stresses that Paul's theological argument was not inconsistent or contradictory but "integrated" and "coherent" (e.g., 1993: 174, 263, 266). Wright accounts for what has been characterized by some scholars to be Paul's "muddle-headedness" and "arbitrary" arguments by contending that Paul's "over-arching (or underlying) scheme of thought is large and subtle enough to provide him with many varied starting-points depending on the argument to be advanced and the audience to be addressed" (1993: 260). The implication of Wright's discourse is, apparently, that Paul's revelation was absolutely complete and of heavenly origin.

Wright's view of Pauline theology leaves no room for the transformation or development of Paul's thought. Rather, for Wright, Paul's theology was fully formulated at the beginning of his missionary activities, and apparently negligibly affected by the diverse socio-historical contexts or the various opposition he encountered during his apostolic journeys. Consequently, Wright frequently employs quotations from one letter to illuminate passages in another, notwithstanding their differing destinations. He asserts, for example, that "Paul is arguing from the same basic theological premises" in Galatians, Romans, and 2 Corinthians, despite the differences in the particular circumstances in each community.[36]

In Wright's view, Paul understands Jesus to *be* Israel and, "because the Messiah represents Israel, he is able to take on himself Israel's curse and exhaust it" (1993: 151). As a result of Jesus' death, the covenant, which Wright deems central to Paul's theology, is renewed (1993: 152). Wright argues that, in Galatians, Romans, and Philippians, Paul clearly "has systematically transferred the privileges and attributes of 'Israel' to the Messiah and his people" (1993: 250).[37] This position, Wright asserts, "in no way commits Paul to being anti-Semitic, or even anti-Judaic" (1993: 173). Wright strongly objects to the approach of Gaston, Gager, Davies, and Richardson regarding anti-Judaism in Christian literature (1993: 173-74):

> [t]he whole post-Auschwitz determination to discover 'anti-Judaism' under every possible New Testament bush is no doubt a necessary reaction to the anti-Judaism endemic in much previous New Testament scholarship, but at the moment it is, frankly shedding just as much darkness on serious historical understanding as did its predecessor.

Whether or not one agrees with Wright that the pendulum has now swung too far in the other direction, it is nevertheless the case that the examination of anti-Judaism in early Christian texts by several of the scholars with whom he disagrees has often elucidated the historical context of the anti-Jewish statements—an area in which insufficient light has previously been shed.

Miriam Taylor: Christian Judaizing in the First and Second Centuries CE?

In *Anti-Judaism and Early Christian Identity*, Miriam Taylor argues against Marcel Simon's view—which she refers to as "conflict theory"—that Christians and Jews competed for power and proselytes in the Greco-Roman world, and that Christian anti-Judaism was a reaction to this rivalry (1995: 2). In her monograph, Taylor explores the presuppositions and implications of the various explanations for the development of Christian anti-Judaism, which she claims are based on Simon's model. She contends that, once

analyzed, these theories "reveal themselves to be based on dubious historical assumptions that lead to hasty and unjustified conclusions" (Taylor
1995: 4). One such theory, which she refers to as "defensive anti-Judaism,"
is the one espoused by Gaston and Gager—that is, that the existence of
Christian judaizers in the first and second centuries CE provoked anti-
Judaic reactions by ecclesiastical leaders who deemed judaizing a threat to
Christian identity and testified to the attractiveness of Judaism (1995:
21).

Taylor claims that "misconceptions in modern scholarship about the
judaizing phenomenon have led to a fundamental misrepresentation of
anti-judaizing in the early church, and to a misunderstanding of the moti-
vations behind it" (1995: 26). The most common misconception about
judaizing, from her perspective, is that it occurred at all during the early
period of church history. She contends that early evidence for judaizing
among Gentile Christians is lacking, and that most evidence for this
phenomenon is from the fourth century (e.g., John Chrysostom's vitu-
peration against the judaizers of his congregation) (1995: 29). Taylor
(1995: 31) claims that such scholars as Meeks, Wilken, Gager, and
Gaston

> assume that if Judaism still managed to exert its influence over Christianity,
> through the intermediary of judaizers in the fourth century, then the prob-
> lem must have seemed all the more acute in the earlier period when the
> church was in a weaker position, and the synagogue in a relatively stronger
> one. I would argue that, to the contrary, such a progressive, uninterrupted
> development in Jewish-Christian relations cannot be assumed unless it is
> proven and backed by solid evidence. Such evidence is lacking. If anything,
> there seem to be more reasons for assuming a lack of continuity in the pre-
> and post-Constantinian periods.

Furthermore, she accuses scholars who argue that judaizing occurred in the
first and second centuries of making fallacious assumptions: "[t]he sparseness of the evidence for judaizing in the pre-Constantinian period has
forced scholars to formulate their theories on the basis of the later evidence
which is then read back and presumed to apply in the earlier period as
well" (1995: 30).[38] In this study, I challenge Taylor's argument that "most
of the main anti-judaizers in the early church, whose writings are quoted
to supplement the evidence found in Chrysostom, also date from the post-
Constantinian period." Instead, this study contends that literary evidence
is available in documents that date from the first and second centuries
CE.[39]

Taylor also argues that Christian anti-Jewish polemic was for internal
consumption alone, and provided the early church with "historically trans-

mitted (and transmissible) symbols"; it has no basis whatsoever, then, in contemporary reality (1995: 54). She contends that there is no real evidence that debates between Jews and the Church Fathers (e.g., Justin Martyr) ever occurred, and asserts that "the Jewish oppressors portrayed in the church's literature represent *an intellectual and not a literal reality*" (1995: 55, emphasis added). Consequently, Taylor denies (1995:141) that judaizing behaviour among Christians has anything to do with a living Jewish community:

> [t]o the extent that the Judaism portrayed by the church fathers is recognized as a figurative entity which emerges out of Christian theorizing about Christianity, it cannot simultaneously be interpreted as referring to a living Judaism from which useful information can be gleaned about Jewish-Christian interaction. Unfortunately, though, most scholars seem oblivious of the need to make interpretive choices of this kind.[40]

For Taylor, judaizing "does not necessarily imply an attraction to Judaism, just as anti-judaizing does not necessarily imply a reaction to such an attraction," because both are "directed at something quite separate from Judaism" (1995: 29). She suggests that "judaizing appears to have been chiefly an internal phenomenon with no apparent connection either to the drawing power of contemporary Judaism, or to positive pressures exerted by the Jews" (1995: 29).[41] Throughout her study, Taylor stresses that anti-Judaism is theoretical and symbolic in nature: it was an intellectual exercise, a way for Christian thinkers to work out their issues. The anti-Jewish perspectives reflected in early Christian literature were, for Taylor, theological points that served the theoretical process of identity formation in Christianity. According to Taylor, the "Jews" of anti-Jewish rhetoric in early Christian texts were strictly symbolic; thus, this rhetoric is entirely abstract and provides no insight into contemporaneous Jewish–Christian relations. Her argument is, ultimately, unpersuasive.[42] She applies her theory too universally and makes sweeping and often unjustified generalizations about diverse scholarly approaches to the material.

Judith Lieu

In contrast, Judith Lieu, in *Image and Reality: The Jews in the World of the Christians in the Second Century* (1996), takes a subtler approach in her exploration of the ways in which Jews and Judaism are presented in second-century texts from Asia Minor. She examines how both image and reality are reflected in the texts, "image" being "that which each text projects concerning Jews or Judaism," and "reality" being "the actual position of Jews and Jewish communities in the context from which the literature comes, both in themselves and in relation to their Christian contemporaries" (Lieu 1996: 2). In Lieu's view, image and reality interact in the texts: "When this literature speaks of Jews and Judaism there is a contemporary reality, one of which, in differing degrees, its authors are aware. Yet their own needs, the logic of their own argument, and the tradition they draw on, especially the 'Old Testament,' help create and mould the terms in which they speak—to create an 'image'" (1996: 12). She argues for a more complex interrelationship between the two than does Taylor: "'image' does not belong to the literary world alone, and 'reality' to the external." Lieu has warned that it is not possible "to maintain a simple contrast between these, for each helps construct the other" (Lieu 1996: 279).

◄○►

Notes

◄○►

Chapter 1

1 This point is made by, among others, Anthony Saldarini (1992: 26), where he provides a succint and insightful summary of how New Testament research has depicted Jewish-Christian relations in antiquity.

2 The reasons for this change are associated with the effect the Holocaust had on New Testament scholars' investigation into how anti-Jewish teachings in the church might have contributed to the Nazi attempt to destroy European Jewry. See the Appendix for a fuller discussion of these issues.

3 This is an important part of Walter Bauer's provocative thesis in *Orthodoxy and Heresy in Earliest Christianity* (1971). Discussion of the strengths and weaknesses of this thesis as it pertains to the understanding of Jewish-Christian relations in the early centuries is found in the Appendix.

4 I use the term "Gentile Christian" to denote Christians of Gentile, non-Jewish, or pagan origin. The word "pagan" bears no derogatory meaning in this study, but is employed in the standard manner adopted by scholars of the ancient world to distinguish Jews and early Christians from others in the Greco-Roman world.

5 For convenience, throughout this study I use the term "Jew" to refer to someone of Jewish origin who does not identify Jesus of Nazareth as one or more of the following: the Messiah, God's Son, or a divine being. The term "Jewish Christian" denotes someone of Jewish birth who does hold one or more of these beliefs.

6 In his earlier publication (1987: 418), Cohen argues that the passage's reference to an "equivocal" element was a reference to the group of judaizers present in the Syrian cities; in a later work he argues that there are instead two "liminal" groups: the "judaizers" and the "ambiguous element" (1999: 184).

7 This point has been emphasized by Gaston, who notes that while the verb "to judaize" sometimes was used to refer to the forced conversion of Gentiles to Judaism (Esth. 8:17 LXX; Josephus, *War* 2.454), it more properly means "to live as a Jew, in accordance with Jewish customs" (Gaston 1986: 35). In other words, it describes the phenomenon of Gentiles' observing various components of the Mosaic law, such as keeping the Sabbath or certain food laws, without converting fully to Judaism (Gal. 2:14; Josephus, *War* 2.463; Plutarch, *Cic.* 7.6; *Acts of Pilate* 2.1; and Council of Laeodicea, Canon 29; also Gaston 1986: 35 and Cohen 1989: 13-33). According to Cohen, "Aside from a small number of passages in which *ioudaizein* might mean to give political support to the Jews…, the verb always means to adopt the customs and manners of the Jews…, it means to abstain from pork, to refrain from work on the Sabbath, or to attend synagogue. What makes Jews distinctive, and consequently

what makes 'judaizers' distinctive, is the observance of the ancestral laws of the Jews" (1993: 32).

8 Some of the "anti-Jewish" rhetoric in the documents discussed in this study addresses Gentile Christians, not Jews. I agree with Taylor that this rhetoric was *intra muros* but for different reasons.

9 My initial goal was to survey early Christian documents dating up to 200 CE, however no extant documents relevant to the issue were found between the period of 160 to 200 CE. For maps of Syria and Asia Minor, see pages xi and xii respectively.

10 In addition, interpretations ought not to be based on ambiguous words or phrases, nor, likewise, on a suspiciously distorted phrase (Barclay 1987: 84).

--◄o►--

Chapter 2

1 Flavius Josephus emphasizes the antiquity of the Jews throughout his writing, and claims, e.g., in *Against Apion,* that Moses is the oldest of all legislators in the world (2.154-56). Even adversaries of the Jews were willing to acknowledge the antiquity of their existence: Tacitus, for one, set the origin of the Jews in Greek pre-history (Feldman 1993: 184).

2 Segal argues that the statement attests "to the success that Judaism had in proselytism" (Segal 1990: 86). Tacitus' remark says nothing, however, about whether the Jews sought the converts or whether non-Jews came of their own initiative. Receiving converts is one thing; actively seeking them is another.

3 Stern (1976: 323) states that Horace's words imply "strong Jewish missionary activity in Rome." But there is nothing here about Jews compelling Gentiles to become Jewish. Cicero from the previous generation attests to how the Jews would use mass intimidation to get their way when lawsuits were in progress (*Flac.* 28). John Nolland argues that Horace does indeed attest to "the Jews pushing their point of view forward—but it is in the realm of politics and personal advantage that Horace sees this occurring, not in the realm of the propagation of religious ideas" (1979: 353).

4 A.T. Kraabel (1981: 113-26) has taken a strong position against the existence of a large number of "God-fearers" who attached themselves to the synagogues of Diaspora Judaism, arguing that there is no epigraphical evidence that proves the existence of Gentile adherents to Judaism (also L. Robert 1964: 43-45).

5 One of the inscriptions mentions a πάτελλα, which may refer either to a soup kitchen itself (so, Reynolds and Tannenbaum 1987: 27) or to some type of dish used for dispensing food.

6 As Feldman notes, "[t]he fact that Josephus singles out specific observances as having spread among non-Jews, citing as two of his four examples the laws pertaining to the Sabbath, apparently the most popular Jewish practice among the 'sympathizers,' and referring to many of the dietary laws (rather than all of them, the observance of which is required of converts) shows that we are dealing not with full proselytes but with 'sympathizers'" (Feldman 1993: 352). This statement of Josephus is discussed more fully below.

7 The Greek is difficult to understand at points in this section. This translation is that of Henry St. John Thackeray in the Loeb Classical Library edition. Cohen, following Otto Michel and Otto Bauernfeind (1959: 275), in Cohen 1999: 184 translates the last sentence as "and it was feared as if it were truly foreign, although it was mixed."

8 For ὑπηγμένας τῇ Ἰουδαϊκῇ θρησκείᾳ H.S. Thackeray renders "become converts to the Jewish religion," but the context of the statement should dictate how the statement is understood. Thus the women, who are not part of the Jewish community and who remain married to their Gentile husbands, are more likely adherents to Judaism than converts (see Cohen 1987: 417; 1999: 185). Margaret Williams's understanding of Josephus' use of the verb "to judaize" (ἰουδαΐζειν) is erroneous. She says that he used it "for those whose public life made them outwardly indistinguishable from Jews but whose avowed attachment to Judaism was somewhat suspect" (Williams 1988: 108). As an example, she points to Josephus' reference, discussed above, to the "non-Jewish residents of certain Syrian cities who practised a Jewish way of life but whose loyalty to their co-religionists on the eve of the Jewish War was a matter of doubt" (Williams 1988: 109). According to the text, however, it was the *Syrians* and not the Jews of the city who were suspicious of the judaizers (*War* 2.559–60): the Syrians could not trust these judaizers even though they were fellow Syrians. I am not aware of evidence that indicates how Jews felt about judaizers, nor whether they were specifically suspicious of them; one possible text that might indicate their attitude is the *Birkat ha-Minim*, although the usual understanding is that this curse was directed toward Jewish Christians to prevent them from being presenters in synagogue, and not toward Gentile Christians. The extant evidence suggests that the phenomenon of Gentile Christian judaizing was primarily a *Christian* problem, not a Jewish one.

9 Lieu understands this description of Poppaea to be an expression of "appreciation of her support or patronage rather than a claim for any overt allegiance to Judaism on her part, and only serves to demonstrate the wide usefulness and reference of the term" (1995: 495).

10 In what may be a similar example of this kind of thinking in another Jewish writer of the first century CE, Philo suggests that Petronius, the governor of Syria who refused to erect a statue of Caligula in the Jerusalem temple, was attracted to Judaism: "Indeed it appears that he himself had some rudiments of Jewish philosophy and religion acquired either in early lessons in the past through his zeal for culture or after his appointment as governor in the countries where the Jews are very numerous in every city, Asia and Syria, or else because his own soul was so disposed, being drawn to things worthy of serious effort by a nature which listened to no voice nor dictation nor teaching but its own" (Philo, *Legation to Gaius* 33.245).

11 Another aristocratic woman who belongs to this list is Queen Helena of Adiabene. Her conversion (and that of her son) are discussed later.

12 Williams notes, "as far as most of our ancient authorities were concerned, Poppaea was nothing if not obsessed with fashion" (1988: 111). See Juvenal, *Satires* 6.462.

13 Berenice's sister Drusilla married Felix, a Roman governor of Judaea (Josephus, *Ant*. 20.142–44). Agrippa II, the brother of the two sisters, had earlier refused to allow Drusilla to marry Epiphanes, the son of King Antiochus of Commagene, when Epiphanes refused to be circumcised (*Ant*. 20.139). Felix, apparently, did not undergo the rite, but Drusilla married him despite this and thereby, according to Josephus, "transgress[ed] the ancestral laws" (*Ant*. 20.143). After the death of Herod IV, who was both her uncle and her husband, Berenice married Polemo, the king of Cilicia, when he agreed to be circumcised (*Ant*. 20.145). Josephus states that she took this step in order to quell rumours that she and her brother had been involved in an incestuous relationship (*Ant*. 20.145-46).

14 Leon states: "the fact that Clemens could be convicted on the ostensible charge of practicing Judaism would suggest that some effort was made to check Jewish proselytizing activity" (1995: 35), suggesting that these Gentiles endured external Jewish pressure or persuasion. There is no indication here, however, of *how* Clemens and Domitilla became exposed to Judaism.

15 Keresztes suggests that "[t]hose 'protected' by this prohibition then had to be gentiles who had turned to Jewish life. They were probably protected only against religious persecution but not against a duty of paying tax to the *fiscus Iudaicus*" (1979: 261).

16 See especially M. Goodman (1994), S. McKnight (1991); also Shaye Cohen (1989, 1999), Louis Feldman (1993), A.T. Kraabel (1982), Judith Lieu (1992), James Carleton Paget (1996: 65–103), A. Segal (1990), and Edouard Will and Claude Orrieux (1992).

17 The most sensible approach to the question "Was Judaism a missionary religion?" is to narrow the application of the question to specific texts, persons and geographical locations (Mason 1996: 1ff). An examination of all of the texts related to this issue would be a book itself; consequently, the ensuing discussion addresses the question in broader terms.

18 Wayne O. McCready (2000) applies Stark's thesis to Jewish sectarians in Second Temple Judaism. Similarly, McKnight suggests that the "most effective and probably unconscious method Jews 'used' to attract Gentiles was the compelling force of a good life" (1991: 67). He also mentions marriage and adoption as "natural means" through which Gentiles were exposed and attracted to Judaism (1991: 68).

19 One family member's attachment to Judaism could have an effect on another: Josephus notes that Izates' brother Monobazus considered conversion to Judaism when he observed the positive experience of Izates (*Ant*. 20. 75).

20 Sifre to Deuteronomy 313 (Deut. 32:10), a rabbinic text which was probably compiled sometime in the third century, describes the patriarch Abraham as so effective a missionary that he causes God to be known not only as king of earth but also of heaven. This third-century document emphasizes his skill as a converter as one of the most important features of his career, whereas such earlier writers as Philo and Josephus stress Abraham's status as a pious convert, rather than as a converter. Sifre Deuteronomy, similar to the statement attributed to Dio Cassius, may reflect an interest in missionary activity among Jews in the third century CE that is not found in the earlier centuries (Goodman 1994: 83).

21 Louis Feldman, who strongly argues that Judaism in antiquity was a missionary religion, admits in a study on the topic that "[o]ne of the questions that
   has always puzzled students of Jewish proselytism is how to explain a movement of such magnitude when we do not know of any missionaries as such"
   (1992: 33).

22 In an interesting modern parallel to our concerns about the definition of "to
   judaize," Hallowel notes the following: "'Indianize,' in the sense of 'to adopt
   the ways of Indians,' is an Americanism dating back to the late seventeenth
   century. Cotton Mather asked: "How much do our people Indianize?" While
   the word has sometimes been used in a collective sense, in its later usage it
   seems to have been employed primarily with reference to individuals *who
   adopted the ways of Indians*" (Hallowel 1963: 520, emphasis added).

23 Perhaps the missionary impulse of early Christians should be questioned as
   well. The concept of the practice of Christian proselytism is taken from the
   Book of Acts, where the presentation of the spread of Christianity (primarily
   through Paul) serves the theological agenda of its author.

—◖◗—

Chapter 3

1 Where to place Galatians among Paul's letters is a much debated issue among
  scholars. I identify the second Jerusalem visit mentioned in Galatians 2:1-10
  with the "apostolic council" of Acts 15 and understand the letter to the Galatians to be written before his letters to Philippi and Rome. The tone of Galatians betrays an emotional, urgent, first-time response to the problem of
  judaizing. That it was written prior to Romans is evident by the fact that the
  latter is a more extensive and methodical piece of writing than the letter to the
  Galatians, and reflects a more developed form of Paul's thought. As Lightfoot
  states: "The Epistle to the Galatians stands in relation to the Roman letter, as
  the rough model to the finished statue" and is of a more "personal and frag-
  mentary" form than Romans (1910: 49).

2 In recent years, scholars have effectively applied models from the social sciences
  to gain new insight into the Pauline corpus, e.g., John Gager (1975); Howard
  Clark Kee (1989); Bruce Malina (1981); Rodney Stark (1996).

3 The usual identification of Paul's opponents in Galatia is as Jewish Christians:
  F.C. Baur (1876); H.D. Betz (1979); F.F. Bruce (1982); E.D. Burton (1921);
  Gager (2000); G. Howard (1979); R. Jewett (1971); J.B. Lightfoot (1865);
  J. Murphy O'Connor (1996).

4 This may have been hinted at earlier in the letter, for example in Gal. 3:3:
  "Are you so foolish? Having started with the Spirit, are you now ending with
  the flesh?"

5 According to Burton (1921: 273), "[t]he form of the conditional clause ἐὰν
  περιτέμνησθε, referring to a future possibility, reflects the fact that the question whether they will be circumcised is still pending. The use of the present
  tense, at first thought surprising, indicates that the apostle is not thinking of

circumcision as a simple (possible future) fact, or result accomplished, but of the attempt or decision to be circumcised, the verb being substantially cona- tive in force." Significantly, in his commentary on Galatians, J.B. Lightfoot states, "the present tense is more appropriate than the past. It is not the fact of their *having been circumcised* which St Paul condemns ... but the fact of their *allowing themselves to be circumcised*" (1890: 204, his emphasis).

6 The remaining parts of the two verses, whose grammatical and exegetical problems have sparked much debate, are addressed later in this chapter in a discussion of the identity of the agitators who exercised the pressure.

7 Burton astutely summarizes the importance of this section of the letter (1921: 112): "[t]he words ἀναγκάζεις Ἰουδαΐζειν are of crucial importance for the understanding of Paul's position. They show what he regarded as the signifi- cance if not the deliberate intent of Peter's conduct in refusing any longer to eat with the Gentile Christians. Under the circumstances this amounted not sim- ply to maintaining the validity of the Jewish law for Jewish Christians, but involved the forcing of Jewish practices upon the Gentile Christians. By his refusal any longer to eat with them and by the adoption under his influence of the same course on the part of the Jewish members of the Antioch church, he left to the Gentiles no choice but either to conform to the Jewish law of foods, or suffer a line of division to be drawn through the church. It was this element of coercion brought to bear on the Gentile Christians that made the matter one of direct concern to Paul. Against efforts to maintain the observance of the Jew- ish law on the part of Jewish Christians, he would doubtless have had noth- ing to say so long as they were confined to Jewish communities, concerned the Jews only, and did not affect the Gentiles." The events described in Galatians 2 may have been the genesis of the Christian judaizing phenomenon in the region of Syria, which I explore further in chapter 4.

8 Esler rightly suggests that "Ἰουδαΐζειν" is "the culmination and climax of this whole historical interlude" (1994: 61). Esler is confident that 2:15-21 is not part of what Paul said to Peter at Antioch. It is, however, impossible to determine this with any certainty.

9 According to Shaye Cohen, "Metilius realized that 'judaising' was a broad concept, and was willing to go as far as circumcision, that is, conversion" (1987: 416). It is not certain, however, that circumcision equalled conversion to Judaism during the first century. Circumcision was possibly only *one* of the steps for male converts to Judaism during the first century. In the argument between the schools of Shammai and Hillel concerning the degree of impurity of a convert from paganism, it is clear that proselyte immersion is another element in the conversion process (*Pesah.* 8.8; *Ed.* 5.2). It seems likelier that, by having baptism as a step in their conversion process, Christians copied an already existing Jewish practice than the other way around, and the debate between Shammai and Hillel in c.80 CE seems to presuppose a well-estab- lished rite. An offering at the Temple is understood to have been the third component of the conversion process, for both males and females. If this was practised, it obviously was carried out prior to 70 CE.

10 Two other non-Christian sources that use the term include Plutarch and the Sep- tuagint's version of the book of Esther. In *Life of Cicero,* Plutarch writes about

a certain freedman named Caecilius "who was accused of Jewish practices (ἔνοχος τῷ ἰουδαΐζειν)" (7.6), and Esther states that "many of the Gentiles were circumcised and judaized (καὶ ἰουδαΐζων) for fear of the Jews" (8.17 LXXX).

11 In his letter to the Galatians, Paul differentiates between his opponents and the Gentile Christians in the Galatian community who are being targeted by his opponents. He disdainfully addresses the former as "some" (1:7), "anyone" (1:9), "they" (4:17; 6:13), and "those" (6:12), and the latter as "you" (e.g., Gal. 3:1-5).

12 This is consistent with Lewis Coser's theory on how social conflict functions, for the closer the ties between opponents, the more intense the conflict between them will be (1956: 69).

13 John Gale Hawkins (1971a) offers a thorough presentation of the various options offered by scholars from the patristic period through the modern period.

14 See a more thorough discussion of Baur's thesis in the Appendix. As for interpretations of other scholars: J.B. Lightfoot (1890: 222) argues that Paul's adversaries in Galatia were Jewish Christians who did not have the support of the Jerusalem church; J.H. Ropes (1929: 27), following Wilhelm Lütgert (1919), suggests that Paul encountered two groups of opponents, a group of Gentiles who focused on the part of Paul's teaching that was founded on Jewish elements, and a libertine, pneumatic group that took literally Paul's teaching on freedom; Walter Schmithals (1972: 29) maintains that Paul's opponents were Jewish Christian Gnostics; Betz (1979: 316) suggests that οἱ περιτεμνόμενοι should be understood as "the circumcised," the "same people whom [Paul] discusses in 6:12" whom Betz takes to be Jews; R. Jewett's thesis "that Jewish Christians in Judea were stimulated by Zealotic pressure into a nomistic campaign among their fellow Christians in the late forties and early fifties" (1971: 205) is lauded by Bruce (1982: 31-32) and Richard Longnecker (1990).

15 A. Neander (1847) first argued that the troublemakers were Gentile Christians who had submitted to the Mosaic law, including circumcision, and then tried to convince Gentile Christians in Galatia to do the same, but (as noted by Hawkins 1971: 22) this theory is usually associated with the work of Johannes Munck (1959), who argued that Gentile Christians applied the Septuagint to their own lives in order to become the people of God; other scholars who identify Paul's opponents as Gentiles who have accepted circumcision and are now pressuring others to be circumcised include Emmanuel Hirsch (1930); Richardson (1969: 89ff).

16 Paul's other postscripts are found in 1 Corinthians 16:21, Philemon 19, Colossians 4:18, and II Thessalonians 3:17, if the last two are genuine.

17 The argument for approaching the Galatians as a whole through the conclusion has convincingly been made by Richardson (1969: 74-76). More recently, Jeffrey Weima asserts that "every one of the closing conventions of 6:11-18 appears to have been adapted and reshaped to echo better the major tensions and essential concerns expressed throughout the letter" (1994: 160).

18 Barclay reminds scholars not to "underestimate the distorting effects of polemic," and observes that Paul was "likely to caricature his opponents, espe-

cially in describing their motivation: were they really *compelling* the Galatians to be circumcised? And was it really *only* in order to avoid persecution
for the cross of Christ?" (1987: 75). And one could add, did Paul's opponents
themselves really not keep the law? But again, as Barclay points out, Paul
could not have *completely* garbled his account of his opponents, or the Galatians would not have known about whom he wrote.

19 The present participial is found in the following manuscripts: א A C D K P 33
88 104, etc., while the perfect participle is in P⁴⁶, B, Ψ, 330, 451, 614, 630,
etc. P⁴⁶ dates to about 200 CE and so is the earliest text.

20 Burton states that "transcriptional probability favours" the present participle
"since the perfect would have been a wholly unobjectionable reading" (1921:
353); also J.B. Lightfoot (1890: 223); Barclay also states that the perfect participle is "undoubtedly the weaker reading" (1988: 42); Metzger (1971: 598)
concurs with this view.

21 Burton logically argues that the people pressuring the Galatian Gentile Christians to submit to circumcision are the "principal subject of the discourse from
the beginning of v.12, and all possible ambiguity is excluded by the close par-
allelism between θέλουσιν ὑμᾶς περιτέμνεσθαι, v.13b and ἀναγκάζουσιν ὑμᾶς
περιτέμνεσθαι of v.12" (1921: 353-54); see also Richardson (1969: 87).

22 Hall likewise proposes: "although not Jewish themselves, the early Gentile
Christians in Galatia felt a particular kinship to the people of Israel and wanted
the Jewish community to accept them as beloved and legitimized children"
(1993: 80).

23 Jerome Murphy-O'Connor argues that Paul's opponents are intruders from
Antioch who "had the best interests of the Gentiles deeply at heart" (1996:
193-94).

24 As Munck suggests, "It is quite understandable that the Gentile Christians
could have doubts about the promises which Israel had received but which had
not been fulfilled for Israel; how then could the promises be fulfilled for the
Gentile Christians" since these Gentile Christians observed how most Jews
rejected Paul's message and "only a part of the God-fearing Gentiles accepted
baptism" and they may have "longed for Jerusalem, of which Paul spoke so
warmly, where the Christians lived as Jews, formed a part of the chosen people, and at the same time believed in Christ" (1959: 133). Their conclusion
might have been that it was "better and safer for a Gentile to become not
merely a Christian but also a Jewish Christian" and thereby cover all the bases
(Munck 1959: 133).

25 Paul understood circumcision to be unnecessary for Gentile Christians; indeed,
it was detrimental to their salvation. But what was his view concerning circumcision of the male children of Jewish Christians? Although arguing from silence
is risky, given Paul's numerous and vigorous protestations regarding circumcision for Gentile Christians, his silence on the topic for Jewish Christians is
striking and perhaps significant. If Jewish Christians continued to circumcise
their sons, and Paul did not condemn this, it is plausible that Gentile Christians,
who were members of communities founded by Paul, might have desired to bear
similar external markings to signify being a member of God's people. The
reliance of Paul's Gentile converts to Christianity on the Septuagint for instruc-

tion, as discussed above, would have made undergoing circumcision—and observance of other Jewish customs as well—compelling and logical for them.

26 Betz states, "[w]hat the Apostle has precisely in mind will in all likelihood always be hidden from our knowledge. Presumably, he refers to matters known to the Galatians as well as to himself, but unknown to us" (1979: 268). Caution in interpretation is required here, since not every statement that Paul makes in this polemical letter is necessarily a response to an argument made by his adversaries. Barclay correctly suggests that verse 11 "could also be no more than a simple contrast between Paul and his opponents, reminding the Galatians that he, Paul, is in a totally different category from them; in this case *no explicit accusation* need be posited" (1987: 80). Peder Borgen (1980) postulates that this verse is Paul's response to people who perceived themselves to be Paul's associates in preaching the necessity of circumcision for converts to Christianity (also Borgen 1982: 37-46; Howard 1979: 7-11).

27 Gauls were members of Celtic tribes who had penetrated Anatolia early in the third century BCE from central Europe (Joukowsky 1996: 385). Tribal feeling and loyalty remained strong in the first century CE; Mitchell notes that "[t]he Celtic origins of the Galatian provincial community continued to be emphasized by its title, the *koinon* of Galatia or of the Galatians, in contrast to the other well-known provincial *koina* in Asia Minor, which were associations of the Greeks in Asia and Bithynia respectively" (1993: 100).

28 Scholarly opinion is divided on the question. Supporters of the North Galatia hypothesis include Gaston (1987: 209 n.8) and Murphy-O'Connor (1996: 162) and of the South Galatia theory include: Bruce (1982: 55); Longnecker (1990: lxxxviii); Ramsay (1949) and Richardson (1969).

29 Mitchell, in 1993: 4, n.14, further notes that "in the mid-first century it was normal to refer to the whole province, quite simply, as Galatia," e.g., Eutropius from the late 20s BCE: "Galatia...provincia facta est...eam M. Lollius pro praetore administravit"; Rutilius Gallicus of the Neronian period is referred to as *legatio provinceae Galaticae*; L. Pupius Praesens in 53/4 CE is referred to as ἐπίτροπος Γαλατικῆς ἐπαρχείας.

◄○►

Chapter 4

1 For example, Prigent and Kraft assert: "[s]'il est possible de proposer une exégèse de ces paragraphes, il faut bien se souvenir qu'on explique non pas l'épître de Barnabé, mais sa source" (1971: 97; also Harnack 1897: 418ff; Prigent 1961).

2 Hippolytus, in *De Antichristo*, has a reading of Daniel 7:8 with the word παραφυάδιον but does not have the other changes that Barnabas does, and in Eusebius, *Dem Ev* 15 there is a reading of Daniel with καὶ τρια κέρατα ὑφ̓ ἑνος συντριβόμενα but, as Paget notes, this parallel "is not exact" (1994: 10-14).

3 Paget suggests that "the words υφ̓ ἕν should be translated as 'at the same time' (approximating to the Latin 'simul'), indicating that the abasement of the three βασιλεῖαι /κέρατα happens at a single stroke" (1994: 11).

4 Vespasian, who reigned after the three emperors Galba, Otho, and Vitellius, is often considered a possibility, but his successful political and military career hardly fits the descriptor "excrescent horn." On the other hand, Nerva came to power when Domitian was assassinated and did not even have the support of the army (Richardson and Shukster 1983:40).

5 Others who hold this view include: Goodspeed 1966: 20; Harnack 1897 (1958): 423-427; Schürer 1973-87: I: 536; Windisch 1920: 388-390.

6 LXX of Isaiah 49:17: καὶ ταχὺ οἰκοδομηθήσῃ ὑφ' ὧν καθῃρέθης, καὶ οἱ ἐρημώσαντές σε ἐξελεύσονται ἐκ σοῦ.

7 Interestingly, 2 Baruch (32.2-3), a text that is also dated to the late first century CE, indicates anticipation of the rebuilding of the Temple in the near future, and the restoration of both the Temple and its sacrificial system (Bar. 68.5).

8 This verse is key to an accurate understanding of the purpose of the epistle and is discussed in greater detail below.

9 W. Horbury states that: "there is a good case for supposing that the assimilation feared in iii 6 was encouraged not just by the attraction of the old paths and the more honoured society, but also by active propaganda" (1992: 226). In my view, Barnabas is indeed responding defensively to a situation where local Christians are adopting Jewish customs, but there is no evidence in the epistle that Jews were actively pursuing Christians to engage in this type of behaviour (contra Hvalvik 1996: 268-321).

10 Clement states in Strom 2.20.116: "And how we say that the powers of the devil, and the unclean spirits sow into the sinner's soul requires no more words from me, on adducing as a witness the apostolic Barnabas who speaks these words (οὔ μοι δεῖ πλειόνων λόγων παραθεμένῳ μάρτυν τὸν ἀποστολικὸν Βαρνάβαν)."

11 Horbury (1992: 329 n.36) suggests further that the Syrians were disliked by the Greeks in Egypt, as the mocking of Agrippa I as a "Syrian king" in Philo, Flacc 39 by the Alexandrians shows; the reference to "all the priests of the idols" can be understood to be Egyptian priests; "and the crowning absurdity of pride in circumcision here is the fact that 'even Egyptians'—particularly despised by Greeks and Jews in Egypt—are circumcised."

12 Prigent (1961) argues that Barnabas, in part, depended on early Christian testimonia from Syria; Richardson and Shukster (1986) postulate a location in Syria-Palestine for the writing of Barnabas.

13 As Paget rightly states, "A document may be written in one place and acclaimed in another" (1994: 32). Prigent and Kraft furthermore note: "Il faut...remarquer que l'accent eschatologique si fortement marqué dans notre épître, ainsi que l'absence de toute théologie du logos sont assez mal explicables dans le cadre de l'hypothèse alexandrine" (1971: 21); furthermore, they suggest that the exegetical interpretation of Barnabas is more similar to rabbinic Judaism than to Philo (esp. Barn. 7 and 8).

14 The argument is based on Windisch's analysis of the structure of the sentence (1920: 354).

15 Wengst 1971: 114-18, argues for a provenance in Asia Minor. One of the reasons given is that he claims to see similarities between Barnabas's theology

and that of Ignatius's opponents in Philadelphia as reflected in the statement: "If I find it not in the charters in the Gospel I do not believe" (*Phil.* 8.2); that is, Barnabas and those against whom Ignatius struggles are people who were preoccupied with scriptural interpretation. I suggest that Barnabas and Ignatius are both fighting the phenomenon of judaizing among Gentile Christians in their respective ecclesiastical communities. I discuss Ignatius and his encounter with Christian judaizing in chapter 5.

16 J.A. Robinson suggests "It is the mind of an Alexandrian Jew, whose Judaism had helped him but little, and had been wholly abandoned in favour of the Christian faith which had really met the needs of his soul" (1920: 24). L.W. Barnard also suggests that Barnabas was "a converted Jew" (1966: 126).

17 As Paget notes, the Gospels of Matthew and John and the letters of Paul are "salutary reminders" of the fact that anti-Judaic comments can come from Jewish authors (1994: 8).

18 Other Gentile Christian writers in antiquity who similarly experienced close familiarity with Judaism include the author of Luke/Acts, Ignatius, Diognetus and Justin Martyr.

19 Kirsopp Lake's text is from a Greek translation of the later Latin text *testamentum illorum et nostrum est. Nostrum est autem, quia illi.* Although there is no Greek text as witness to this reading, it best fits the context and most scholars accept this reading (Paget 1994: 113–14; Hvalvik 1996: 90).

20 Other examples of contrasting pronouns may be found in the following places in the *Epistle*: 2.9-10; 3.1, 3, 6; 4.7, 8; 5.2; 6.8; 7.5; 8.7; 9.1-4; 10.12; 13.1; 14.1, 4, 5; see Wilson 1995: 129; Hvalvik 1996: 137–39.

21 Philo uses it to refer to foreigners elsewhere (*Som.* 1.160; *Spec. Leg.* 1.308), and to refer to proselytes (*Vit. Mos.* 1.7, 147, 148; *Spec. Leg.* 1.52, 53; 2.118, 119; *Virt.* 102, 103, 104, 182, 219).

22 Furthermore it would be odd for him to warn Jewish Christians not to become converts to Jewish law.

23 So Paget concludes as well: "That [the author] chooses to end this chapter with such an unambiguous warning against Christians becoming proselytes is significant for its overall interpretation" (1994: 110). Hvalvik states "Taken at face value, 3.6 clearly shows that *Barnabas* presupposes that Christians may be tempted to become adherents of Judaism," and that the attitude expressed in 4.6b ("the covenant is both theirs and ours") (*Barn.* 4.6) "reflects a theological position which *removed the difference* between the Church and the Synagogue" (Hvalvik 1996: 98, emphasis added). I would argue, however, that for some (most?) of the Christians in Barnabas's community "Judaism" and "Christianity" were undifferentiated; that is, those Gentile Christians who began practising "Jewish" customs did not perceive themselves as crossing any boundaries. It fell to Barnabas, as leader of the community, to teach his congregants about the distinction between Judaism and Christianity.

24 Again, this may not have been a conscious decision on the part of these Christians; that is, they may not have perceived themselves as belonging to something other than Judaism and, thus, from their perspective, they were not crossing any boundary lines. This is a slight departure from Wilson, who suggests that "there were Christians who had begun to rethink their relationship

with Judaism, who wished to create room for coexistence within a single covenant, and who were attracted to Jewish ways" (1995: 139).

25 Barnabas uses the term λαός to refer to Israel four times (9.3; 10.2; 12.8; 16.5) and three times to refer to Christians (3.6; 5.7; 7.5). It is significant that he twice refers to Christians as τὸν λαὸν τὸν καινον (5.7; cf. 7.5). This reference to Christians as a "new people" is consistent with the author's goal of differentiating Christianity from Judaism for his readers and of his desire to persuade them that Christianity is superior to Judaism.

26 Harnack, for example, states: "Von der praktischen Gefahr eines concreten Abfalles zum Judenthum sehe ich in dem Brief keine Spur" (1958 [1897]: 414); likewise Dibelius (1975 [1926]: 130), who states that "[d]ie Erörterung über das Judentum ist völlig akademisch."

27 The misconceived arguments proposed by these scholars remind me of Miriam Taylor's study (1995). Taylor likewise stresses that anti-Judaism is theoretical and symbolic in nature, and emphasizes that it is anchored in the theological perceptions of Christians rather than in actual social exchange among Jews and Christians (see appendix for further discussion of Taylor).

28 See discussion in the appendix of recent scholarship that focuses on the interaction between Jews and Christians.

29 Hvalvik suggests that "[o]ne could…say that his selection of topics seems to be dictated by Jewish rather than by Christian interests. In other words, it seems probable that Barnabas has chosen his topics due to external factors, namely the challenge represented by actual Jewish law observance" (Hvalvik 1996: 97). In my view, however, Barnabas's selection was significantly shaped by what was going on *inside* his own community; that is, among the Jewish observances he chose to discuss were those that some of his Gentile Christian congregation found particularly appealing.

30 Certain scholars (e.g., Windisch 1920: 322–23) who assert that Barnabas' attitude towards Judaism was completely derived from anti-Jewish testimonies incorporated into his writing, point to the discussion of sacrifices and offerings in the epistle as evidence for the theoretical nature of Barnabas' argument with Judaism, since by the time he wrote, the Temple was destroyed and it was impossible for Jews to make sacrifices. It is true that Barnabas did use traditional material from other sources; however, this does not prove that his struggle with Judaism was of an abstract nature. Justin Martyr likewise incorporates traditional sources into his corpus, and discusses sacrifices offered in the Temple (*Dial.* 15–22), even though he is aware that the Temple is destroyed and that Jewish sacrifices there were impossible (*Dial.* 40); certainly, Justin's knowledge of Jews and Judaism was not confined to the theoretical, abstract level, despite his utilization of anachronistic material in his writing. Nor was it so for Barnabas (see Hvalvik 1996: 94-95 and below, chapter 5). Indeed, perhaps discussion of Temple sacrifice in the *Epistle of Barnabas* ought not to be considered anachronistic at all, if, as argued above, it was written during a time when the rebuilding of the Temple was anticipated.

31 There is no scholarly consensus regarding the provenance of this document. A Syrian setting is admittedly speculative, but that is no more uncertain, it seems to me, than any other possible location.

32 Paget suggests that this is because Clement was writing when there were very few Jews living in Alexandria but, when Barnabas wrote, they were a significant and influential force in the city. I agree with Paget that the *Epistle of Barnabas* was written in circumstances where the author felt the presence of a powerful Jewish community but, as argued earlier, I understand Syria to have been the location.

33 The same spiritualization of fasting is found in the second century CE work of the *Shepherd of Hermas* (*Sim.* 5.1.4-5).

34 Ptolemy's *Letter to Flora*, on which there is no consensus regarding its provenance, provides the author's position on the Mosaic law and discusses the significance of Jewish customs for Valentinians (Quispel 1966: 9; Grant 1946: 30). Claiming that he is following Jesus' instruction, Ptolemy divides the law into three, attributing one part of the three to God himself, and then divides this part into three again. The third part of this tripartite division he describes as "figurative and symbolic:" it is that component of God's law that has been "transposed from the level of the sensible and of appearance to that of the spiritual and invisible" by Jesus (33.5.2). Readers of the letter would understand that the Jewish customs of offering sacrifices, performing circumcision, keeping the Sabbath, fasting in imitation of the Jews, abstaining from yeast during Passover, were not to be physically engaged in, but instead were to be understood as moral directives on how to live life as a Valentinian Christian. Perhaps Ptolemy's proscription of the literal interpretation of these commandments indicates that it was current practice among some Christians to observe these customs, while his prescription of a spiritual understanding of these customs reflects the attitude that he hoped to instil among members of his community.

35 Philo states that "not only the Jews but also the Egyptians, Arabs, and Ethiopins and nearly all those who inhabit the southern regions near the torrid zone are circumcised, [while] the nations which are in the northern regions … are not circumcised" (*Questions on Genesis* 3.48). In *Against Apion* 2.141, Josephus states that the Egyptian *priests* were circumcised, while Jerome asserts that, even in his day (the fifth century CE), Arabs practised circumcision. Shaye Cohen suggests that "we may assume that in the first century CE in portions of Asia Minor, Syria, Arabia, and perhaps Egypt, circumcision will not have been unusual and certainly will not have been a Jewish peculiarity" (1993: 19). The information concerning Jewish circumcision practices provided by Strabo is rather shocking, as he mentions female circumcision as among those practices (*Geog.* 16.2.37). He describes how the successors of Moses practised "circumcisions and excisions (καὶ αἱ περιτομαὶ καὶ αἱ ἐκτομαὶ)" and in 16.4.9 he describes how the Creophagi males "have their sexual glands mutilated and the women are excised in the Jewish fashion (καὶ αἱ γυναῖκες Ἰουδαϊκῶς ἐκτετμημέναι)." In his description of the Egyptians, Strabo states that: "One of the customs most zealously observed among the Egyptians is this, that they rear every child that is born, and circumcise the males, and excise the females, as is also customary among the Jews (καὶ τὰ θήλεα ἐκτέμνειν, ὅπερ καὶ τοῖς Ἰουδαίοις νόμμον), who are also Egyptians in origin" (16.4.17). Was Strabo mistaken, or was female circumcision practised by some Jews?

36 Audet, for example, suggests the *Didache* underwent four developmental stages, aside from the pre-existing Two Ways material (1958: 104-120) and others have suggested a variety of formulations (e.g., Kraft 1965: 63-65; Niederwimmer 1989; Rordorf and Tuilier 1978: 16).

37 *Didache* (2.2ff) gives a list of prohibitions in the following sequence: murder (φονεύσεις), adultery (μοιχεύσεις), stealing (κλέψεις), coveting (ἐπιθυμήσεις), bearing false witness (ψευδομαρτυρήσεις). This follows the sequence of Exodus 20:13-16 in the Masoretic text and Deuteuronomy 5:17-21 in the Codex Alexandrinus; the same order is found in Matthew 19:18, though Matthew does not include ἐπιθυμήσεις [*coveting*] (Jefford 1989: 55; Kloppenborg 1995: 92). The *Didache* inverts ἐπιθυμήσεις and ψευδομαρτυρήσεις and so the order is not exactly the same as in the Masoretic text and the Codex Alexandrinus. Despite this, the use of οὐ with the second person singular future indicative as well as the way the list of prohibitions is presented without conjunctions—which is characteristic of the decalogue in Exodus 20 and Deuteronomy 5—make it "safe to assume that the reader of the *Didache* would have recognized the source" (Kloppenborg 1995: 100).

38 The Two Ways teaching may go back to a Jewish prototype, likely utilized in the instruction of Jewish proselytes. Audet dates the entire document of the *Didache* to an earlier period (c. 50-60 CE) but such a view is not widely held (see Audet 1958; Draper 1991).

39 Harnack (1884: 76-82) argued that the *Didache* derived from a group of Gentile Christians that had separated itself completely from its Jewish roots, and obtained its Two Ways material from *Barnabas* and the *Shepherd of Hermas*. Charles Taylor, in his 1885 lecture in London (published as Taylor 1886), was the first to posit a common Jewish *Vorlage* for the *Didache* and the *Epistle of Barnabas*. Reversing Harnack's position, Taylor argued that not only Barnabas and the *Shepherd* use the *Didache*, but so did Justin Martyr in his *Apologies*. Opinion was divided on this topic, with some scholars affirming Harnack's view that the *Didache* was dependent on *Barnabas,* such as Adam Krawutzcky (1884: 547-606) and Adolf Hilgenfeld (1884: 88-94), while others argued that *Barnabas* borrowed the Two Ways material from the *Didache*, such as Francis Xavier Funk (1905). Taylor's argument caused Harnack to change his opinion, as reflected in Harnack (1886/89: 14, 27-30).

40 Draper notes that the *Didache* did not simply fall into disuse but "continued to be modified and used, particularly by the communities of the *Apostolic Constitutions*, the *Liber Graduum* and the Coptic and Ethiopic churches" (1991: 349). John Kloppenborg (1979) suggests that the *Didache* (16.2-8) reflects an apocalyptic tradition which Matthew later incorporated into his gospel (1979).

41 Draper asks the question, "Why should any Christian document continue to advocate such a Jewish teaching?" and argues that the "yoke *of the Lord*" of 6.2 refers "to the Torah as interpreted by the Lord, i.e. by the Christian community under the influence of the Jesus tradition" (Draper 1991: 362, my emphasis). The question about a "Christian" document advocating a "Jewish" teaching seems anachronistic, however, since the Two Ways material probably was incorporated by a community that was so closely intertwined with Judaism it did not necessarily perceive itself to be something other than Judaism.

42 For example, Lev. 15:13 instructs a person with a discharge to "wash his clothes and bathe his body in fresh water (מים חיים)," cf. Num. 19:17, etc. Perhaps Jewish Christians initially "baptized" Gentile converts to Christianity in *mikvaoth*.

43 For example, Daniel 6:10 and Psalms 55:17. Within Rabbinic Judaism, the custom was prayer in the morning, afternoon, and evening (cf. *Ber.* 4:1). But there were other Jewish traditions regarding times of prayer: the Theraputae, described by Philo (*De Vita Contemplativa* 27), prayed twice daily—in the morning and the evening—and the Qumran sect also might have prayed only twice a day (cf. 1QS 10.1-3a and 1QH 12.4-7 in Vermes 1987: 76 and 197).

44 Wilson observes: "That the Lord's Prayer is thoroughly Jewish in tone and content none would deny, though it is not patterned precisely on any Jewish prayer known to us" (1995: 225). See also Bradshaw (1981: 27).

45 As far as I can tell, Rordorf uses the phrase *chrétiens judaisants* to refer to Jewish Christians and Gentile Christians who observe Jewish law, without distinguishing between the two.

46 Bauckham stated: "[w]hile there is unambiguous evidence that Sunday was called κυριακὴ from the second half of the second century onwards, there is no unambiguous evidence that Easter was ever called simply κυριακὴ" (1982: 230).

47 Bauckham suggests that κυριακὴ was a technical term used for Sunday particularly in Syria and Asia Minor (1982: 240).

48 As we will discuss in chapter 5, worship on the Sabbath by Gentile Christians also occurred in Asia Minor.

49 The original Greek of H is extant in two manuscripts from the eleventh, twelfth, or fourteenth centuries, while the Greek rendition of R has been lost except for bits and pieces found in the literature of the church fathers. A Latin translation of R does survive; it was written by Rufinus in the fifth century CE. In addition to this, there is a portion of R in a Syriac translation made a little earlier than the fifth century (see Jones 1991: 1061).

50 Henry Dodwell was the first to argue that there was a source that he called "Kerygma Petrou" (Dodwell 1689: 440-42 in Jones 1982: 14). K.A. Credner argued that the *Homilies* express a different view and attempt to suppress the KP, while Mayerhof suggested that the Pseudo-Clementines were not related to the *Kerygmata Petrou* (Credner 1832: 351ff and Mayerhoff 1835: 313-17 in Jones 1982: 15). Hilgenfeld averred that a different *Kerygmata Petrou* was embedded in the Pseudo-Clementine literature (PC), and used the table of contents in R. 3.75 to reconstruct the contents of the *Kerygmata Petrou*, and suggested that the source is found in R. 1.27-72 and in parts of R. 1-3 (in Jones 1982: 15).

51 Schneemelcher dates the KP to the first half of the second century, stating "Egypt has doubtless to be accepted as its homeland, even though this conjecture is not strictly demonstrable" (1992: 34). Strecker's view that the document originated in the area of Coele-Syria in c. 200 CE is more convincing. He notes that the author quotes only Galatians and 1 Corinthians from the Pauline corpus, and observes that the Syrian compilation of the Pauline letters begins with these two letters. He argues that it was originally written in Greek, not

Aramaic, "hence for its land of origin we may think of the Greek-speaking Syria which bordered on Osrhoene" (in Irmscher and Strecker 1989: 492–93).

52 For a recent comprehensive break-down of scholarly positions regarding the literary layers of this literature, see F. Stanley Jones (1982: 1–33, 63–95). Schoeps argues that the KP relies on the Ebionite "Acts of the Apostles" which Epiphanius mentions in *Pan.* 30.16. He argues that the KP was an anti-Marcionite document produced by Jewish Christians whom he identifies as Ebionites (he identifies all Jewish Christians as Ebionites!) (1969: 16–17).

53 Wilson points out that "[i]f the evidence is approached with extreme skepticism, it is always possible to throw doubt on its reliability. If it is approached more positively, then, even though subjected to a properly critical and cautious analysis, it is possible to piece together the broad outlines of various Jewish Christian groups" (1995: 144). Likewise Lüdemann questions whether sources embedded within the Pseudo-Clementines can be specified with confidence, but recognizes that different themes can be differentiated within the work (1989: 169). While there is considerable disagreement about which material belongs to KP, there is a strong consensus regarding the second century CE date of the material (Smith 1985: 59; Wilson 1995: 152).

54 The *Contestatio* and the *Epistula Petri* are fictitious texts. The *Epistula Petri* discuss the transmission of Peter's teachings to "bishop" James, and requests cautionary measures to prevent the falsification of the teaching by followers of the "hostile man" (Paul) (Strecker 1965: 106). The *Contestatio* describes the transmission of the *Epistula Petri* to seventy church elders, and the establishment of the required precautions (e.g., "we should pass on the books of his preachings…only to a good and religious candidate for the position of a teacher, a man who as one who has been circumcised is a believing Christian" [1.1]).

55 Female prophecy accompanies the true prophet throughout his various physical manifestations as a "negative, left-hand syzygy-partner" who leads all of her followers into error and death (J. 3.24.3f. in Strecker 1965: 107).

56 A stronger version is found in H. 8.6–7 (see Strecker 1981: 164–65; Strecker in Bauer 1971: 261; Wilson 1995: 151–52). According to Strecker, "the absence of an anti-Jewish polemic, which was so freely practiced in the 'great church' of the same period, also suggests that the Jewish Christianity of the *Kerygmata Petrou* existed in close relationship to Judaism" (in Bauer 1971: 261).

57 The description of "Simon" as a missionary to the Gentiles (H. 2.17; 11.35), that he taught the Gentiles a "lawless and absurd doctrine" (H. 2.3), and where Peter's apostolicity is contrasted with that of Paul (17. 13–19), is a more appropriate portrayal of the historical Paul rather than Simon (Smith 1985: 59–61).

58 As Meeks notes, since Simon Magus did not preach "in the name of the Lord," the original *Kerygmata* could not have meant him (Meeks 1972: 181).

◄○►

Chapter 5

1 During the nineteenth and early twentieth centuries numerous scholars argued that Revelation was written while Nero was emperor, including Lightfoot (1890), B.F. Westcott (1881), and F.J.A. Hort (1908); John A.T. Robinson (1976) has recently revived the argument supporting a Neronian date. Most twentieth-century scholars, however, hold that Revelation was written during Domitian's reign, and this is the dating assumed in this study. A recent exception is John W. Marshall, who argues that the Apocalypse was written from Patmos during the Jewish war against Rome in 69 CE (2001).

2 Elsewhere in the document the term βλασφημία is used in reference to behaviour of the beast (cf. Rev. 13:1, 5, 6; 17:3) or in reference to the actions of people who curse God (Rev. 16:9, 11, 21). See Thompson (1986: 149).

3 John Sweet, for example, writes that: "Smyrna was a city of great wealth, second only to Pergamum as a centre of the emperor cult, and had a large Jewish community. The letter shows the church to be in imminent danger, from the Roman authorities probably, but at the instigation of the Jews" (1990: 84). David Frankfurter argues that these "so-called Jews" are Jews, including "Pauline and neo-Pauline proselytes to the Jesus movement [who were] *within* the Jesus movement who were claiming the label 'Jew' in a manner that John finds illegitimate" (2001: 403).

4 Some scholars have taken this posture to the extreme, seeing "the Jews" as responsible for all opposition that Christians experienced: e.g., Frend states that "one only needs to peruse the later books of the New Testament and the apostolic fathers to realize that the churches were being perpetually harassed by enemies who could only be orthodox Jews and their allies" (1984: 123ff). An earlier expression of this perspective was made by Harnack, who argues that "wherever bloody persecutions are afoot in later days the Jews are either in the background or the foreground" (1904: 66).

5 Kirsopp Lake makes the rather naive suggestion that: "The writer desires to bring out the points of resemblance to the Passion of Christ. The coincidences are remarkable, but none are in themselves at all improbable" (1985 [1912]: 319 n.2). The cumulative effect of these "coincidences" makes the historicity of the description extremely improbable.

6 Sanders points out that "with one accord" is one of Luke's favourite terms (1993: 319 n.95).

7 As Wayne McCready noted recently: "It is hard to imagine why Jews in the mid-second century would be concerned about Christians worshipping Polycarp and hence abandon[ing] Christ;" he suggests that "Jews play a minor but important support role in a literary endeavour struggling with a self-definition process that is primarily if not exclusively Christian" (1999: 13–14). While McCready is probably correct that the text does not reflect "the historical situation of Jews at Smyrna" (1999: 12), I wonder how such a text may have affected existent Jewish/Christian relations in that city; e.g., how did the reading of this document shape Christian perceptions of and attitudes toward their Jewish neighbours?

8 Yarbro Collins, for example, argues that "the vilification in Rev. 2:9 and 3:9 ... has a social function. On a basic level, it defines who the Christians are. They are the genuine Jews, the heirs of the promises to Israel" (1986: 314). Yarbro Collins is correct that John's passionate outcry against the "synagogue of Satan" and "those who say that they are Jews and are not" in these two letters is related to the establishment of self-identity. Whereas she is convinced that the conflict is between Christians and Jews from the Jewish synagogues in Smyrna and Philadelphia, in my view the polemic is between two Christian groups. Expressing a similar argument to Yarbro Collins, Harvey asserted: "Whilst it is possible that these people are gentiles who have 'Judaized' in some sense, it is more likely that they are ethnically Ἰουδαῖοι but are being denied the use of their ancestral name in a polemic which asserts that Christians are 'true Jews'" (1996: 94). See also Hemer (1986: 67).

9 E.g., "For the scripture concerning him relates partly to Israel, partly to us [Christians]." (*Barn.* 5.2; also 5.8; 6.7; 8.1, 3; 9.2 etc.)

10 Zeitlin gets the term correct but the momentum backward when he suggests that, after the Bar Kochba revolt, the Jews adopted the name Israel "because the Christians had held that they themselves were the true Israelis" (1952: 377). In Jewish literature, "Israel" is the term used to indicate the "people of God." Where one group's point of view opposes the rest of Judaism, in Jewish documents it tends to claim that it is Israel. As Richardson notes, "[a]n exclusivist tendency within Judaism nearly always involves the implication that the particular group represented 'Israel'" (1969: 217). For example, in 1 Maccabees, there are several places where polemic is directed against part of the population that follows the wrong leader or behaviour: "in those days certain renegades came out from Israel and misled many (ἐξ Ἰσραὴλ υἱοὶ παράνομοι)" (1 Macc. 1:11) to castigate those who were led by Alcimus as "the renegade and godless men of Israel (ἄνομοι καὶ ἀσεβεῖς ἐξ Ἰσραήλ)," where ἐξ "implies both origin and separation, with more emphasis on the latter" (Richardson 1969: 218). In the Qumran documents, the name "Israel" is applied to the sect and there is the tendency to deny the name to those who were not considered part of this exclusivistic group (Richardson 1969: 228).

11 Indeed, the term Ἰουδαῖοι was applied to Gentiles who followed Jewish religious rites, as Dio Cassius reports at the end of the second century CE (*Roman History* 66.1.4; see Wilson 1995: 359 n.84). Marshall, who argues that John is criticizing opponents who hold "less stringent scruples than he does about participating in the polyreligious milieu of the Greco-Roman world" (2001: 132), suggests that this group of people "consists of a mixture of Pagan Godfearers and comfortably Hellenizing Jews who welcome Godfearers without requiring a substantial (in John's eyes) separation from Greco-Roman culture in either themselves or their adherents" (2001: 134).

12 Feldman suggests that there may be later (mid-third century CE) evidence of this in the *Martyrdom of Pionios* (13.1), where the author allegedly describes how Christians took refuge from persecution in local synagogues (1993: 371). This detail, however, is found only in a tenth-century version of the story written by Simeon Metaphrastes, a composer of martyrologies; consequently, its authenticity is questionable.

13 Leonard Rutgers explains that Roman magistrates passed several decrees during the approximately fifty-year period between Caesar and Augustus, which
facilitated unencumbered Jewish worship, including the right to "gather freely
in *thiasoi*, observe the Sabbath and the Jewish festivals, send money to the
Temple in Jerusalem, and enjoy autonomy in their communal affairs"; in addition Jews were released from the obligation of serving in the Roman military
(Josephus, *Ant.* 14.190–264; Rutgers 1998: 94). Josephus presents numerous
decrees issued during the reign of Augustus, which describe how Jews living
in the diaspora were able to collect and transport their Temple tax, and were
not forced to attend court on the Sabbath.

14 Richardson notes that the significance of these two decrees is that both "confirmed a range of rights, both were set in Sardis, one of the places that has
remarkable archaeological evidence of a synagogue" (1996: 96). That evidence attests to the existence of a prominent, wealthy Jewish community in
Sardis. The largest excavated synagogue in the world, dating to the third and
fourth centuries CE, was discovered in the heart of ancient Sardis (Kraabel
1971; Crawford 1990; Crawford 1996), as discussed in chapter 6.

15 While expulsions of Jews from particular areas of the empire occurred in the
first century CE (in 19 CE under Tiberius and in 41 CE under Claudius), they
seemed not to affect negatively the position of Jews generally (see Rutgers
1998: 93-116).

16 Of the three recensions of Ignatius's work presently extant—the short, middle,
and long—the middle recension is considered by modern scholars to be the
authentic version; from this version, the information about Ignatius is taken
(Lake 1912; also Zahn 1873; Lightfoot 1989; Schoedel 1993).

17 Docetic Christians, whose name comes from a Greek word meaning "to seem"
or "to appear," believed that Christ's humanity was apparent, not real.

18 There may be evidence that at least one Jewish custom was observed in the Pastoral community. The author's complaint that the opponents "demand abstinence from foods" (1 Tim. 4:3) could refer to the practice of Jewish dietary laws
(Ward 1974: 68). It is less clear, however, whether Gentile Christians or Jews
(or Jewish Christians) are behind the promotion of Jewish customs. Titus 10
and 11 refer to "those of the circumcision" (οἱ ἐκ τῆς περιτομῆς) who "must
be silenced, since they are upsetting whole families by teaching for sordid gain
what is not right to teach." This seems to point to the Jewish origin of the opponents, since οἱ ἐκ περιτομῆς most naturally refers to Jews (or Jewish Christians).

19 While Lightfoot understands this phrase to be an allusion to the docetics who
denied the reality of Jesus' death and resurrection (1989: 130), it is more likely
that this is a "purely parenthetical" expression and does not point to the presence of docetic Christians (Schoedel 1985: 125; also Grant 1966: 63). The
closest Ignatius comes to addressing docetic beliefs is in his statement that he
wants his readers "to be convinced of the birth and passion and resurrection
which took place at the time of Pontius Pilate; for these things were truly and
certainly done by Jesus Christ" (*Magn.* 11.1). But this is a warning in advance.
That is, as Schoedel states, "the reason for writing disclosed by Ignatius is not
that he wanted to criticize the Magnesians for actually having fallen prey to
the erroneous opinions discussed but that he desired to warn them against

possible dangers" (1985: 129). As noted above, it seems that Ignatius feared that the corollary of judaizing was disbelief in the reality of Jesus' human existence.

20 The meaning of ἑρμηνεύω is "explain," "interpret," or "translate" (Bauer 1979: 310).

21 Robert G. Hall discusses how the practice of epispasm (the reversal of circumcision) reached a plateau in the first century and suggests that "it is as likely that Ignatius speaks of Jews or Judaizers who thought circumcision unnecessary" (1988: 80).

22 Schoedel goes on to suggest that "we could assume that the gentile Christians would not have been circumcised because circumcision was not always required of proselytes" (1985: 202). In my view, however, it is unlikely that Ignatius is referring to proselytes actively seeking conversion to Judaism based on the other comments he makes about these opponents.

23 Schoedel points out how Josephus and Philo refer to the Jewish scriptures as "public records" (ἀναγραφαί) and that this "should remove any lingering doubt that Ignatius's opponents in Philadelphia could have referred to the Bible as 'archives'" (1978: 101).

24 This is contrary to C.K. Barrett's understanding of the statement; he suggests that "Ignatius was trapped in his own rhetoric: he meant to say that there was no harm in hearing Christianity from a Christian Jew, but having begun the sentence with ἄμεινον he constructed a comparison that he did not really intend" (1976: 234).

25 Wilson suggests that Ignatius "initially found [the Judaizers'] arguments quite plausible" (1995: 165).

26 Perhaps he was accused of sending people ahead of him as spies to see how the congregation was operating. The circumstances of Ignatius's arrest and subsequent journey through Asia Minor are rather baffling. It seems as though he had a large amount of freedom, given the fact that he was able to meet with Christians, and visit congregations, along the way. Did his ten Roman guards simply "escort" him in this journey? In Schoedel's view, "[t]here are features of the situation for which it is difficult to find exact analogies, for we do not often see life from the prisoner's point of view in antiquity. What we do know about such matters indicates that there is finally nothing impossible or seriously improbable here" (1985: 11).

27 Sanders makes the plausible suggestion that the existence of a separate eucharist implies concern for Jewish dietary laws (1993: 189).

28 Donahue, who believes that Ignatius's opponents are Jewish Christians only, suggests that this group "traces its roots back to those who with Peter accepted the dictates from James; they accepted Gentile Christianity, but did not accord it equal status with Jewish Christianity; they did not believe that it had displaced Israel. In the end, this group was unable to preserve its theological identity; it was absorbed in a synthesis more influenced by Paul than by Peter" (1978: 92-93). While in my view Donahue's identification of the opponents is mistaken, he might be on to something nonetheless. Perhaps the genesis of the Gentile judaizing opponents whom Ignatius encounters in Asia Minor can be traced to the group who opposed Paul in Galatia (especially Gal. 6).

29 An example of Justin's lack of Hebrew knowledge is usually understood to be evident where he asks about the etymology of "Israel" (*Dial.* 125.1). He receives no suggestions from the Jews in his presence, and proceeds to give an incorrect answer, although, admittedly, "Israel" is a difficult term to define even if one *does* know Hebrew (see Margalith 1990: 225-74).

30 Remus (1986: 73) and Horbury (1992: 343) point out the different ways in which the narrative reflects the reality of Jewish/Christian contact in the second century CE. Many scholars understand Justin's references to cursing in the synagogue as the contemporary practice of the *Birkat ha-Minim*, the imprecation against heretics added to the Eighteen Benedictions by the Yavnaen sages in the late first century CE, e.g., Herford (1903: 379-81); S. Krauss (1893); Moore (1927: 426-32); and M. Simon (1986: 234-36).

31 The text in its present form does not indicate the location of the dispute—an introduction might have been part of the original but is no longer attached—but, as Lieu states, "it seems reasonable to follow Eusebius in setting the debate in Ephesus" (*H.E.* IV. 18.6; Lieu 1996: 103).

32 C. Foss (1979: 3-4), describes Ephesus as "the greatest city of Roman Asia Minor....It was the terminus of two great highways connecting the Aegean coast with the interior of Asia Minor and the lands to the east: the ancient Persian Royal Road, and the *koine hodos*, the main trade route of the Romans which led up the Maeander valley to the plateau....In addition, Ephesus was a great seaport, the largest in the Aegean, a place where the trade routes of Asia Minor and the whole eastern Mediterranean met. Under the *Pax Romana*, therefore, Ephesus had grown to become a great center of trade, finance and industry."

33 Foss acknowledges that "no synagogue has been located; the 'basilica' north of the Theater Gymnasium may have been one, but the evidence is slight," consisting of a Jewish lamp of either the second or third century CE which was found in this building (1979: 45 n.47).

34 Justin argues that, although Jesus was circumcised, he was not made righteous by this (*Dial.* 67.6).

35 In chapter 4 I discussed how *Barnabas* 10 interprets the food laws in an innovative, allegorical way by arguing that each restricted food represented a vice and each food permitted represented a moral virtue.

36 Justin does not explicitly state that the members he describes in the last group are Gentiles, but, as Wilson points out, "the context favours this view and, if he had Jewish Christians in mind, we might have expected him to say that they 'returned to' rather than 'switched over to' (μεταβαίνω) the Jewish community" (1992: 609 n.16).

37 Wilson postulates that: "the way in which he discusses the issue, and in particular the casual allusion to disagreements in the Christian community about how to evaluate and relate to Jewish Christians (*Dial.* 47.1-2), indicates most naturally a situation known to him firsthand," so it was not a case of Justin applying what he knew from apostolic tradition to his contemporary situation (1995: 166).

38 Stephen Wilson's unpublished 1998 paper was a helpful resource for this discussion; later Wilson focuses on epigraphic evidence for Jewish apostates and defectors (2000: 354-67).

39 Justin tells Trypho that Jewish Christians who do not try to persuade Gentile Christians to Judaize "will be saved," a point of view that apparently was not held by some of Justin's Christian colleagues, some of whom, writes Justin, refused to eat or converse with Jewish Christians (*Dial.* 47.2).

40 The letter to the Colossians, which deviates from the genuine Pauline letters in theology, vocabulary and style, was probably written about twenty years or so after Paul's death by someone familiar with the tradition and perhaps the letters of Paul (Roetzel 1998: 134-137). It contains warnings about yielding to teachings which promoted Jewish ritual practices, and since the community was predominantly Gentile (1:21, 27; 2:13, but particularly 3:5-7), if the teaching were accepted, Christian judaizers would have resulted. Colossians 2:16 states: "Therefore do not let anyone condemn you in matters of food and drink or of observing festivals, new moons, or sabbaths"; this instruction implies that Gentile Christians who are not observing these Jewish practices are being denounced by advocates of such practices. The program being promoted in Colossae also encouraged the practice of circumcision. In 2:11-12, the author reminds his readers that they "were circumcised with a spiritual circumcision, by putting off the body of the flesh in the circumcision of Christ" and that this was achieved when they "were buried with him in baptism." The statement in that "there is no longer Greek and Jew, circumcised and uncircumcised" (*Col.* 3:11) can also be understood as an attack intended to undermine the promotion of circumcision for Gentiles.

41 While Justin elsewhere uses the term προσηλύτος to refer to Jewish converts to Christianity (cf. *Dial.* 28.2; 123.5) here he refers to Jewish proselytes (cf. *Dial.* 122.1-123.2): see Skarsaune (1987: 258-59).

42 Skarsaune notes that "Trypho's friends become particularly engaged when Justin says that Is 42:6ff does not refer to the (Jewish) proselytes, *Dial.* 122.4: It looks as if they are personally involved!" (1987: 258). He concludes that "It is a very reasonable surmise that the *Dialogue* itself is addressed primarily to the same kind of people, or at least that these were the original addressees of the exegetical exposition of the *Dialogue*" (Skarsaune 1987:258). Also see Lieu (1996: 106-108).

◄○►

Chapter 6

1 May admits, despite his skepticism, "the writing of the old witnesses must in any case serve as the substantial basis for the reconstruction of Marcion's doctrine" (1987-88: 134). Michel Desjardins points out that the Church fathers "have often reproduced the words of their opponents far more extensively and probably far more literally than the author of Acts ever did of Paul" (1990: 10).

2 Hoffmann argues that Marcion was born in c.70 CE—thirty years earlier than the usually accepted chronology—suggesting that Polycarp, Ignatius and even the author of the Pastorals and II Peter combatted the Marcionite movement.

He states that "there is…good reason to believe that the earliest anti-Marcionite polemic emanated from a particular circle of orthodoxy, in which Polycarp, Ignatius, and the author of the Pastorals, played key roles" (Hoffmann 1984: 73). Wilson has pointed out the circular nature of this argument, "for it is the identification of the obscure heretics opposed by Ignatius et al. as Marcionites that proves that Marcion came earlier" (1995: 377, n.52).

3 Grant plausibly postulates that Marcion might have desired to distance Christianity from Judaism in light of the unsuccessful Jewish revolt under Bar Kochba (1959: 121–28).

4 Tertullian correspondingly states that "We too claim that the primary epistle against Judaism is that addressed to the Galatians" (*adv. Marc.* 5.2).

5 The manner in which he identifies the Jews as separate from himself in this statement strongly implies that Marcion was of Gentile, and not Jewish origin.

6 Leviticus 19:2, e.g., is quoted in 1 Peter 1:16 and paraphrased in 1:15, while 1 Peter 2:9-10 conflates references from Exodus 19:5-6 and Isaiah 43:20-21, calling the readers "a chosen race, a royal priesthood, a holy nation, God's own people (γένος ἐκλεκτόν, βασίλειον ἱεράτευμα, ἔθνος ἅγιον, λαὸς εἰς περιποίησιν)."

7 Likewise Richardson suggests that "it is a mixed Church, preponderantly Gentile with perhaps a good number previously being God-fearers or proselytes" (1969: 173). John Elliott (1981: 66) states: "It is likely that among their number were those pagans whose contact with Christianity was mediated through an earlier association with the synagogue as proselytes to Judaism. This is suggested by the attraction which the Christian movement had for such Gentile proselytes to Judaism in general, the knowledge and persuasive force of the Old Testament which 1 Peter assumes, the Greek version of the Old Testament which the letter quotes, and the use of metaphors for conversion which were common to Jewish as well as Christian missionary propaganda."

8 Epiphanius (*De Mens. et pond.* 14) says that Aquila was a Greek from Sinope, Pontus and a relation (πενθερίδης) of Hadrian by marriage. There are a number of Talmudic legends pertaining to a certain "Onkelos the Proselyte," a Tanna at the end of the first century CE. Frequently the name "Onkelos" and "Aquila" are interchanged. At Babylon, little was known about the proselyte Aquila, but Onkelos was well known in Talmudic tradition. Thus legends related to Aquila became associated with Onkelos, (e.g., "Onkelos translated the Pentateuch into Aramaic according to the instructions of R. Eliezer and R. Joshua" [*b. Meg.* 3a]).

9 Werner states that "they were anything but Judaeo-Christians, most of them were gentiles through and through" (1966: 200); as far as I am aware, there is no evidence that "most" were Gentiles.

10 There is a range of opinions concerning the authenticity of the letters and decrees presented by Josephus, with some scholars skeptical (such as Moehring 1975: 124-58 and Barclay 1996: 262-64) and others more accepting (Tcherikover 1970: 306-309; Smallwood 1976: 127-43; Rajak 1985: 19-35; Trebilco 1991: 8-19; Richardson 1996: 90-109). While Josephus's representation of these texts should not be accepted at face value, their content on the whole is probably genuine.

11 The author of Revelation may have drawn on the local memory of the disaster in some of that book's apocalyptic imagery (e.g. 6: 14-16; 8:8; 11:13; 16: 18-20; Hemer 1986: 134).

12 The structure shows evidence of having undergone repairs until at least the middle of the sixth century, despite the law of Theodosius II in 438 CE prohibiting the restoration and construction of synagogues. This suggests, as Crawford asserts, "that actual relations between Christians and Jews were not as hostile as literary sources claim" (1996: 44). For a recent examination of Crawford's claims regarding the relations among Jews, Christians, and pagans in the city of Sardis, see Hammer and Murray [in press].

13 This inscription has been published only in English transliteration (Hanfmann 1963: 43-44; Trebilco 1991: 44); its original location is not known, but it was later placed in a third-century wall (Seager 1983: 171).

14 The religious affiliation of the occupants of ten other shops is not apparent, and one shop was left unexcavated for control purposes (Crawford 1996: 40; Hammer and Murray [in press]).

15 Noakes suggests that "there was constant strife between Jews and Christians in the province [of Asia Minor]" and mentions the alleged participation of Jews in the *Martyrdom of Polycarp* (1975: 245). As I argued in chapter 5, however, the death of Polycarp, the bishop of Smyrna, is described in such a way as to conform to the pattern of Jesus' death in the gospels, thereby undermining what one may learn about Jews in Smyrna from this text. There is, furthermore, little evidence for "constant strife" between Jews and Christians in Asia Minor; in fact, the existence of judaizing practices among Christians indicates that close interaction occurred between Jews and Christians in Asia Minor.

16 Hall further notes that the manuscript is in Greek, and other fragments in Greek, Syriac, and Coptic are extant. Werner suggests that "it is an open question in which language the homily was first written" (1966: 200), and seems to lean toward Syriac because the suffix-rhymes found in the homily are more natural in Syriac poetry than in Greek.

17 Eusebius also states that Clement of Alexandria quoted from Melito's book on the Pascha, and was in fact prompted to write his own book on the topic "because of" this work by Melito (*Hist. eccl.* 4.26; 6.13). Some scholars argue that this suggests that Clement wrote to counter Melito in a polemical sense, and they conclude that Melito's work was a defence of Quartodeciman practices. This, however, casts doubt on whether Bonner's version of the *Peri Pascha* is indeed by Melito, since it does not seem to have been written with the purpose of defending Quartodeciman practices. Hall (1979: xx) rightly suggests that the reference in Clement should not be taken as an indication that Clement wrote his work to attack Melito.

18 Halton (1970: 251) notes that "there is considerable theatricality in the description of the mourning scenes in Egypt," which is similar to Bacchic rites: e.g., Melito describes how Egypt was devastated after every firstborn child had been killed, and depicts a frenzied mourning scene of "people beating themselves here, and wailing there" (l. 120).

19 Analogous passages are found in the writings of Melito's contemporary, Maximus of Tyre, but the *Peri Pascha* is "la première oeuvre chrétienne où nous

trouvons l'usage de cette prose d'art. L'image elle-meme est typiquement hel-lénistique" (Daniélou 1962: 286). Cf. also *Barn.* 1.7; 5.3; 17.2.

20 S.G. Wilson accurately observes: "insofar as the attributes of Judaism have con-tinuing value it is by absorption into the Christian reality alone" (1995: 246).

21 Melito usually employs the term λαος to refer to the Jews. The one time that he uses it to refer to the new people, the church (ll. 494-95), there are indica-tions that the verses are not authentic: one important textual witness (B) omits them altogether, and there is a lacuna in another (L) (Noakes 1975: 249).

22 Hall notes how "the false etymology of the Aramaic *pascha*, as if it came from the root of the Greek *páschein*, is widespread in early Christianity" (1979: 23).

23 K.W. Noakes notes that Pilate "is mentioned only once, despite the great prominence given to the events of the Passion. Pilate's washing of his hands is given as an example of the exemplary behaviour of the Romans towards Jesus, in contrast to the ingratitude of the Jews" (1975: 247; cf. Matt. 27:24; the *Gospel of Peter* 1.1; the *Acts of Pilate* 9.4, 12.1).

24 S.G. Wilson observes, "the notion that the Jews were responsible for the death of Jesus had a long pedigree in Christian thinking, stretching back at least to the early accounts of Jesus' Passion. Prior to Melito, however, no one had made the accusation with such boldness and dramatic skill, and no one had transformed the 'crime' of the Jews from responsibility for the death of Jesus to responsibility for the death of God" (1995: 248).

25 Numerous factors no doubt influenced how Melito expressed himself, includ-ing certain theological conventions reflected already in the New Testament. Taylor rightly highlights the theological dimension of Melito's homily against the Jews but she overstates her case by suggesting that he does not have con-temporaneous Sardis Jews in mind at all. Her argument is further weakened by the rather ingenuous suggestion that "the extent to which the condem-nation of historical Jews would have manifested itself in the attitudes of Sar-dian Christians towards their Jewish contemporaries is not a given. In this instance, therefore, we cannot simply take for granted that such a spill-over effect took place" (1995: 64). Surely Melito's harsh critique of "Israel" would colour how his Christian listeners would view their Jewish neighbours.

26 In a more recent publication, Kraabel alters his view somewhat and explains that the *Peri Pascha* "does not mean a Jewish Christian conflict in late second century Sardis; there is no evidence from the Jewish side for that....There is no firm evidence that Sardis Jews were even aware of Melito, or that a direct hostility on their part provoked his attacks" (cited in Overman 1992: 264; see also Norris 1986: 246).

27 Feldman notes that "the Judaism of Asia Minor was hardly learned...there is no mention in the entire rabbinic corpus of even a single Torah academy in all of Asia Minor. Nor is there any mention in the Talmudic and midrashic writ-ers of a single student from Asia Minor who studied in the academies of either Palestine or Babylonia during the entire Talmudic period (first through fifth centuries CE), when rabbinic Judaism was at its height, even though the Tal-mud usually gives the place of origin of those from abroad" (1993: 72).

Notes to Chapter 7

1 Circumcision is discussed with respect to Gentile Christians in Galatians 2:3; 5:2–12; 6:12, 15; Colossians 2:11–12; 3:11; the *Dialogue with Trypho* 47.2, 4 and the *Epistle of Barnabas* 9.4. Sabbath observance is addressed in Galatians 4.10; Colossians 2:16; *Magnesians* 9.152; Justin's *Dialogue* 47.2, 4; the *Didache* 14.1; *Barnabas* 15.6–9, and observance of food laws in Colossians 2:16; the *Didache* 6.3 and *Barnabas* 10.2, 9.

2 Taylor argues that "[b]asing themselves primarily on post-Constantinian evidence, [scholars] describe the judaizing phenomenon as one of the main problems posed for the church by a vital and aggressive Judaism" (1995: 40). The phenomenon of Christian Judaizing indicates that Judaism was indeed "vital" but not "aggressive." See my discussion of how Gentiles were drawn to Judaism in chapter 2.

3 In *War* 7.43 Josephus explains that Syria's proximity to Judea is why the largest concentration of Jews lived there.

4 Jews in Antioch, Syria, according to Josephus, "were constantly attracting to their religious ceremonies multitudes of Greeks" in the pre-Christian period (*War* 7.45).

5 Similarly, Barnabas's argument that the covenant belonged to the Christians and never to the Jews expresses a radical position not typical of the Syrian documents (13.1).

6 Of course, the ultimate purpose of the *Dialogue* was to convince Gentile Christians not to judaize. Full abstention was preferable to only passable conduct. See chapter 5.

7 According to Stark, "the function of a leader is to make a latent conflict conscious, to give form to a pre-existing movement, to impart direction to its energies, and to help it to focus on definite ends" (1967: 48).

8 Ignatius writes a letter to the church in Magnesia, where he observes that Gentiles are "living according to Judaism" (*Magn.* 8:1), a lifestyle which apparently includes observing the Sabbath (*Magn.* 9:1). In his letter to Philadelphia, he states that he is hearing Judaism interpreted by Gentiles, whom I identify as Gentile Christians (*Phld.* 6:1). Ignatius admits that he was nearly deceived by them, and he appears to have stood alone in his protest against judaizing: see chapter 5.

◄o►

Notes to Appendix

1 Whether Jews of the first and second centuries CE engaged in missionizing is discussed in chapter 2.

2 According to Poliakov, "[i]n Germany anti-Semitism was led by the Lutherans, as in Austria and France it was led by the Catholics" (1985: 19).

3 Two other nineteenth-century scholars who present the Jews of antiquity as actively participating in missionary efforts to secure converts to Judaism are E. Schürer et al. 1973 (1890) and J. Wellhausen 1958 (1897).

4 My analysis of certain post-apostolic Syrian documents in chapter 4 demonstrates that the issue of Gentile Christian observance of Torah was far from settled and that the allegorical understanding of the law may not have been the "popular" view among Gentile Christians as Harnack suggests.

5 See A. Ritschl (1857), also Philip Hefner (1962). Ritschl began his career as an adherent of the Tübingen School and, in the 1840s, defended F.C. Baur's thesis that the conflict in the early church was between Gentile Christian Paulinists and Jewish Christian Petrinists; by the late 1850s he had rejected the Tübingen doctrines. The "Ritschlian School" attracted a number of prominent Protestant scholars—Harnack among them—and was characterized by a focus on ethics, community, and a rejection of metaphysics and religious experience. Harnack's espousal of Ritschlian views—i.e., in his *Lehrbuch der Dogmengeschichte* (1886-89; trans. 1894-99) where he treats Christian teachings critically—provoked strong antagonism from conservative theologians.

6 According to Harnack, the relationship between Jewish Christians and non-Jews became more strained as the result of the destruction of the Temple: "Undoubtedly the catastrophe decimated the exclusive Jewish Christianity of Palestine and drove a considerable number either back into Judaism or forward into the Catholic church" (1908: 63). Additionally, he states "[w]e do not know when Jewish Christians broke off, or were forced to break off, from all connection with the synagogues; we can only conjecture that if such connections lasted till about 70 A.D., they ceased then" (Harnack 1908: 63 n.2).

7 Harnack notes that Paul "held that the day of the Jews...was past and gone, yet he could not believe in a final repudiation of God's people" and that this position was "a Pauline idiosyncrasy" (1908: 65). For the majority of Christians, who interpreted the content and obligations of "Old Testament religion" allegorically, Paul's view was unacceptable "since the legitimacy of the allegorical conception, and inferentially the legitimacy of the Gentile church in general, was called in question, if the Pauline view held good at any single point" (Harnack 1908: 65). Harnack opines that "the attitude consistently adopted by the Gentile church" was that Jews "were always in error" regarding their literal interpretation of the law, and that the Jews "*never were the chosen people*," but at the same time "most people admitted vaguely that in earlier days a special relation existed between God and his people, though at the same time all the Old Testament promises were referred even by them to Christian people" (1908: 66-67).

8 Harnack explains that there was "one vital omission in the Jewish missionary preaching: viz., that no Gentile, in the first generation at least, could become a real son of Abraham. His rank before God remained inferior" and his future uncertain (1908: 13). Christian missionaries superseded Jewish efforts because in Christianity, Gentile converts were fully accepted; Christian missionaries won "thousands where the previous missionary preaching won but hundreds" (Harnack 1908: 13). In his *History of Dogma*, Harnack states that "nearly all the Gentile Christian groups that we know are at one in the detachment of Christianity from empiric Judaism," and asserts that early Christian communities "were far superior to the synagogue in power of attraction" (1899: 148-49). He surmises that "the great mass of the earliest Gentile Christians

became Christians" because they had found in Christianity what they had formerly been looking for in Judaism, but had not found (Harnack 1900: 17).

9 The English translation of Harnack's monograph, entitled *What is Christianity?*, was first published in 1901. The translation used here is the newer (1957) edition by Thomas Bailey Sauders; in his introduction to this edition, Rudolf Bultmann observes that "Though [Harnack's] conception of history is otherwise dominated to a great extent by the idea of evolution...it is nevertheless quite clear that for him the Christian faith is neither a product of evolution, nor, as such, something with a history subject to development" (in Harnack 1957: xiii).

10 E.g., Donfried and Richardson (1998); Kraabel (1971); Wilken (1976). Bauer's thesis has also received much criticism, as demonstrated by Georg Strecker's appendix (later augmented by Robert A. Kraft) called "The Reception of the Book" (Bauer 1971: 286–316) which surveys reviews and criticisms of *Orthodoxy and Heresy in Earliest Christianity*. One of the most frequent criticisms is that Bauer too often argued from silence.

11 L. Michael White observes that Bauer implicitly introduced "a model of expansion different from the 'great church' notion espoused by Harnack" (1985/86: 121).

12 Other works on the topic of Jewish Christianity by Georg Strecker include the following: *Das Judenchristentum in den Pseudoklementinen* (1958; 2nd ed. 1981), where he argues that scholars frequently overestimate the effect of the destruction of the Temple in 70 CE on Judaism and Jewish Christianity; Strecker provides an extensive bibliography on Jewish Christianity at the end of "Le Judéo-Christianisme entre la Synagogue et l'Église," *Orthodoxie et Hérésie Dans L'Église Ancienne* (1993).

13 Other studies on Jewish Christianity include: Daniélou (1958; trans. 1964; 1970); Lüdemann (1989); Schoeps (1969; 1965: 53–75); Visotzky (1989); Wilson (1995: 143–59; bibliography: 351 n.1).

14 Parkes' view regarding Jewish proselytes is as insightful as it is rare in its time: he suggests that converts to Judaism "were made by the attractive power of the local synagogue, not by trained missionaries going out singly or in groups to cities and regions where settled Jewish communities did not exist," (1969: 12). See G.F. Moore (1921; 1927/30); and A.L. Williams (1935).

15 E.g., A.T. Davies, ed. (1979); A. Roy Eckardt (1967); W. Eckert, N.P. Levinson, M. Stöhr (1967); Craig A. Evans, and Donald A. Hagner, ed. (1993); J.G. Gager (2000); Sidney G. Hall III (1993); Charlotte Klein (1975; trans. 1978); Judith Lieu (1996); Peter Richardson (1969); Peter Richardson and Stephen Westerholm (1991); Stephen G. Wilson, ed. (1986); Stephen G. Wilson (1995).

16 David Daube (1973); W.D. Davies (1980; 1962); David Flusser (1979; 1990); J. Jeremias (1962; trans. 1969); E.P. Sanders (1977; 1992); Samuel Sandmel (1969); H.J. Schoeps (1961); M. Simon and A. Benoit (1968); Pieter W. van der Horst (1990); G. Vermes (1973).

17 Sanders undercuts this post-Reformation theory of Jewish identity by suggesting a new theory of his own: "covenantal nomism." This theory emphasizes two foci crucial to Judaism: the Mosaic law and the covenant, with the under-

standing that the law is kept in order to express the covenantal relationship with
God, not to earn that relationship.

18 Moore notes that "[n]o doubt there was an abundance of real controversy
between Jews and Christians, through which the apologists were acquainted
with the points of their opponents' argument" (1921: 198).

19 A.L. Williams likewise recognized how Christian writers in antiquity "blamed
the obstinate Jews for not accepting the evidence which seemed to them so
strong. But in reality, this was only because they themselves misconceived the
case" (1935: 417).

20 Simon furthermore argues that theological controversy, as expressed in
Aphraates and Eusebius, cannot "properly be described as manifestations of
anti-Semitism," since "[b]oth one and the other have Judaizing Christians just
as much in mind, and perhaps even more in mind, than the Jews themselves.
Ecclesiastical authorities could not be expected to encourage or even to toler-
ate practices that called in question the autonomy and integrity of Christianity" (1986: 401).

21 Simon suggests that Hellenistic Judaism "in its missionary endeavors, went
out to meet the pagans. Conversions were the result of a mutual effort of
adaptation. But from now on Israel was to demand of its recruits total commitment, and expected from them an effort it made no move to reciprocate"
(1986: 376-77).

22 The details of Munck's argument from Galatians are discussed in chapter 3.

23 Munck argues that the judaizing opponents of Paul in Galatia were not Jewish Christians because Jewish Christians simply were not interested in converting Gentile Christians. He explains that there was a clear distinction
between the plan of salvation held by Jewish Christians and that held by Gentile Christians. Since Jewish Christians believed that salvation would come to
the Jews first and to the Gentiles second, Gentiles were not their immediate concern and thus the Jerusalem church did not advocate circumcision or any other
obligations from the Mosaic law for Gentiles wishing to become Christians.
Paul, on the other hand, held that salvation would come first to the Gentiles
and then to the Jews, so Gentiles were his primary concern (Munck 1959:
120). Because their proselytizing strategies were so different, Munck insists that
mixed communities of Gentile Christians and Jewish Christians were rare
(1959: 123).

24 Munck explains that, "[w]hat the Gentile Christian churches know of Jewish
Christianity they know only through Paul," not from Jewish Christians themselves (1959: 131).

25 The background of some of the Gentile converts might have influenced their
attitudes and views; Munck rightly suggests that prior to becoming Christians, some of the Gentiles might have attended synagogue services "and had
learnt there to read the Old Testament as a Jewish book, so that when the
Bible was used in these newly converted Gentile communities there was a great
risk of misunderstandings; they could very easily drop into *habitual Jewish ways
of thought*" (Munck 1959: 132, emphasis added).

26 Elsewhere, Munck states that "this Gentile Christian heresy" is met "only
within the Galatian churches" (1959: 279-80).

27 Leo Baeck (1966: 164) states that "[t]he eleventh chapter in the Letter to the Romans is the most moving thing Paul has ever written. The sincerity of this man, the depth of his feeling rooted in his Jewish people, are all revealed here."

28 E.g., A.T. Davies, ed. (1979); Gager (2000); Richardson and Westerholm (1991); E.P. Sanders (1983); Alan F. Segal (1990); S.G. Wilson, ed. (1986).

29 James Parkes espoused a perspective similar to the dual covenants view, as Jocz notes: "Parkes's theology operates on the premise of a double Covenant: two religions, two chosen peoples with different tasks and missions. Judaism can in no way be a substitute for Christianity, nor Christianity for Judaism. Both are right and both must acknowledge the rightness of the other" (1981: 86; Parkes 1969: 12, 30). Roy A. Ekardt builds on Parkes's idea of the dual covenant: both Judaism and Christianity serve different purposes, and both are equally legitimate. The Jews need the Torah, and the Gentiles need the Gospel, and Christian missionizing of Jews is completely unnecessary. The Christian is the "younger brother" who should not presume to imply that the elder brother "is not already a member of the household of salvation" (1967: 152ff).

30 Gaston discusses several Christian texts which polemicize against Gentile Christian interest in Judaism (e.g., Rev. 2:9 and 3:9; Ignatius' letter to Philadelphia 6:1 and to Magnesia 10.3 [Gaston 1986: 33–44]). A fuller discussion of these comments and other texts is in chapter 5.

31 Gager incorrectly refers to both Jewish Christians and Gentile Christians as "Judaizers," lumping both together under this category in a confusing manner.

32 According to Gager, within the New Testament are passages that "convey a sense of the logic which seemed so apparent to the earliest Christian Judaizers" (1985: 133).

33 Gager states that: "No matter what form it took...Judaizing among Christians regularly provoked anti-Jewish polemic on the part of ecclesiastical leaders" (1985: 118).

34 Gager identifies a functional similarity between Christian and pagan anti-Jewish polemic; both strove to prevent attachment to Judaism: "Both were bent on making Judaism seem unattractive to potential or actual converts and sympathizers" (1985: 118).

35 As Saldarini aptly puts it, by comparison with the typical scholarly portrayal of Judaism and Christianity in antiquity as separate religions with defined, impenetrable boundaries, "reality is not so uniform or tidy....Christian communities and writers of the first two centuries lived in varied relationships with Jewish communities" (1992: 26).

36 While Wright warns against the "reductionism that makes everything a matter of speculative theology," he seems most opposed to "the reductionism that refuses to recognize a theological argument when (as in Galatians) it jumps up and bites the reader on the nose, insisting instead on everything in terms of sociological or cultural forces or agenda" (1993: 260).

37 Richardson notes that this perspective "flies in the face of Paul's reluctance— along with that of virtually all early Christian literature—to make this equation so precisely" (1994: 233). Indeed, as noted earlier, the complete appropriation of the term "Israel" is not explicit in any of the New Testament documents.

38 According to Taylor, some scholars mistakenly read second and third century literature "as a mere prelude to Chrysostom," adding that "[i]f we do not assume a priori that these texts necessarily relate back to the influence and power of a living Judaism, then the judaizing phenomenon that they reveal appears in quite a new light" (1995: 32).

39 Taylor notes that Simon states that judaizing has an "uninterrupted tradition" (Simon 1986: 330). She also mentions Gager (1983: 133); Gaston (1986: 166); Meeks and Wilken (1978: 36), and Shukster and Richardson (1986: 30-31) as scholars who assert the long-standing existence of judaizers, including the period before Chrysostom. To this she objects, declaring that these scholars "make this affirmation despite their admission that the lack of evidence from the earlier period severely restricts their findings, allowing them to do no more than speculate about active contact between Christians and Jews" (Taylor 1995: 30).

40 In Taylor's view, advocates of the conflict theory have missed the mark on this because they have been swayed by two trends in modern scholarship: the emphasis on a deconfessional approach to early Christian literature which has effectively discouraged theological interpretation at all levels, and the application of "sophisticated theories of conflict" to interpret early church discourse (1995: 151-53).

41 As discussed in early chapters of this study, some of the "anti-Jewish" rhetoric in early Christian documents addresses Gentile Christians, not Jews; consequently, I agree with Taylor that this rhetoric was *intra muros* but for a different reason.

42 As Alan Davies suggests, "[t]o say that early Christian anti-Judaism had no basis in Jewish-Christian conflicts during the patristic period is similar to saying that the white-devil myths of the Black Muslims of America have no basis in black-white conflicts in contemporary America" (1997: 236).

Bibliography

━◄◦►━

I. Primary Sources

Barnabas, Epistle of. "The Epistle of Barnabas." In Kirsopp Lake (trans.), *The Apostolic Fathers.* vol. 1, 340-409. Loeb Classical Library. Cambridge: Harvard University Press, 1912.

Dead Sea Scrolls. In Geza Vermes (trans.), *The Dead Sea Scrolls in English.* 4th. ed. London: Penguin, 1995.

Didache. "The Didache, or Teaching of the Twelve Apostles." In Kirsopp Lake (trans.), *The Apostolic Fathers.* vol. 1, 308-33. Loeb Classical Library. Cambridge: Harvard University Press, 1912.

Dio Cassius. *Roman History.* Trans. Earnest Cary. 9 vols. Loeb Classical Library. London: Heinemann, 1914-1927.

Diognetus, Epistle to. "The Epistle to Diognetus." In Kirsopp Lake (trans.), *The Apostolic Fathers.* vol. 2, 350-79. Loeb Classical Library. Cambridge: Harvard University Press, 1912.

Epiphanius. *The Panarion of Epiphanius of Salamis.* F. Williams, ed. 2 vols. Nag Hammadi Studies. Leiden: Brill, 1987.

Eusebius. *The History of the Church.* Trans. G.A. Williamson. New York: Dorset Press, 1984.

Ignatius. "Ignatius to the Magnesians." In Kirsopp Lake (trans.), *The Apostolic Fathers.* vol. 1, 197-212. Loeb Classical Library. Cambridge: Harvard University Press, 1912.

———. "Ignatius to the Philadelphians." In Kirsopp Lake (trans.), *The Apostolic Fathers.* vol. 1, 239-49. Loeb Classical Library. Cambridge: Harvard University Press, 1912.

Irenaeus. *Adversus haereses.* Ed. A. Rousseau, L. Doutreleau, B. Hemmerdinger and C. Mercier. Sources Chrétiennes. Paris: Cerf, 1965-82.

Josephus. "Against Apion." In H. St. J. Thackery (trans.), *Josephus: The Life, Against Apion,* 161-411. Loeb Classical Library. Cambridge: Harvard University Press, 1926.

———. *The Jewish War.* Trans. H. St. J. Thackery. 2 vols. Loeb Classical Library. Cambridge: Harvard University Press, 1927-28.

———. *Jewish Antiquities.* Trans. H. St. J. Thackery, Ralph Marcus, Allen Wikgren, Louis H. Feldman. 6 vols. Loeb Classical Library. Cambridge: Harvard University Press, 1930-65.

————. "Life." In H. St. J. Thackery (trans.), *Josephus: The Life, Against Apion*, 1-159. Loeb Classical Library. Cambridge: Harvard University Press, 1926.

Justin Martyr. *Dialogue with Trypho*. Trans. A.L. Williams. London: Society for Promoting Christian Knowlege, 1930.

Juvenal. *The Sixteen Satires*. Trans. Peter Green. Harmondsworth: Penguin, 1974.

Melito. *On Pascha and Fragments*. Trans. Stuart G. Hall. Oxford: Clarendon Press, 1979.

Mishnah. Trans. H. Danby. London: Oxford University Press, 1964.

Oracula Sibyllina. Ed. J. Geffcken, *Komposition und Entstehungszeit der Oracula Sibyllina*. Leipzig: Zentral-Antiqariat der Deutschen Demokratischen Republik, 1967; orig. 1902.

Philo of Alexandria. *Philo*. Trans. F.H. Colson, G.H. Whitaker, J.W. Earp and R. Marcus. 10 vols. and 2 supplements. Loeb Classical Library. London: Heinemann.

Pliny the Elder. *Natural History*. Trans. H. Rackham, D.E. Eichholz and W.H.S. Jones. 10 vols. Loeb Classical Library. London: Heinemann, 1938-1962.

Pliny the Younger. *The Letters*. Trans. Betty Radice. London: Penguin, 1969.

Polycarp, Martyrdom of. "The Martyrdom of Polycarp." In Kirsopp Lake (trans.), *The Apostolic Fathers*. vol. 2, 312-45. Loeb Classical Library. Cambridge: Harvard University Press, 1912.

Pseudo-Clementines. "The Pseudo-Clementines." In *New Testament Apocrypha*, ed. W. Schneemelcher. Trans. G. Strecker. rev. ed., vol. 2, 483-541. Westminster: John Knox Press, 1992.

————. "Pseudo-Clementine Literature." In W.A. Meeks (trans.), *The Writings of St. Paul*, 176-84. New York: Norton, 1972.

Sibylline Oracles. "Sibylline Oracles." In J.H. Charlesworth (ed.), *The Old Testament Pseudepigrapha*, vol. 1, 317-472. Trans. John J. Collins. New York: Doubleday, 1983.

Suetonius. *The Twelve Caesars*. Trans. Robert Graves. New York: Penguin, 1957.

Tacitus. *The Annals and the Histories*. Trans. A.J. Church and W.J. Brodribb. New York: Washington Square Press, 1964.

Talmud, Babylonian. E. Epstein, ed. London: Soncino, 1971-87.

Tertullian. *Adversus Marcionem*. Trans. Ernest Evans. vols. 1 and 2. Oxford: Clarendon Press, 1972.

◄○►

II. Secondary Sources

Alon, G. "Halacha in the Epistle of Barnabas [in Hebrew]." *Tarbiz* 12 (1940/1941): 23-38.

Angerstorfer, I. *Melito und das Judentum: Dissertation zur Erlangung des Doktorgrades der Katholisch-Theologischen Fakultät der Universität Regensburg.* Regensburg, 1986.

Ascough, R.S. "Voluntary Associations and Community Formation: Paul's Macedonian Christian Communities in Context." Ph.D. diss., St. Michael's College, 1997.

Audet, J.P. "Affinités littéraires et doctrinales du 'Manuel de Discipline.'" *Revue biblique* 59 (1952): 219-38.

———. La Didaché. Instructions des Apôtres, 1958.

Aune, D.E. "The Social Matrix of the Apocalypse of John." *Biblical Research* 26 (1981): 16-32.

Baeck, L. *Judaism and Christianity*. Trans. Walter Kaufmann. Philadelphia: The Jewish Publication Society of America, 1966 (1958).

Barclay, J. "Mirror Reading a Polemical Letter: Galatians as a Test Case." *Journal for the Study of the New Testament* 31 (1987): 73-93.

———. *Jews in the Mediterranean Diaspora: From Alexander to Trajan (323 BCE-117 CE)*. Edinburgh: T. & T. Clark, 1996.

———. *Obeying the Truth. A Study of Paul's Ethics in Galatians*. Edinburgh: T. & T. Clark, 1988.

Barnard, L.W. "The Old Testament and Judaism in the Writings of Justin Martyr." *Vetus Testamentum* 14 (1964): 394-406.

———. *Studies in the Apostolic Fathers and Their Background*. New York: Schocken Books, 1966.

Barrett, C.K. *The Pastoral Epistles*. Oxford: Clarendon Press, 1963.

———. "Jews and Judaizers in the Epistles of Ignatius." In *Jews, Greeks, and Christians, Essays in Honor of William Davies*, ed. R. Hammerton-Kelly and R. Scroggs, 220-44. Leiden: E.J. Brill, 1976.

———. *Essays on Paul*. Philadelphia: Westminster Press, 1982.

Bauckham, R.J. "The Lord's Day." In *From Sabbath to Lord's Day*, ed. D.A. Carson. Grand Rapids: Zondervan Corporation, 1982.

Bauer, W. *Kritische Untersuchungen über die kanonischen Evangelien: ihr Verhältnis zueinander, ihren Charakter und Ursprung*. Tübingen: Fues, 1847.

———. *Das Christentum und die christliche Kirche der drei ersten Jahrhunderte*, v. 1, Tübingen: Fues, 1853.

———. *Orthodoxy and Heresy in Earliest Christianity*. Trans. R. Kraft and G. Krodel. Philadelphia: Fortress Press, 1971. Originally published as *Rechtgläubigkeit und Ketzerei im ältesten Christentum* Tübingen: Mohr, 1934.

———. *A Greek-English Lexicon of the New Testament and Other Early Christian Literature*. Trans. William F. Arndt and F. Wilbur Gingrich. 2nd. ed. University of Chicago Press, 1979.

Baur, F.C. *Paul the Apostle of Jesus Christ: His Life and Work, His Epistles and His Doctrine*. London: Williams and Norgate, v. 1, 1876; v. 2, 1875. Originally published as *Paulus, der Apostel Jesu Christi, sein Leben und Wirken, seine Briefe und seine Lehre*. 2 vols. Leipzig: Reisland, 1866-67.

Beare, F.W. *A Commentary on the Epistle to the Philippians*. London: Adam & Charles Black, 1959.

Benko, S. "The History of the Early Roman Empire." In *The Catacombs and the Colosseum*, ed. Stephen Benko and John J. O'Rourke, 37-80. Valley Forge: Judson Press, 1971.

Best, E. *1 Peter*. London: Oliphants, 1977.

Betz, H.D. *Galatians*. Philadelphia: Fortress Press, 1979.

———. *2 Corinthians 8 and 9: A Commentary on Two Administrative Letters of the Apostle Paul*. Philadelphia: Fortress, 1985.

Billerbeck, P. *Kommentar zum Neuen Testament aus Talmud und Midrasch*. München: Beck, 1922-1928.

Birnbaum, P. *Daily Prayer Book [Ha-Siddur Ha-Shalem]*. New York: Hebrew Publishing, 1977.

Bockmuehl, M. *The Epistle to the Philippians*. London: Adam & Charles Black, 1997.

Bokser, B.Z. "Justin Martyr and the Jews." *The Jewish Quarterly Review* 64 (1973/74): 97-122.

Borgen, P. "Observations on the Theme 'Paul and Philo.' Paul's Preaching of Circumcision in Galatia (Gal. 5:11)." In *Die Paulinische Literatur und Theologie*, ed. by S. Pedersen, 85-102. Arhus: Forlaget Aros, 1980.

———. "Paul Preaches Circumcision and Pleases Men." In *Paul and Paulinism. Essays in Honour of C.K. Barrett*, ed. M.D. Hooker and S.G. Wilson, 37-46. London: Society for Promoting Christian Knowlege, 1982.

———. "Militant and Peaceful Proselytism and Christian Mission." In *Early Christianity and Hellenistic Judaism*, 45-69. Edinburgh: T. & T. Clark, 1996.

———. "Polemic in the Book of Revelation." In *Anti-Semitism and Early Christianity: Issues of Polemic and Faith*, ed. C.A. Evans and D.A. Hagner, 199-211. Minneapolis: Fortress, 1993.

Bousset, W. *Nachrichten von der Königlichen Gesellschaft der Wissenscaften zu Göttingen; Philologische-historische Klasse*. Berlin: Reuther, 1916.

Bouyer, L. *Eucharist: Theology and Spirituality of the Eucharistic Prayer*. Trans. C.U. Quinn. University of Notre Dame Press, 1968.

Bradshaw, P.F. *Daily Prayer in the Early Church*. London: Society for Promoting Christian Knowledge, 1981.

Brändle, Rudolf. *Die Ethik der Schrift an Diognet: eine Wiederaufnahme paulinischer und johanneischer Theologie am Ausgang des zweiten Jahrhunderts*. Zürich: Theologischer Verlag, 1975.

Broadhurst, L. "Rhetoric and Reality in Melito's Homily." Paper presented at the Canadian Society of Biblical Studies, Bishop's University, Lennoxville, QC, 1999.

Brooten, B.J. *Women Leaders in the Ancient Synagogue. Inscriptional Evidence and Background Issues*. Brown Judaic Studies 36. Chico, CA: Scholars Press, 1982.

Bruce, F.F. *Commentary on Galatians*. Grand Rapids: William B. Eerdmans, 1982.

———. *Philippians*. Peabody: Hendrickson, 1989.

Bultmann, R. *Theology of the New Testament I*. Trans. Kendrick Grobel. London: SCM Press, 1952.

Burton, E.D. *A Critical and Exegetical Commentary on the Epistle to the Galatians*. Edinburgh: T. & T. Clark, 1921.

Caird, G.B. *Paul's Letters from Prison*. Oxford: Oxford University Press, 1976.

Carson, R. *Coins of the Roman Empire*. Cambridge University Press, 1990.

Casson, L. *Travel in the Ancient World*. London: George Allen & Unwin, 1974.

Chadwick, H. "Justin Martyr's Defence of Christianity." *The Bulletin of the John Rylands University Library* 47 (1964/65): 275-97.

Charlesworth, J.H., ed. *The Old Testament Pseudepigrapha*. 2 vols. Garden City, NY: Doubleday, 1983-85.

Cohen, S.J.D. "Conversion to Judaism in Historical Perspective: From Biblical Israel to Postbiblical Judaism." *Conservative Judaism* 36, 4 (1983): 31-45.

———. "Respect for Judaism by Gentiles according to Josephus." *Harvard Theological Review* 80, 4 (1987): 409-30.

———. "Crossing the Boundary and Becoming a Jew." *Harvard Theological Review* 82, 1 (1989): 13-33.

———. "Adolph Harnack's 'The Mission and Expansion of Judaism': Christianity Succeeds Where Judaism Fails." In *The Future of Early*

Christianity, ed. B.A. Pearson, 163–69. Minneapolis: Fortress Press, 1991.

———. "Was Judaism in Antiquity a Missionary Religion?" In *Jewish Assimilation, Acculturation and Accommodation: Past Traditions, Current Issues and Future Prospects*, ed. Menachem Mor. Landham: University Press of America, 1992.

———. "Those Who Say They Are Jews and Are Not': How Do You Know a Jew in Antiquity When You See One?" In *Diasporas in Antiquity*, ed. Shaye J.D. Cohen and Ernest S. Frerichs. Atlanta: Scholars Press, 1993.

———. *The Beginnings of Jewishness: Boundaries, Varieties, Uncertainties*. Berkley: University of California Press, 1999.

Corwin, V. *St. Ignatius and Christianity in Antioch*. New Haven: Yale University Press, 1960.

Coser, L. *The Functions of Social Conflict*. Glencoe, IL: Free Press, 1956.

Crawford, J.S. *The Byzantine Shops at Sardis*. Cambridge: Harvard University Press, 1990.

———. "Multiculturalism at Sardis." *Biblical Archaeology Review* 22, 5 (1996): 38–47.

Crook, J.A. "Titus and Berenice." *American Journal of Philology* 72 (1951): 162–75.

Daniélou, J. "Figure and Événement chez Méliton de Sardes." *Neotestamentica et Patristica* 6 (1962): 282–92.

———. *The Theology of Jewish Christianity, The Development of Christian Doctrine before the Council of Nicaea*. vol. 1. Trans. and ed. John Baker. Chicago: Henry Regnery Company, 1964; orig. 1958.

———. *L'église des apôtres*. Paris: Seuil, 1970.

Darnell, D.R., trans. "The Old Testament Pseudepigrapha." In J.H. Charlesworth, *The Old Testament Pseudepigrapha*, vol. 2, 671–97. New York: Doubleday, 1985.

Daube, D. *The New Testament and Rabbinic Judaism*. London: Athlone Press, 1973; orig. 1956.

Davies, A.T., ed. *Anti-Semitism and the Foundations of Christianity*. New York: Paulist Press, 1979.

———. "Review of Anti-Judaism and Early Christian Identity: A Critique of the Scholarly Consensus by Miriam Taylor." *Studies in Religion* 26, 2 (1997): 235–36.

Davies, W.D. *Christian Origins and Judaism*. London: Darton, Longman & Todd, 1962.

———. *Paul and Rabbinic Judaism*. Philadelphia: Fortress Press, 1980; orig. 1948.

Desjardins, M. *Sin in Valentinianism*. Atlanta: Scholars Press, 1990.

Delitzsch, F. *Babel und Bibel: ein Vortrag*. Leipzig: Hinrich, 1902.

Dibelius, M., and H. Conzelmann. *The Pastoral Epistles*. Philadelphia: Fortress Press, 1972.

————. *Geschichte der urchristlichen Literatur*. repr. Munich: Chr. Kaiser, 1975; orig. 1926.

Dohm, Christian Wilhelm von. *Concerning the Amelioration of the Civil Status of the Jews*. Trans. Helen Lederer. Cincinnati: Hebrew Union College, 1957; orig. 1781.

Donahue, P. "Jewish Christanity in the Letters of Ignatius." *Vigiliae Christianae* 32 (1978): 81-93.

Donaldson, T.L. "Jerusalem Ossuary Inscriptions and the Status of Jewish Proselytes." In *Text and Artifact in the Religions of Mediterranean Antiquity*, ed. Stephen G. Wilson and Michel Desjardins, 372-88. Waterloo: Wilfrid Laurier University Press, 2000.

Donfried, K.P. and P. Richardson, eds. *Judaism and Christianity in First-Century Rome*. Grand Rapids: William B. Eerdmans, 1998.

Draper, J.A. "The Jesus Tradition in the *Didache*." In *Gospel Perspectives: The Jesus Tradition outside the Gospels*, ed. David Wenham, 269-89. Sheffield: JSOT, 1985.

————. "Torah and Troublesome Apostles in the Didache Community." *Novum Testamentum* 33, 4 (1991): 347-72.

————. "Christian Self-Definition Against the 'Hypocrites' in Didache VIII." In *The Didache in Modern Research*, ed. Jonathan A. Draper, 223-43. Leiden: E.J. Brill, 1996.

Dunn, J.D.G. *The Epistles to the Colossians and to Philemon*. Grand Rapids: William B. Eerdmans, 1996.

Eckardt, A.R. *Elder and Younger Brothers: The Encounter of Jews and Christians*. New York: Scribner's Sons, 1967.

Eckert, W., N.P. Levinson, and M. Stöhr, eds. *Antijudaismus im Neuen Testament?* München: Chr. Kaiser Verlag, 1967.

Elliott, J.H. *A Home for the Homeless*. Philadelphia: Fortress Press, 1981.

Enslin, M.S. "Justin Martyr: An Appreciation." *The Jewish Quarterly Review* 34 (1943-44): 179-205.

Esler, P.F. *The First Christians in Their Social Worlds: Social-Scientific Approaches to New Testament Interpretation*. London: Routledge, 1994.

Evans, C.A. and D.A. Hagner, eds. *Anti-Semitism and Early Christianity: Issues of Polemic and Faith*. Minneapolis: Fortress Press, 1993.

Ewald, H. *The History of Israel*. Trans. J. Estlin Carpenter. vol. 5. 2nd. ed. London: Longmans, Green, 1880.

————. *The History of Israel.* Trans. J. Frederick Smith. vol. 7. London: Longmans, Green, 1885.

Feine, P. "Das Christentum Jesu und das Christentum der Apostel in ihrer Abgrenzung gegen die Religionsgeschichte." *Christentum und Zeitgeist* 1 (1904): 44-57.

Feldman, L. "Proselytism by Jews in the Third, Fourth and Fifth Centuries." *Journal for the Study of Judaism* 24 (1992): 1-58.

————. *Jew & Gentile in the Ancient World.* Princeton, NJ: Princeton University Press, 1993.

Ferguson, E. *Backgrounds of Early Christianity.* 2nd. ed. Grand Rapids: William B. Eerdmans, 1993.

Fiensy, D.A. *Prayers Alleged to Be Jewish.* Chico: Scholars Press, 1985.

Flusser, D. *Yahadut u-mekorot ha-natsrut: mehkarim u-ma'asot.* Tel Aviv: Sifriyat Po'alim, 1979.

————. *Das Christentum: eine jüdische Religion.* München: Kösel, 1990.

————. "Paul's Jewish-Christian Opponents in the Didache." In *The Didache in Modern Research*, ed. Jonathan A. Draper, 195-211. Leiden: E.J. Brill, 1996.

Foss, C. *Ephesus After Antiquity: A Late Antique, Byzantine and Turkish City.* Cambridge, UK: Cambridge University Press, 1979.

Frankfurter, D. "Jews or Not? Reconstructing the 'Other' in Rev 2:9 and 3:9." *Harvard Theological Review* 94, 4 (2001): 403-25.

Fredriksen, P. "Judaism, the Circumcision of Gentiles, and Apocalyptic Hope: Another Look at Galatians 1 and 2." *Journal of Theological Studies* 42 (1991): 532-64.

Frend, W.H.C. *The Rise of Christianity.* London: Darton, Longman & Todd, 1984.

————. *Martyrdom and Persecution in the Early Church: A Study of a Conflict from the Maccabees to Donatus.* New York: New York University Press, 1967.

Frey, J.B. *Corpus of Jewish Inscriptions: Jewish inscriptions from the third century BC to the seventh century AD.* New York: Ktav Publishing House, 1975.

Funk, F.X. *Doctrinae duodecim apostolorum, Canones ecclesiastici ac religuae doctinae duarum viarum expositiones veteres.* Tübingen: Henrici Laupp, 1887.

————. "Die Doctrina Apostolorum." *Theologische Quartalschrift* 87 (1905): 161-79.

————. *Didascalia et Constitutiones Apostolorum.* Paderbornae: F. Schöningh, 1905b.

Furnish, V.P. "The Plan and Purpose of Philippians III." *New Testament Studies* 13 (1963/1964): 80-88.

Gager, J.G. *Moses in Greco-Roman Paganism*. Nashville: Abingdon Press, 1972.

——. *Kingdom and Community: The Social World of Early Christianity*. Englewood Cliffs, NJ: Prentice-Hall, 1975.

——. *The Origins of Anti-Semitism: attitudes toward Judaism in Pagan and Christian Antiquity*. Oxford, UK: Oxford University Press, 1983.

——. *Reinventing Paul*. Oxford, UK: Oxford University Press, 2000.

Gaston, L. "Judaism of the Uncircumcised in Ignatius and Related Writers." In *Anti-Judaism in Early Christianity: Separation and Polemic*, ed. Stephen Wilson, 33-44. Waterloo: Wilfrid Laurier University Press, 1986.

——. *Paul and the Torah*. Vancouver: University of British Columbia Press, 1987.

Georgi, D. *The Opponents of Paul in Second Corinthians*. Philadelphia: Fortress Press, 1986.

Gibbon, E. *History of the Decline and Fall of the Roman Empire*. London: A. Strahan and T. Cadell, 1791-92.

Gingrich, F.W., and F.W. Danker. *A Greek-English Lexicon of the New Testament and Other Early Christian Literature*. 2nd. ed. Chicago: University of Chicago Press, 1979.

Gnilka, J. *Der Kolosserbrief*. Frieburg: Herder, 1980.

Gooch, P. *Dangerous Food: 1 Corinthians 8-10 in its Context*. Waterloo: Wilfrid Laurier University Press, 1993.

Goodenough, E.R. *The Theology of Justin Martyr*. Jena: Frommanische Buchhandlung, 1923.

——. *By Light, Light*. New Haven, CT: Yale University Press, 1935.

Goodman, M. "Jewish Proselytizing in the First Century." In *The Jews among Pagans and Christians in the Roman Empire*, ed. John North, Tessa Rajak, and Judith Lieu, 53-78. London: Routledge, 1992.

——. *Mission and Conversion*. Oxford, UK: Clarendon Press, 1994.

Goodspeed, E.J. *An Introduction to the New Testament*. University of Chicago Press, 1937.

——. *A History of Early Christian Literature*. rev. and enl. Robert M. Grant. Chicago: University of Chicago Press, 1966.

——. *Problems of New Testament Translation*. Chicago: University of Chicago Press, 1945.

Grant, R.M. *Second-Century Christianity; a collection of fragments*. London: Society for Promoting Christian Knowledge, 1946.

——. *Gnosticism and Early Christianity*. New York: Columbia University Press, 1959.

——. *The Apostolic Fathers: A New Translation and Commentary. Ignatius of Antioch*. vol. 4. London: Thomas Nelson, 1966.

———. "Marcion and the Critical Method." In *From Jesus to Paul*, eds. Peter Richardson and John C. Hurd, 207-15. Waterloo: Wilfrid Laurier University Press, 1984.

Grenfell, B.P. and A.S. Hunt. *The Oxyrhynchus Papyri* 15. London: Egyptian Exploration Society, 1922.

Gunther, J.J. "The Epistle of Barnabas and the Final Rebuilding of the Temple." *Journal for the Study of Judaism* 7 (1976): 143-51.

Hall, R. "Epispasm and the Dating of Jewish Writings." *Journal for the Study of the Pseudepigrapha* 2 (1988): 71-86.

———. *Melito of Sardis on Pascha*. Oxford: Oxford University Press, 1979.

———. *Christian Anti-Semitism and Paul's Theology*. Minneapolis: Fortress Press, 1993.

Hallowel, A.I. "American Indians, White and Black: The Phenomenon of Transculturalization." *Current Anthropology* 5, 5 (1963): 519-31.

Halton, T. "Stylistic Device in Melito, ΠΕΡΙ ΠΑΞΧΑ." In *Kyriakon Festschrift Johannes Quasten*, 249-55. Munsterwestf: Verlag Aschendorff, 1970.

Hammer, K. and M. Murray. "Aquaintances, Supporters and Competitors: Evidence of Interconnectedness and Rivalry among the Religious Groups in Sardis." In *Religious Rivalries and the Struggle for Success in Sardis and Smyrna*. ed., Richard A. Ascough. Waterloo: Wilfrid Laurier University Press, in press.

Hanfmann, G.M.A. "The Fifth Campaign at Sardis." *Bulletin of the American Schools of Oriental Research* 170: 1-65.

Hanson, A.T. *The Pastoral Letters*. Cambridge, UK: Cambridge University Press, 1966.

Hare, D.R.A. *The Theme of Jewish Persecution of Christians in the Gospel According to St. Matthew*. Cambridge, UK: Cambridge University Press, 1967.

Harnack, A. von. *Die Lehre der zwölf Apostel nebst Untersuchungen zur ältesten Geschichte der Kirchenverfassung und des Kirchenrechts*. Leipzig: Hinrichs, 1884.

———. *Lehrbuch der Dogmengeschichte*. 3 vols. Freiburg I.B. and Leipzig: Mohr, 1886-89.

———. *History of Dogma*. 7 vols. London: Williams and Norgate, 1894-1899.

———. *Die Apostellehre und die jüdische beiden Wege*. Leipzig: J.C. Hinrichs, 1896.

———. *Geschichte der altchristlichen Literatur bis Eusebius: Die Chronologie*. vol. 1, pt. 2. Leipzig: J.C. Hinrichs, 1958; orig. 1897.

————. *Ist die rede des Paulus in Athen ein ursprünglicher bestandteil der Apostelgeschichte? Judentum und Judenchristentum in Justins dialog mit Trypho.* Leipzig: J.C. Hinrichs, 1913.

————. *The Mission and Expansion of Christianity in the First Three Centuries.* Trans. James Moffat. 2nd ed., enl. and rev. 2 vols. London: William & Norgate, 1908.

————. *The Expansion of Christianity in the First Three Centuries.* vol. 1. London: Williams and Norgate, 1904.

————. *What Is Christianity?* Trans. Thomas Baily Saunders. Gloucester, MA: Harper & Brothers, 1957; orig. 1901.

————. *Marcion, The Gospel of the Alien God.* Trans. John E. Steely and Lyle D. Bierma. Durham: The Labyrinth Press 1990; orig. 1921.

Harris, M.J. *Colossians and Philemon.* Grand Rapids: William B. Eerdmans, 1991.

Harvey, G. *The True Israel.* Leiden: E.J. Brill, 1996.

Hasler, V. *Die Brief an Timotheus und Titus.* Zürich: Theologischen Verlag, 1978.

Hastings, J., ed. *Encyclopedia of Religion and Ethics.* vol. 10, 1919.

Hawkins, J.G. "The Opponents of Paul in Galatia." Ph.D. diss., Yale University, 1971.

Hawthorne, G.F. *Philippians.* Waco, TX: Word Books, 1983.

Hefner, P. "Baur Versus Ritschl on Early Christianity." *Church History* 31 (1962): 259-78.

Hemer, C.J. *The Letters to the Seven Churches of Asia in Their Local Setting.* Sheffield: JSOT Press, 1986.

Henderson, B.W. *The Life and Principate of the Emperor Nero.* Philadelphia: J.B. Lippincott, 1903.

Herford, T. *Christianity in Talmud and Midrash.* New York: Ktav, 1903.

Hilgenfeld, A. *Novum Testamentum extra canonem receptum, Evangeliorum 4,2.* Leipzig: Weigel, 1884.

Hirsch, E. "Zwei Fragen zu Galater 6." *Zeitschrift für die neutestamentliche Wissenschaft* 29 (1930): 192-97.

Hoffmann, R.J. *Marcion: On the Restitution of Christianity.* Chico, CA: Scholars Press, 1984.

Horbury, W. "Jewish-Christian Relations in Barnabas and Justin Martyr." In *Jews and Christians*, ed. James D.G. Dunn, 315-45. Tübingen: J.C.B. Mohr (Paul Siebeck), 1992.

Horner, G. *The Statutes of the Apostles or Canones Ecclesiastici.* London: Williams & Norgate, 1904.

————. "A New Fragment of the Didache in Coptic." *Journal of Theological Studies* 25 (1924): 225-31.

Hort, F.J.A. *The Apocalypse of St. John, I-III.* Minneapolis, MN: James and Klock Publishing, 1908.

Houlden, J.L. *Paul's Letters from Prison.* Harmondsworth, UK: Penguin, 1970.

Howard, G. *Paul: Crisis in Galatia. A Study in Early Christian Theology.* Cambridge, UK: Cambridge University Press, 1979.

Hurd, J. *The Origin of I Corinthians.* New York: Seabury, 1965.

———. "Pauline Chronology and Pauline Theology." In *Christian History and Interpretation: Studies Presented to John Knox*, ed. C.F.D. Moule, W.R. Farmer, and R. Niebuhr, 225-48. Cambridge, UK: Cambridge University Press, 1967.

Hvalvik, R. *The Struggle for Scripture and Covenant.* Tübingen: J.C.B. Mohr (Paul Siebeck), 1996.

Jefford, C.A. *The Sayings of Jesus in the Teaching of the Twelve Apostles.* Leiden: E.J. Brill, 1989.

Jeremias, J. *Jerusalem in the Time of Jesus.* Philadelphia: Fortress Press, 1962.

———. *Jesus' Promise to the Nations.* London: SCM Press, 1986.

Jewett, R. "The Epistolary Thanksgiving and the Integrity of Philippians." *Novum Testamentum* 12 (1970): 40-53.

———. "Agitators and the Galatian Congregation." *New Testament Studies* 17 (1971): 198-212.

Jocz, J. *The Jewish People and Jesus Christ after Auschwitz.* Grand Rapids, MI: Baker Book House, 1981.

Jones, F.S. "The Pseudo-Clementines: A History of Research." *Second Century* 2 (1982): 1-33, 63-95.

———. "Clementines, Pseudo-." *Anchor Bible Dictionary* 1 (1991): 1061-62.

———. *An Ancient Jewish Christian Source on the History of Christianity: Pseudo-Clementine Recognitions 1.27-71.* Atlanta, GA: Scholars Press, 1995.

Joukowsky, M.S. *Early Turkey.* Dubuque, IA: Kendall/Hunt, 1996.

Judge, E.A. *The Social Pattern of the Christian Groups in the First Century.* London: Tyndale Press, 1960.

Kee, H.C. *Knowing the Truth: A Sociological Approach to New Testament Interpretation.* Minneapolis: Fortress Press, 1989.

Kelly, J.N.D. *A Commentary on the Pastoral Epistles.* London: Adam & Charles Black, 1963.

Keresztes, P. "The Imperial Roman Government and the Christian Church." *Aufstieg und Niedergang der römischen Welt* II 23, 1 (1979): 247-314.

Kilpatrick, G.D. "*Blepete*, Philippians 3:2." In *In Memoriam Paul Kahle*, eds. M. Black and G. Fohrer, 146-48. Berlin: Töpelmann, 1968.

Klausner, T. "Taufet in Lebendigem Wasser! Zum religions und kultur-geschichtlichen Verständnis von Didache 7: 1-3." In *Pisciculi. Studien zur Religion und Kultur des Altertums*, eds. T. Klauser and M. Rükker, 157-64. Münster: Aschendorff, 1939.

Klein, C. *Theologie und Anti-Judaismus*. München: Chr. Kaiser Verlag, 1975.

Kloppenborg, J. "*Didache* 16: 6-8 and Special Matthaean Tradition." *Zeitschrift für die neutestamentliche Wissenschaft* 70 (1979): 54-67.

———. "The Transformation of Moral Exhortation in *Didache* 1-5." In *The Didache in Context: Essays of Its Text, History and Transmission*, ed. Clayton N. Jefford, 88-109. Leiden: E.J. Brill, 1995.

Knight, G. *The Pastoral Epistles*. Grand Rapids: William B. Eerdmanns, 1992.

Knox, J. *Chapters in a Life of Paul*. 2nd. ed. London: Adam & Charles Black, 1954; 1st. ed. Nashville: Abingdon Press, 1950.

Köster, H. *History and Literature of Early Christianity*. vol. 2. Philadelphia: Hermeneia, 1982.

———, ed. *Ephesos: Metropolis of Asia*. Valley Forge, PA: Trinity Press International, 1995.

Kohler, K. "Über die Ursprünge und Grundformen der synagogalen Liturgie." *Monatschrift fur die Geschichte und Wissenschaft des Judentums* 37 (1893): 441-51, 489-97.

———. "The Origin and Composition of the Eighteen Benedictions with a Translation of the Corresponding Essene Prayers in the Apostolic Constitutions." *Hebrew Union College Annual* 1 (1924): 387-425.

Kraabel, A.T. "Melito the Bishop and the Synagogue at Sardis: Text and Context." In *Diaspora Jews and Judaism: Essays in Honour of, and in Dialogue with, A. Thomas Kraabel*, ed. J. Andrew Overman and Robert S. MacLennan, 257-68. Atlanta: Scholars Press, 1992.

———. "Paganism and Judaism: The Sardis Evidence." *Mélanges oferts à Marcel Simon: Paganisme, Judaïsme, Christianisme: Influences et affrontements dans le monde antique*, 13-33. Paris: De Boccard, 1978.

———. "The Roman Diaspora: Six Questionable Assumptions." *Journal of Jewish Studies* 33 (1982): 445-64.

Kraemer, R.S., ed. *Maenads, Martyrs, Matrons, Monastics: A Sourcebook on Women's Religions in the Greco-Roman World*. Philadelphia: Fortress Press, 1988.

———. "On the Meaning of the Term 'Jew' in Greco-Roman Inscriptions." *Harvard Theological Review* 82, 1 (1989): 35-53.

Kraft, R.A. "Review of Prigent's L'Épître de Barnabé I–XVI et ses sources." *Journal of Theological Studies n.s.* 13 (1962): 401–408.

———. *The Apostolic Fathers: Barnabas and the Didache.* vol. 3. New York: Thomas Nelson & Sons, 1965.

———. "Judaism on the World Scene." In *The Catacombs and the Colosseum*, ed. Stephen Benko and John J. O'Rourke, 81–98. Valley Forge: Judson Press, 1971.

Krauss, S. "The Jews in the Works of the Church Fathers." *Jewish Quarterly Review* 5 (1893): 122–57.

Krawutzcky, A. "Über die sogenannte Zwölfapostellehre, ihre hauptsächlichsten Quellen und ihre erste Ausnahme." *Theologische Quartalschrift* 4 (1884): 547–606.

Kümmel, W.G. *The New Testament: the History of the Investigation of Its Problems.* Trans. S.M. Gilmour and H.C. Kee. Nashville: Abingdon Press, 1972.

Lake, K. *Apostolic Fathers.* 2 vols. Loeb Classical Library. Cambridge: Harvard University Press, 1912.

Lea, T.D. "Unscrambling the Judaizers: Who Were Paul's Opponents?" *Southwestern Journal of Theology* 37 (1994): 28–42.

Lefort, L.T. *Les Pères apostoliques en copte I.* Louvain: Durbecq, 1952.

Leon, H.J. *The Jews of Ancient Rome*, ed. Carolyn A. Osiek. London: Hendrickson, 1960; rev. ed. 1995.

Levinskaya, I. *The Book of Acts in Its Diaspora Setting.* vol. 5. Grand Rapids, MI: William B. Eerdmans, 1996.

Liddell, H.G., and R. Scott, H.S. Jones and Roderick McKenzie, eds. *A Greek-English Lexicon.* 9th. ed. Oxford: Clarendon Press, 1940; orig. 1843.

Lieu, J.M. *The Jews among pagans and Christians in the Roman Empire.* London: Routledge, 1992.

———. *Image and Reality: The Jews in the World of the Christians in the Second Century.* Edinburgh: T. & T. Clark, 1996.

Lifshitz, B. *Donateurs et fondateurs dans les synagogues juives, répertoire des dédicaces grecques relatives à la construction et à la réfection des synagogues.* Paris: J. Gabalda et Cie, 1967.

Lightfoot, J.B. *St. Paul's Epistle to the Galatians.* 10th ed. Andover, MA: Warren F. Draper, 1890; orig. 1865.

———. *St. Paul's Epistles to the Colossians and to Philemon.* Peabody: Hendrickson Publishers, 1987; orig. 1875.

———. *The Apostolic Fathers: S. Ignatius, S. Polycarp.* vol. 2. London: Macmillan, 1989; orig. 1889.

Lindeskog, G. *Das jüdisch-christliche Problem: Randglossen zu einer Forschungsepoche.* Stockholm: Almqvist & Wiksell, 1986.

Littell, F.H. *The Crucifixion of the Jews*. New York: Harper & Row, 1975.

Lohse, E. *Colossians and Philemon*. Trans. William R. Poehlmann and Robert J. Karris. Philadelphia: Fortress Press, 1971.

Longnecker, R. *Galatians*. Dallas: Word Books, 1990.

Louth, A. *Early Christian Writings*. London: Penguin, 1987.

Lowy, S. "The Confutation of Judaism in the Epistle of Barnabas." *Journal of Jewish Studies* 11 (1960): 1-33.

Lüdemann, G. *Paul, Apostle to the Gentiles*. Trans. F. Stanley Jones. Philadelphia: Fortress Press, 1984.

———. *Opposition to Paul in Jewish Christianity*. Trans. M. Eugene Boring. Minneapolis: Fortress Press, 1989.

Lütgert, W. *Gesetz und Geist: eine Untersuchung zur Vorgeschichte des Galaterbriefes*. Gütersloh: C. Bertelsmann, 1919.

Lyons, G. *Pauline Autobiography: Toward a New Understanding*. Atlanta: Scholars Press, 1985.

Magie, D. *Roman Rule in Asia Minor*. vol. 1. Princeton: Princeton University Press, 1950.

Malherbe, A.J. "The Beasts at Ephesus." *Journal of Biblical Literature* 87 (1968): 71-80.

———. *Social Aspects of Early Christianity*. Baton Rouge: Louisiana State University Press, 1977.

Malina, B. *The New Testament World: Insights from Cultural Anthropology*. Atlanta: John Knox Press, 1981.

Marcus, J. "The Circumcision and the Uncircumcision in Rome." *New Testament Studies* 35 (1989): 67-81.

Margalith, O. "On the Origin and Antiquity of the Name 'Israel.'" *Zeitschrift für die Alttestamentliche Wissenschaft* 102 (1990): 225-74.

Marshall, J.W. *Parables of War: Reading John's Jewish Apocalypse*. Waterloo: Wilfrid Laurier University Press, 2001.

Martin, R.P. *Colossians and Philemon*. 2nd. ed. London: Marshall, Morgan & Scott, 1978.

Martyn, J.L. "A Law-Observant Mission to Gentiles: the Background of Galatians." *Scottish Journal of Theology* 38 (1985): 307-24.

Mason, S. "Josephus the Missionary? The *Contra Apionem* in Social and Literary Context: An Invitation to Judean Philosophy." Paper presented at the Canadian Society of Biblical Studies, Brock University, St. Catharines, ON, 1996.

Mattingly, H., and E.A. Sydenham. *The Roman Imperial Coinage*. vol. 2. London: Spink & Son, 1926.

May, G. "Marcion in Contempory Views: Results and Open Questions." *The Second Century* 6 (1987-88): 129-51.

MacLennan, R.S. *Early Christian Texts on Jews and Judaism*. Atlanta: Scholars Press, 1990.

McCready, W.O. "Martyrdom—In Accordance with the Gospel." Paper presented at the Canadian Society of Biblical Studies, Bishop's University, Lennoxville, QC, 1999.

———. "Friendship and Second Temple Jewish Sectarianism." In *Text and Artifact in the Religions of Mediterranean Antiquity*, ed. Stephen G. Wilson and Michel Desjardins, 402–22. Waterloo: Wilfrid Laurier University Press, 2000.

McKnight, S. *A Light among the Gentiles*. Minneapolis: Fortress Press, 1991.

Meeks, W.A. *The Writings of St. Paul*. New York: Norton, 1972.

Meeks, W.A. and R.L. Wilken. *Jews and Christians in Antioch in the First Four Centuries of the Common Era*. Missoula, MT: Scholars Press for the Society of Biblical Literature, 1978.

Meshorer, Y. *A Treasury of Jewish Coins: From the Persian Period to Bar-Kochba* [in Hebrew]. Jerusalem: Yad Izhak Ben-Zvi Press, 1997.

Metzger, B.M. *A Textual Commentary on the Greek New Testament*. London: United Bible Societies, 1971.

Mitchell, N. "Baptism in the Didache." In *The Didache in Context*, edited by N. Jefford. Leiden: E.J. Brill, 1995.

Mitchell, S. "Population and the Land in Roman Galatia." *Aufstieg und Niedergang der römischen Welt* II 7, 2 (1980): 1053–81.

———. *Regional Epigraphic Catalogues of Asia Minor* II. The Ankara District. The Inscriptions of North Galatia. Oxford: British Archaeological Reports International Ser. 135, 1982.

———. *Anatolia: Land, Men and Gods in Asia Minor*. 2 vols. Oxford: Clarendon Press, 1993.

Moehring, H.R. "The *Acta pro Judaeis* in the *Antiquities* of Flavius Josephus: A Study in Hellenistic and Modern Apologetic Historiography." In *Christianity, Judaism and other Greco-Roman Cults: Studies for Morton Smith at Sixty*, ed. Jacob Neusner. Leiden: E.J. Brill, 1975.

Molland, E. "The Heretics Combatted by Ignatius of Antioch." *Journal of Ecclesiastical History* 5 (1954): 1–6.

Moore, G.F. "Christian Writers on Judaism." *Harvard Theological Review* 14 (1921): 197–254.

———. *Judaism in the First Centuries of the Christian Era: The Age of the Tannaim*. 3 vols. Cambridge, UK: Cambridge: Harvard University Press, 1927.

Moule, C.F.D. *The Epistles of Paul the Apostle to the Colossians and to Philemon*. Cambridge, UK: Cambridge University Press, 1957.

Munck, J. *Paul and the Salvation of Mankind.* Trans. Frank Clarke. London: SCM, 1959. Originally published as *Paulus und die Heisgeschichte.* Aarhus: Universitetforlaget, 1954.

Munier, C. "Où en est la question d'Ignace d'Antioche?" *Aufstieg und Niedergang Der Römischen Welt* II 27, 1 (1993): 359-484.

Murphy-O'Connor, J. "Lots of God-Fearers? *Theosebeis* in the Aphrodisias Inscription." *Revue biblique* 99 (1992): 418-24.

———. *Paul: A Critical Life.* Oxford: Clarendon Press, 1996.

Neander, A. *Geschichte der Pflanzung und Leitung der christlichen Kirche durch die Apostel.* vol. 1. 4th, rev. ed. Hamburg: Friedrich Verthes, 1847.

Niederwimmer, K. *Die Didache.* Göttingen: Vandenhoeck & Ruprecht, 1989.

Nilson, J. "To Whom Is Justin's *Dialogue with Trypho* Addressed?" *Theological Studies* 38 (1977): 538-46.

Noakes, K.W. "Melito of Sardis and the Jews." *Studia Patristica* 13 (1975): 244-49.

Nock, A.D. *Conversion.* Oxford, UK: Oxford University Press, 1933.

Nolland, J. "Proselytism or Politics in Horace?" *Vigiliae Christianae* 33 (1979): 347-55.

Norris, F.W. "Melito's Motivation." *Anglican Theological Review* 68, 1 (1986): 16-24.

Noy, D. *Jewish Inscriptions of Western Europe.* 2 vols. New York: Cambridge University Press, 1993.

Overman, J.A. "The God-Fearers: Some Neglected Features." In *Diaspora Jews and Judaism: Essays in Honor of, and in Dialogue with, A. Thomas Kraabel,* ed. J. Andrew Overman and Robert S. MacLennan, 145-52. Atlanta: Scholars Press, 1992.

Overman, J.A. and R.S. MacLennan, eds. *Diaspora Jews and Judaism: Essays in Honor of, and in Dialogue with, A. Thomas Kraabel.* Atlanta: Scholars Press, 1992, 145-52.

Paget, J.C. *The Epistle of Barnabas.* Tübingen: J.C.B. Mohr (Paul Siebeck), 1994.

———. "Jewish Proselytism at the Time of Christian Origins: Chimera or Reality?" *Journal for the Study of the New Testament* 62 (1996): 65-103.

Parkes, J. *Prelude to Dialogue: Jewish-Christian Relationships.* London: Vallentine, Mitchell, 1969.

———. *Antisemitism.* London: Vallentine, Mitchell, 1963.

———. *The Foundations of Judaism and Christianity.* London: Vallentine, Mitchell, 1960.

———. *The Conflict of the Church and the Synagogue. A Study in the Origins of Antisemitism.* London: Soncino, 1985; orig. 1934.

Pasto, J. "'He is not really a Jew, he is only acting the part': Jewish and non-Jewish Identity in Antiquity." Paper presented at the Annual Meeting of the Society of Biblical Literature, Chicago, IL, 1994.

Pilhofer, P. *Philippi.* vol. 1. Tübingen: J.C.B. Mohr (Paul Siebeck), 1995.

Poliakov, L. *The History of Anti-Semitism.* Trans. George Klim. vol. 4. New York: The Vanguard Press, 1985.

Prigent, P. *L'Épître de Barnabé I–XVI et ses sources.* Paris: J. Gabalda, 1961.

———. *L'Apocalypse de Saint Jean.* Lausanne: Delachaux et Niestlé, 1981.

Prigent, P., and R.A. Kraft. *L'Épître de Barnabé.* Paris: Les Éditions du Cerf, 1971.

Quispel, G. *Lettre à Flora.* Paris: Les Editions du Cerf, 1966.

Rajak, T. "Jewish Rights in the Greek Cities under Roman Rule: A New Approach." In *Approaches to Ancient Judaism: Studies in Judaism and its Greco-Roman Context,* ed. William Scott Green. Atlanta: Scholars Press, 1985.

Ramsay, W.M. *The Letters to the Seven Churches,* ed. Mark W. Wilson. 2nd. ed. Peabody, MA: Hendrickson, 1994; orig. 1904.

Reicke, B. *Neutestamentliche Zeitgeschichte.* Berlin: Alfred Töpelmann, 1965.

Remus, H. "Justin Martyr's Argument with Judaism." In *Anti-Judaism in Early Christianity: Separation and Polemic,* ed. Stephen G. Wilson, vol. 2: 59–80. Waterloo: Wilfrid Laurier University Press, 1986.

Rengstorf, K.H., ed. *A Complete Concordance to Flavius Josephus.* vol. 2. Leiden: E.J. Brill, 1975.

Rengstorf, K.H., and S. von Kortzfleisch. *Kirch und Synagoge: Handbuch zur Geschichte von Christen und Juden.* vol. 1. Stuttgart: Klett, 1968.

Reynolds, J. and R. Tannenbaum. *Jews and God-Fearers at Aphrodisias: Greek Inscriptions with Commentary.* Cambridge, UK: Cambridge Philological Society, 1987.

Richardson, P. *Israel in the Apostolic Church.* Cambridge, UK: Cambridge University Press, 1969.

———. "Review of The Climax of the Covenant: Christ and the Law in Pauline Theology by N.T. Wright." *Studies in Religion* 23, 2 (1994): 232–33.

———. "Early Synagogues as Collegia in the Diaspora and Palestine." In *Voluntary Associations in the Graeco-Roman World,* ed. John S. Kloppenborg and Stephen G. Wilson, 90–109. London: Routledge, 1996.

———. "Augustan-Era Synagogues in Rome." In *Judaism and Christianity in First-Century Rome*, ed. Karl P. Donfried and Peter Richardson, 17-29. Grand Rapids, MI: William B. Eerdmans, 1998.

Richardson, P., ed. *Anti-Judaism in Early Christianity*. vol. 1. Waterloo: Wilfrid Laurier University Press, 1986.

Richardson, P. and M. Shukster. "Barnabas, Nerva, and the Yavnean Rabbis." *Journal of Theological Studies* 34 (1983): 31-55.

Richardson, P. and S. Westerholm, eds. *Law in Religious Communities in the Roman Period: The Debate Over Torah and Nomos in Post-Biblical Judaism and Early Christianity*. Waterloo: Wilfrid Laurier University, 1991.

Richter Reimer, I. *Women in the Acts of the Apostles: A Feminist Liberation Perspective*. Trans. Linda M. Maloney. Minneapolis: Fortress Press, 1995.

Ritschl, A. *Die Entstehung der altkatholischen Kirche*. Göttomgen: Vandenhoöck & Ruprecht, 1857.

Robinson, J.A.T. *Barnabas, Hermas and the Didache*. London: Society for Promoting Christian Knowlege, 1920.

———. *Redating the New Testament*. London: SCM, 1976.

Roetzel, C.J. *The Letters of Paul: Conversations in Context*. 4th ed. Louisville, KY: Westminster John Knox Press, 1998.

Ropes, J.H. *The Singular Problem of the Epistle to the Galatians*. Cambridge: Harvard University Press, 1929.

Rordorf, W. "Baptism according to the Didache." In *The Didache in Modern Research*, ed. Jonathan A. Draper, 148-64. Leiden: E.J. Brill, 1996.

Rordorf, W. and A. Tuilier. *La Doctrine des Douze Apôtres (Didaché)*. Paris: Les Éditions du Cerf, 1978.

Rowley, H.H. *Israel's Mission to the World*. London: SCM Press, 1939.

Ruether, R. *Faith and Fratricide: The Theological Roots of Anti-Semitism*. New York: Seabury, 1974.

Rutgers, L.V. "Roman Policy toward the Jews: Expulsions from the City of Rome during the First Century CE." In *Judaism and Christianity in First-Century Rome*, ed. Karl P. Donfried and Peter Richardson. Grand Rapids, MI: William B. Eerdmans, 1998.

Saldarini, A. "Jews and Christians in the First Two Centuries: The Changing Paradigm." *Shofar* 10 (1992): 16-34.

Sanders, E.P. *Paul and Palestinian Judaism: A Comparison of Patterns of Religion*. Philadelphia, PA: Fortress Press, 1977.

———. *Paul, the Law, and the Jewish People*. Minneapolis, MN: Fortress Press, 1983.

———. *Judaism: Practice and Belief 63 BCE-66 CE.* Philadelphia: Trinity Press, 1992.

Sanders, J.T. *Schismatics, Sectarians, Dissidents, Deviants.* London: SCM Press, 1993.

Sandmel, S. *The First Christian Century in Judaism and Christianity: Certainties and Uncertainties.* New York: Oxford University Press, 1969.

———. *Judaism and Christian Beginnings.* New York: Oxford University Press, 1978.

Sappington, T.J. *Revelation and Redemption at Colossae.* Sheffield: JSOT Press, 1991.

Scarsaune, O. *The Proof from Prophecy.* Leiden: E.J. Brill, 1987.

Schlecht, J. *Doctrina XII Apostolorum, die Apostellehre in der Liturgie der katholischen Kirche.* Freiburg im Brreisgau: Herder, 1901.

Schlier, H. *Der Brief an die Galater.* Göttingen: Vandenhoeck & Ruprecht, 1949, 1971.

Schmithals, W. *Paul and the Gnostics.* Trans. John E. Steely. Nashville: Abingdon Press, 1972.

———. *Neues Testament und Gnosis.* Darmstadt: Wissenschaftliche Buchgesellschaft, 1984.

Schneemelcher, W., ed. *New Testament Apocrypha.* Trans. R. McL. Wilson. vol. 2, rev. Westminster: John Knox Press, 1991. Originally published as *Neutestamentliche Apokryphen,* E. Hennecke, vol. 2. Tübingen: Mohr, 1964.

———. "The Kerygma Petri." In *New Testament Apocrypha,* ed., W. Schneemelcher, vol. 2, 34-41. Westminster: John Knox Press, 1991.

Schneider, H.P. "Some Reflections on the Dialogue of Justin Martyr with Trypho." *Scottish Journal of Theology* 15 (1962): 164-75.

Schoedel, W.R. "Ignatius and the Archives." *Harvard Theological Review* 71 (1978): 97-106.

———. *Ignatius of Antioch.* Philadelphia: Fortress Press, 1985.

———. "Polycarp of Smyrna and Ignatius of Antioch." *Aufstieg und Niedergang Der Römischen Welt* II 27, 1 (1993): 272-358.

Schoeps, H.J. *Paul: The Theology of the Apostle in the Light of Jewish Religious History.* Trans. Harold Knight. Philadelphia: Westminster, 1961.

———. *Jewish Christianity.* Philadelphia: Fortress Press, 1969.

Schöllgen, G. "The Didache as a Church Order: An Examination of the Purpose for the Composition of the Didache and Its Consequences for Interpretation." In *The Didache in Modern Research,* ed. Jonathan A. Draper, 43-71. Leiden: E.J. Brill, 1996.

Schürer, E. *The History of the Jewish People in the Age of Jesus Christ* (175 B.C.–A.D. 135), ed. G. Vermes and F. Millar et al. Rev. ed. 4 vols. Edinburgh: T. & T. Clark, 1973-87; orig. 1890.

Schüssler Fiorenza, E. "Apocalyptic and Gnosis in the Book of Revelation and Paul." *Journal of Biblical Literature* 92 (1973): 565-81.

Schutter, W.L. *Hermeneutic and Composition in 1 Peter*. Tübingen: J.C.B. Mohr (Paul Siebeck), 1989.

Schweizer, E. *The Letter to the Colossians*. Trans. Andrew Chester. Minneapolis: Augsburg Publishing House, 1982.

Seager, A.R. "The Synagogue and the Jewish Community." In *Sardis from Prehistoric to Roman Times: Results of the Archaeological Exploration of Sardis 1958-1975*, ed. G.M.A. Hanfmann, 169-78. Cambridge, UK: Cambridge University Press, 1983.

Segal, A. *Paul the Convert*. New Haven: Yale University Press, 1990.

Setzer, C. *Jewish Responses to Early Christians*. Minneapolis: Fortress Press, 1994.

Shukster, M.B. and P. Richardson. "Temple and Bet Ha-midrash in the Epistle of Barnabas." In *Anti-Judaism in Early Christianity: Separation and Polemic*, ed. Stephen G. Wilson, vol. 2: 17-31. Waterloo: Wilfrid Laurier University Press, 1986.

Siegert, F. "Gottesfurchtige und Sympathisanten." *Journal for the Study of Judaism* 4 (1973): 109-64.

Sigal, P. "An Inquiry into Aspects of Judaism in Justin's *Dialogue with Trypho*." *Abr-Nahrain* 18 (1978/79): 74-100.

Simon, M. *Verus Israel*. Trans. H. McKeating. London: Oxford University Press, 1986.

Simon, M., and A. Benoit. *Le Judaïsm et le Christianisme antique*. Paris: Presses universitaires de France, 1968.

Skarsaune, O. *The Proof from Prophecy. A Study in Justin Martyr's Proof Text Tradition: Text-type, Provenance, Theological Profile*. Leiden: Brill, 1987.

Skeat, T.C. "'Especially the Parchments': A Note on 2 Timothy IV.13." *Journal of Theological Studies* (1979): 173-77.

Smallwood, E.M. *The Jews under Roman Rule: From Pompey to Diocletian*. Leiden: E.J. Brill, 1976.

———. "The Alleged Jewish Tendencies of Poppaea Sabina." *The Journal of Theological Studies* 10 (1959): 329-35.

Smith, T.V. *Petrine Controversies in Early Christianity*. Tübingen: J.C.B. Mohr (Paul Siebeck), 1985.

Soden, von D.H. "Der erste Brief des Petrus." In *Hand-Commentar zum Teuen Testament*. Freiburg: J.C.B Mohr, 1893.

Spicq, C. *Saint Paul: les Épitres Pastorales*. Paris: J. Gabalda, 1947.

Stanton, G. "Aspects of Early Christian-Jewish Polemic and Apologetic."
New Testament Studies 31 (1985): 377-92.

———. "Other Early Christian Writings: 'Didache,' Ignatius, 'Barnabas,'
Justin Martyr." In *Early Christian Thought in Its Jewish Context*, ed.
John Barclay, 174-90. Cambridge, UK: Cambridge University Press,
1996.

Stark, W. *The Sociology of Religion: A Study of Christendom*. Vol. 2. New
York: Fordham University Press, 1967.

Stark, R. *The Rise of Christianity: A Sociologist Reconsiders History*.
Princeton, NJ: Princeton University Press, 1996.

Stendahl, K. *Paul among Jews and Gentiles, and Other Essays*. Philadelphia: Fortress Press, 1976.

Stern, M. "Sympathy for Judaism in Roman Senatorial Circles in the Early
Empire [in Hebrew]." *Tsiyon* 29 (1964): 155-67.

Stern, M. *Greek and Latin Authors on Jews and Judaism*. 3 vols. Jerusalem:
Israel Academy of Sciences and Humanities, 1974-84.

Strecker, G. "The Kerygma Petrou." In W. Schneemelcher, ed., *New Testament Apocrypha*. vol.2, 102-27. London: Lutterworth Press, 1965.

———. "The Problem of Jewish Christianity." In *Orthodoxy and Heresy
in Earliest Christianity*, ed. W. Bauer, 241-85. Philadelphia: Fortress
Press, 1971.

———. "The Reception of the Book." In *Orthodoxy and Heresy in Earliest Christianity*, by W. Bauer, 286-316. Philadelphia: Fortress Press,
1971.

———. *Das Judenchristentum in den Pseudoklementinen*. 2nd. ed. Berlin:
Akademie-Verlag, 1981; orig. 1958.

———. "Introduction to the Pseudo-Clementines," in W. Schneemelcher,
ed., *New Testament Apocrypha*. vol.2, 483-92. Westminster: John
Knox Press, 1992.

———. "Le Judéo-Christianisme entre la Synagogue et l'Église." In *Orthodoxie et Hérésie Dans L'Église Ancienne*, 3-20. Lausanne: Neuchâ-
tel, 1993.

Sweet, J. *Revelation*. London: SCM Press, 1990; orig. 1979.

Synge, F.C. *Philippians and Colossians*. London: SCM Press, 1958.

Taylor, C. *The Teaching of the Twelve Apostles*. Cambridge: Deighton
Bell, 1886.

Taylor, M.S. *Anti-Judaism and Early Christian Identity*. Leiden: E.J. Brill,
1995.

Tcherikover, V. "Jewish Apologetic Literature Reconsidered." *Eos* 48
(1956): 169-93.

———. *Hellenistic Civilization and the Jews*. New York: Atheneum, 1970.

Tellbe, M. "The Sociological Factors Behind Philippians 3. 1-11 and the Conflict at Philippi." *Journal for the Study of the New Testament* 55 (1994): 97-121.

Thompson, L. "A Sociological Analysis of Tribulation in the Apocalypse of John." *Semeia* 36 (1986): 147-74.

Trakatellis, D. "Justin Martyr's Trypho." *Harvard Theological Review* 79 (1986): 287-97.

Trebilco, P.R. *Jewish Communities in Asia Minor*. Cambridge, UK: Cambridge University Press, 1991.

Van der Horst, P. *Essays on the Jewish World of Early Christianity*. Freiburg, Switzerland: Universitätsverlag, 1990.

Van Unnik, W.C. "Christianity According to 1 Peter." *The Expository Times* 68 (1956-1957): 79-83.

———. "First Letter of Peter." *Interpreters Dictionary of the Bible* (1963): 758-67.

Vermes, G. *Jesus the Jew*. London: Collins, 1973.

———. *The Dead Sea Scrolls in English*. London: Penguin, 1987.

Visotzky, B.L. "Prolegomenon to the Study of Jewish-Christianities in Rabbinic Literature." *The Journal of the Association for Jewish Studies* 14 (1989): 47-70.

Walton, C.S. "Oriental Senators in the Service of Rome." *Journal of Roman Studies* 19 (1929): 38-49.

Ward, T. *Commentary on 1 & 2 Timothy and Titus*. Waco: Word Books, 1974.

Weber, F. *Jüdische Theologie auf Grund des Talmud und verwandter Schriften*. Leipzig: Dörffling, 1897.

Weima, J. *Neglected Endings: The Significance of the Pauline Letter Closings*. Sheffield: JSOT Press, 1994.

Wellhausen, J. *Israelitische und jüdische Geschichte*. 9th. ed. Berlin: De Gruyter, 1958; orig. 1897.

Wengst, K. *Tradition und Theologie des Barnabasbriefes*. Berlin: De Gruyter, 1971.

———. *Didache (Apostellehre), Barnabasbrief, Zweiter Klemensbrief, Schrift an Diognet*. Darmstadt: Wissenschaftliche Buchgesellschaft, 1984.

Werner, E. "Melito of Sardes, the First Poet of Deicide." *Hebrew Union College Annual* 37 (1966): 191-210.

Westcott, B.F. *The Gospel According to St. John*. Grand Rapids, MI: Wm. B. Eerdmans, 1881.

White, M.L. "Adolf Harnack and the 'Expansion' of Early Christianity: A Reappraisal of Social History." *The Second Century* 5, 2 (1985/1986): 97-127.

———. "Visualizing the 'Real' World of Acts 16: Toward Construction of a Social Index." In *The Social World of the First Christians: Essays in Honor of Wayne A. Meeks*, ed. L. Michael White and O. Larry Yarbrough, 234-61. Minneapolis: Fortress Press, 1995.

Wiefel, W. "The Jewish Community in Ancient Rome and the Origins of Roman Christianity." In *The Romans Debate*, ed. Karl P. Donfried. Peabody, MA: Hendrickson, 1991.

Wilken, R. "Melito, the Jewish Community at Sardis, and the Sacrifice of Isaac." *Theological Studies* 37 (1976): 53-69.

———. *John Chrysostom and the Jews*. Berkeley: University of California Press, 1983.

Will, E. and C. Orrieux. *Proselytisme Juif? Une Histoire d'une Erreur*. Paris: Les Belles Lettres, 1992.

Williams, A.L. *Adversus Judaeos. A Bird's-Eye View of Christian Apologiae until the Renaissance*. Cambridge University Press, 1935.

Williams, M.H. "θεοσεβὴ" γὰρ ἦν The Jewish Tendencies of Poppaea Sabina." *Journal of Theological Studies* 39 (1988): 97-111.

———. "Domitian, the Jews, and the 'Judaizers'—a Simple Matter of Cupiditas and Majestas?" *Historia* 39 (1990): 196-211.

Willis, W.W. *Idol Meat in Corinth*. Chico: Scholars Press, 1985.

Wilson, R. *Marcion: A Study of a Second-Century Heretic*. London: James Clarke, 1980; orig. 1933.

Wilson, S.G. *Luke and the Pastoral Epistles*. London: Society for Promoting Christian Knowlege, 1979.

———. "Gentile Judaizers." *New Testament Studies* 38 (1992): 605-16.

———. *Related Strangers: Jews and Christians 70-170 CE*. Minneapolis: Fortress Press, 1995.

———. "Defectors and Apostates among Jews, Christians and Pagans in Late Antiquity: A Neglected Aspect of Religious Rivalry." Paper presented at the Canadian Society of Religious Studies, University of Ottawa, Ottawa, ON, 1998.

———. "Οι Ποτε Ιουδαιοι: Epigraphic Evidence for Jewish Defectors." In *Text and Artifact in the Religions of Mediterranean Antiquity*, ed. Stephen G. and Michel Desjardins Wilson, 354-71. Waterloo: Wilfrid Laurier University Press, 2000.

Wilson, S.G., ed. *Anti-Judaism in Early Christianity*. vol. 2. Waterloo: Wilfrid Laurier University Press, 1986.

Windisch, H. "Der Barnabasbrief." In *Handbuch zum Neuen Testament: Die Apostolischen Vater III*. Tübingen: Mohr, 1920.

Wright, N.T. *The New Testament and the People of God*. Minneapolis: Fortress Press, 1992.

————. *The Climax of the Covenant*. Minneapolis: Fortress Press, 1993.

Yarbro Collins, A. "Persecution and Vengeance in the Book of Revelation." In *Apocalypticism in the Mediterranean World and the Near East: Proceedings of International Colloquium on Apocalypticism, Uppsala, August* 12-17, 1979, 729-49, Tübingen: Mohr, 1983.

————. "Insiders and Outsiders in the Book of Revelation and Its Social Context." In *'To See Ourselves as Others See Us' Christians, Jews, 'Others' in Late Antiquity*, eds. J. Neusner and E.S. Frerichs, 187-218. Chico: Scholars Press, 1985.

————. "Vilification and Self-Definition in the Book of Revelation." *Harvard Theological Review* 79, 1 (1986): 308-20.

Zahn, T. *Ignatius von Antiochien*. Gotha: Perthes, 1873.

Zeitlin, S. "The Names Hebrew, Jew and Israel: A Historical Study." *The Jewish Quarterly Review* 53 (1952): 365-79.

◄○►

Ancient Sources Index

◄◖►

Subject Index

◄○►

Israel, 160n24, 164n25, 172n28,
173n29; Christian claim to, 77, 79,
93, 182n37; and Judaism, 111, 113,
116, 170n10; Paul's teachings about,
142-43, 146, 149

James, 32, 68, 119, 168n54, 172n28
Jerusalem, 5, 32, 38, 44, 81, 113-15,
118, 119, 141-43; destruction of
Jewish Temple in, 1, 6, 119, 137,
164n30, 179n6; rebuilding of
Temple in, 46-47, 48, 59, 162n7,
164n30
Jesus, 67, 69-70, 98, 173n34; death of,
76, 112-13, 169n5, 171n19, 177n23;
laws of, 63; as Messiah, 34, 104,
123, 144, 146, 149; teachings of, 89,
102-5, 133
Jews, 77-78; and contact with
Christians, 47-48, 79, 91-92, 109-
10, 115; and contact with Gentiles,
26-27; and covenant, 3, 50, 51-52,
54, 57, 59, 67-68, 77, 120, 178n5;
and deicide, 112-13, 122, 177n24;
persecution by, 74-76, 98, 132,
169nn3-4; persecution of, 24, 35;
presence of, 92-93, 98, 107-9, 115,
119, 165n32, 178n3, 180n14;
resettlement of, 92, 107; status of,
128-29. See also Christians, Jewish;
Judaism
John (the Baptist), 93
John (the prophet), 75
Judaism: antiquity of, 10-12, 154n1;
customs and traditions of, 3, 4, 5,
12-14, 15, 21, 23, 30-34, 39, 40, 43,
50, 53-58, 80-81, 85-86, 97, 117-18,
119, 154n6, 165n34; conversion to,
79, 96, 97-99, 102, 106, 115, 121-
22, 123-24, 128, 133, 140, 153n7,
156nn19-20, 158n9, 172n22,
174n41, 179n8, 180n14, 181n21;
interaction with Christianity, 6, 9,
79, 105-6, 109-10, 113-14, 119,
120, 124-25, 127, 136-40, 148, 150-
52, 166n41, 169n7, 173n30, 175n7,
176nn12, 15, 181n18, 183nn40, 42;
misconceptions of, 137-39, 141,
181n19; as missionary religion, 10,
12-13, 21-26, 88, 118-19, 127, 129-
30, 140, 154nn2-3, 156nn14, 20,
157n21, 162n9, 175n7, 178n3,
180n14, 181n21; separation from

Christianity, 1, 9, 50, 51-54, 57-60,
63, 90-92, 101, 102-5, 116, 121-23,
125, 128-29, 131, 132, 149, 175n3,
179n6, 182nn29, 35; inferiority to
Christianity, 3, 47, 116, 119-20,
124, 128-29, 140-41, 164n25;
supplanted by Christianity, 76-78,
79, 85, 91, 93, 98, 110-11, 116, 120-
21, 122, 124, 129-30, 132, 133,
170nn8, 10, 177n20, 179n7; status
of, 18, 80-81, 139-40, 171nn13-15;
and taxation, 45-46, 108, 156n15,
171n13; teachings of, 59-60, 87-89,
178n8. See also circumcision;
fasting; food laws; Jews; Sabbath
judaizers, 101, 131; acceptance of, 95-
96, 98-99, 122-23; and conversion,
10, 32, 51, 115, 121-22, 123-24,
155n8; criticisms of, 2-4, 30-31, 34-
36, 50-53, 63-66, 73-74, 81, 83-84,
116, 118, 122, 146-47, 155n8,
163n15; encouragement for, 8, 67-
68, 83; perspective of, 68, 87-88,
120, 122; political danger of, 75,
155n8; presence of, 5-7, 70, 78-79,
82, 83, 89-90, 96, 121, 143-44, 146-
48, 150-51, 153nn6-7, 154n4,
173nn36-37, 174n40, 176n15,
183n39; reasons for, 5, 9, 32-34, 35-
39, 81, 118, 142, 144-45, 147,
156n15, 160n24; religious danger of,
9, 36, 37-38, 39, 40-41, 53, 79-80,
90, 117, 123, 150, 171n19, 181n20;
social status of, 37
judaizers, non-Christian, 119; and
conversion, 12-14, 17, 21, 24-25;
persecution of, 19-20; political
danger of, 4, 14-15; reasons for, 11-
12; social status of, 15-19, 20-21
Judea, 119, 143, 156n13, 178nn3-4
Julius Caesar, 80
Junius Rusticus, 91
Justin Martyr, 73, 77, 91-92, 99, 121-
24, 144, 151, 163n18, 164n30;
Apologies of, 166n39. See also
Dialogue with Trypho

kashruth. See food laws
Kerygamata Petrou, 67, 71-72, 118,
167nn50-51, 168n52; criticism of
Paul in, 68-70; Judaism esteemed in,
67-68, 168n56. See also Pseudo-
Clementine literature

Series Published by Wilfrid Laurier University Press for the Canadian Corporation for Studies in Religion/Corporation Canadienne des Sciences Religieuses

Series numbers not mentioned are out of print.

Series no. Editions SR

2 *The Conception of Punishment in Early Indian Literature*
Terence P. Day / 1982 / iv + 328 pp.

4 *Le messianisme de Louis Riel*
Gilles Martel / 1984 / xviii + 483 p.

7 *L'étude des religions dans les écoles : l'expérience américaine, anglaise et canadienne*
Fernand Ouellet / 1985 / xvi + 666 p.

8 *Of God and Maxim Guns: Presbyterianism in Nigeria, 1846-1966*
Geoffrey Johnston / 1988 / iv + 322 pp.

10 *Prometheus Rebound: The Irony of Atheism*
Joseph C. McLelland / 1988 / xvi + 366 pp.

11 *Competition in Religious Life*
Jay Newman / 1989 / viii + 237 pp.

12 *The Huguenots and French Opinion, 1685-1787: The Enlightenment Debate on Toleration*
Geoffrey Adams / 1991 / xiv + 335 pp.

13 *Religion in History: The Word, the Idea, the Reality / La religion dans l'histoire : le mot, l'idée, la réalité*
Edited by/Sous la direction de Michel Despland and/et Gérard Vallée
1992 / x + 252 pp.

14 *Sharing Without Reckoning: Imperfect Right and the Norms of Reciprocity*
Millard Schumaker / 1992 / xiv + 112 pp.

15 *Love and the Soul: Psychological Interpretations of the Eros and Psyche Myth*
James Gollnick / 1992 / viii + 174 pp.

16 *The Promise of Critical Theology: Essays in Honour of Charles Davis*
Edited by Marc P. Lalonde / 1995 / xii + 146 pp.

17 *The Five Aggregates: Understanding Theravāda Psychology and Soteriology*
Mathieu Boisvert / 1995 / xii + 166 pp.

18 *Mysticism and Vocation*
James R. Horne / 1996 / vi + 110 pp.

19 *Memory and Hope: Strands of Canadian Baptist History*
Edited by David T. Priestley / 1996 / viii + 211 pp.

20 *The Concept of Equity in Calvin's Ethics**
Guenther H. Haas / 1997 / xii + 205 pp.
Available in the United Kingdom and Europe from Paternoster Press.

21 *The Call of Conscience: French Protestant Responses to the Algerian War, 1954-1962*
Geoffrey Adams / 1998 / xxii + 270 pp.

22 *Clinical Pastoral Supervision and the Theology of Charles Gerkin*
Thomas St. James O'Connor / 1998 / x + 152 pp.

23 *Faith and Fiction: A Theological Critique of the Narrative Strategies of Hugh MacLennan and Morley Callaghan*
Barbara Pell / 1998 / v + 141 pp.

24 *God and the Chip: Religion and the Culture of Technology*
    William A. Stahl / 1999 / vi + 186 pp.
25 *The Religious Dreamworld of Apuleius' Metamorphoses: Recovering a Forgotten*
    Hermeneutic
    James Gollnick / 1999 / xiv + 178 pp.
26 *Edward Schillebeeckx and Hans Frei: A Conversation on Method and Christology*
    Marguerite Abdul-Masih / 2001 / vi + 194 pp.
27 *Radical Difference: A Defence of Hendrik Kraemer's Theology of Religions*
    Tim S. Perry / 2001 / x + 170 pp.
28 *Hindu Iconoclasts: Rammohun Roy, Dayananda Sarasvati, and Nineteenth-Century*
    Polemics against Idolatry
    Noel Salmond / 2004 / 192 pp. (est.)
29 *The Biblical Politics of John Locke*
    K.I. Parker / 2004 / 220 pp. (est.)

Comparative Ethics Series /
Series no. # Collection d'Éthique Comparée

2 *Methodist Education in Peru: Social Gospel, Politics, and American Ideological*
   and Economic Penetration, 1888-1930
   Rosa del Carmen Bruno-Jofré / 1988 / xiv + 223 pp.
4 *In Good Faith: Canadian Churches Against Apartheid*
   Renate Pratt / 1997 / xii + 366 pp.
5 *Towards an Ethics of Community: Negotiations of Difference in a Pluralist Society*
   James H. Olthuis, editor / 2000 / x + 230 pp.
6 *Doing Ethics in a Pluralistic World: Essays in Honour of Roger C. Hutchinson*
   Phyllis J. Airhart, Marilyn J. Legge and Gary L. Redcliffe, editors / 2002 /
   viii + 264 pp.
7 *Weaving Relationships: Canada-Guatemala Solidarity*
   Kathryn Anderson / 2003 / xxii + 322 pp.

Studies in Christianity and Judaism /
Series no. # Études sur le christianisme et le judaïsme

2 *Anti-Judaism in Early Christianity Vol. 1, Paul and the Gospels*
   Edited by Peter Richardson with David Granskou / 1986 / x + 232 pp.
   Vol. 2, *Separation and Polemic*
   Edited by Stephen G. Wilson / 1986 / xii + 185 pp.
3 *Society, the Sacred, and Scripture in Ancient Judaism: A Sociology of Knowledge*
   Jack N. Lightstone / 1988 / xiv + 126 pp.
4 *Law in Religious Communities in the Roman Period: The Debate Over* Torah
   and Nomos *in Post-Biblical Judaism and Early Christianity*
   Peter Richardson and Stephen Westerholm with A.I. Baumgarten, Michael Pettem
   and Cecilia Wassén / 1991 / x + 164 pp.
5 *Dangerous Food: 1 Corinthians 8-10 in Its Context*
   Peter D. Gooch / 1993 / xviii + 178 pp.
6 *The Rhetoric of the Babylonian Talmud, Its Social Meaning and Context*
   Jack N. Lightstone / 1994 / xiv + 317 pp.
7 *Whose Historical Jesus?*
   Edited by William E. Arnal and Michel Desjardins / 1997 / vi + 337 pp.
8 *Religious Rivalries and the Struggle for Success in Caesarea Maritima*
   Edited by Terence L. Donaldson / 2000 / xiv + 402 pp.
9 *Text and Artifact in the Religions of Mediterranean Antiquity*
   Edited by Stephen G. Wilson and Michel Desjardins / 2000 / xvi + 616 pp.

10 *Parables of War: Reading John's Jewish Apocalypse*
   by John W. Marshall / 2001 / viii + 262 pp.
11 *Mishnah and the Social Formation of the Early Rabbinic Guild:*
   A Socio-Rhetorical Approach
   by Jack N. Lightstone / 2002 / xii + 240 pp.
12 *The Social Setting of the Ministry as Reflected in the Writings of Hermas,*
   Clement and Ignatius
   Harry O. Maier / 1991, second impression 2002 / x + 234 pp.
13 *Playing a Jewish Game: Gentile Christian Judaizing in the First and*
   Second Centuries CE
   Michele Murray / 2004 / xii + 228 pp.

The Study of Religion in Canada /
Series no. ## Sciences Religieuses au Canada

1 *Religious Studies in Alberta: A State-of-the-Art Review*
  Ronald W. Neufeldt / 1983 / xiv + 145 pp.
2 *Les sciences religieuses au Québec depuis 1972*
  Louis Rousseau et Michel Despland / 1988 / 158 p.
3 *Religious Studies in Ontario: A State-of-the-Art Review*
  Harold Remus, William Closson James and Daniel Fraikin / 1992 / xviii + 422 pp.
4 *Religious Studies in Manitoba and Saskatchewan: A State-of-the-Art Review*
  John M. Badertscher, Gordon Harland and Roland E. Miller / 1993 / vi + 166 pp.
5 *The Study of Religion in British Columbia: A State-of-the-Art Review*
  Brian J. Fraser / 1995 / x + 127 pp.
6 *Religious Studies in Atlantic Canada: A State-of-the-Art Review*
  Paul W. R. Bowlby with Tom Faulkner / 2001 / xii + 208 pp.

Studies in Women and Religion /
Series no. ## Études sur les femmes et la religion

1 *Femmes et religions**
  Sous la direction de Denise Veillette / 1995 / xviii + 466 p.
2 *The Work of Their Hands: Mennonite Women's Societies in Canada*
  Gloria Neufeld Redekop / 1996 / xvi + 172 pp.
3 *Profiles of Anabaptist Women: Sixteenth-Century Reforming Pioneers*
  Edited by C. Arnold Snyder and Linda A. Huebert Hecht / 1996 / xxii + 438 pp.
4 *Voices and Echoes: Canadian Women's Spirituality*
  Edited by Jo-Anne Elder and Colin O'Connell / 1997 / xxviii + 237 pp.
5 *Obedience, Suspicion and the Gospel of Mark: A Mennonite-Feminist*
  Exploration of Biblical Authority
  Lydia Neufeld Harder / 1998 / xiv + 168 pp.
6 *Clothed in Integrity: Weaving Just Cultural Relations and the Garment Industry*
  Barbara Paleczny / 2000 / xxxiv + 352 pp.
7 *Women in God's Army: Gender and Equality in the Early Salvation Army*
  Andrew Mark Eason / 2003 / xiv + 246 pp.
8 *Pour libérer la théologie.* Variations autour de la pensée féministe d'Ivone
  Gebara Pierrette Daviau, dir. / 2002 / 212 pp.
9 *Linking Sexuality & Gender: Naming Violence against Women in The United*
  Church of Canada
  Tracy J. Trothen / 2003 / x + 166 pp.

*Only available from Les Presses de l'Université Laval

Series no. **SR Supplements**

9 *Developments in Buddhist Thought: Canadian Contributions to Buddhist Studies*
   Edited by Roy C. Amore / 1979 / iv + 196 pp.
11 *Political Theology in the Canadian Context*
   Edited by Benjamin G. Smillie / 1982 / xii + 260 pp.
14 *The Moral Mystic*
   James R. Horne / 1983 / x + 134 pp.
16 *Studies in the Book of Job*
   Edited by Walter E. Aufrecht / 1985 / xii + 76 pp.
17 *Christ and Modernity: Christian Self-Understanding in a Technological Age*
   David J. Hawkin / 1985 / x + 181 pp.
19 *Modernity and Religion*
   Edited by William Nicholls / 1987 / vi + 191 pp.

Series discontinued

Available from:

Wilfrid Laurier University Press
Waterloo, Ontario, Canada N2L 3C5
Telephone: (519) 884-0710, ext. 6124
Fax: (519) 725-1399
E-mail: press@wlu.ca
World Wide Web: http://www.wlupress.wlu.ca